The Buddha
was not
a Buddhist

The Buddha
was not
a Buddhist

*A Rational Path to Meditation, Mindfulness,
and the Art of Fighting without Fighting*

陳
志
強

Mushin Press

The Buddha was not a Buddhist

Copyright © 2014 by Chen Zhi-qiang

ISBN-10: 0990923320
ISBN-13: 978-0-9909233-2-9

Mushin Press

www.mushinpress.com

TO JENNIFER, VIVIAN, AND PHOEBE

Contents

INTRODUCTION

This book is not about Buddhism or Taoism, though it refers often to these philosophies, nor is it about meditation or mindfulness, though it describes meditation and mindfulness techniques. No, this book is about how to live engaged with the realities of our humanness, which can be understood by recognizing these four fundamental truths:

1. The true nature of egoistic cravings and the deceits of our conditioned minds;
2. the true nature of non-duality;
3. the true nature of compounded phenomena and impermanence;
4. the true nature of our interconnectedness to the external world.

With this understanding, one can live more present, honest, and patient; kinder, calmer, and gentler; less judgmental, reactionary, fearful, destructive, petty, and everything else. One can live a life with more contentment, freedom, and creativity, and less fear, self-doubt, and anxiety.

I must admit that I have no new ideas. Living and traveling in Asia, studying, discussing, meditating, contemplating, and sitting in the forest have taught me that all knowledge, truth, and practices necessary for a life of contentment have already been taught by others. It is all already out there to be realized. Whenever I thought I might have had a somewhat novel idea about truth or life or the ego, I would later read a book or listen to a speaker and find that some other tradition or philosopher had long ago stated "my" profound idea.

No, this book is not about revealing sage insights or secrets but rather conveying unfamiliar ideas in a logical and rational manner. Can concepts about the true nature of self and of our existence be described so that anyone can understand, without esoteric phrasing, without dogma, without riddles obscuring the meaning?

Coming upon unfamiliar philosophical ideas, I would sometimes think, *Yes, that's right,* as if I were reading or hearing thoughts of my own. Oftentimes, though, I would scratch my head and wonder, *What does that mean?* To the uninitiated, Eastern philosophical concepts sometimes read like perplexing riddles:

Walpola Rahula: "In other words, there is no thinker behind the thought. Thought itself is the thinker."[1]

Jiddu Krishnamurti: "I, who am very earnest, want to dissolve the self . . . The moment I say 'I want to dissolve this,' and in the process I follow for the dissolution of that, there is the experiencing of the self; and so, the self is strengthened."[2]

Zen Master Linji Yixuan: "If you meet the Buddha on the road, kill him."

Tao Te Ching, Chapter One:
道可道非常道名可名非常名無名天地之始
有名萬物之母故常無欲以觀其妙常有欲以觀其徼
此兩者同出而異名同謂之玄玄之又玄眾妙之門
The Tao that can be told is not the eternal Tao.
The name that can be named is not the eternal name.
The nameless is the beginning of heaven and earth.
The named is the mother of the ten thousand things.
Ever desireless, one can see the mystery.

[1] Walpola Rahula, *What the Buddha Taught* (Grove Press, 1974) 26
[2] Jiddu Krishnamurti, *Krishnamurti Foundation Annual Gathering Compilation 1990* (Krishnamurti Foundation Trust Ltd., 1990) 26

Ever desiring, one sees the manifestations.
These two spring from the same source but differ in name;
this appears as darkness.
Darkness within darkness.
The gate to all mystery.[3]

Sometimes when I was first introduced to an Eastern philosophical concept, it felt counterintuitive to acknowledge a fundamental idea. The heart of the Buddha's teaching, for example, known as the Four Noble Truths, begins with the plainspoken First Noble Truth of Dukkha, often translated in English as "Life is suffering."[4] I can't say that I was especially inspired by such a seemingly bleak outlook on life. How could one agree with this dreary sentiment when most of us experience, or have experienced, some measure of happiness and kindness and love and enjoyment in our lives? Maybe I was misinterpreting some word or translation or, as I have often found, the ideas are not related within a context that is easily comprehended by a person from a different cultural upbringing.

I do not claim to be a Buddhist nor a Taoist nor am I interested in religious dogma or doctrines. I have no special powers or authority. Is it necessary to claim spiritual affiliation to find truth and rationality? No, it is not. There is no necessity for believing in or having faith in the Buddha or the Taoists or anybody else. The Buddha himself taught that you need not faith but personal observation to recognize and understand truth for yourself.

> "The Buddha said, 'Do not accept my teaching out of respect for me. Examine it and rediscover the truth in it for yourself.'"—Matthieu Ricard[5]

[3] Lao-zi translated by Gia-fu Feng and Jane English, *Tao Te Ching* (New York: Vintage Books, 1989)
[4] Rahula, *What the Buddha Taught*, 16–18
[5] Jean-Francois Revel & Matthieu Ricard, *The Monk and the Philosopher* (Random House, 1998) 251

"Buddha told the Kalamas, Don't accept anything just because it is said by religion or scripture, or a teacher or guru, only accept it if you see for yourself that it is right; if you see it is wrong or bad, then reject it."—Walpola Rahula[6]

Why "believe" anything? Question and contemplate all knowledge and ideas and values until you see the truth of them, without a trace of doubt. If you have any beliefs, throw them out. They are not your own. They are the thoughts and ideas of some other, thoughts and ideas that you have been conditioned to believe or have blindly assumed. To follow religious or political or philosophical or cultural or traditional dogma, or a cult of personality, is to remain conditioned and mechanical.

When you realize the truth, it is no longer necessary to believe. You need not have faith or belief, just the truth presented in a logical, rational manner, and it does not matter where or how it is discovered. It matters not if you are Buddhist, Christian, Muslim, atheist, agnostic, Republican, Democrat, monied, or destitute. The truth about the nature of the self, the nature of our relationship to the external world, and the nature of our existential reality is universal and can be observed by anyone.

[6] Jiddu Krishnamurti in Dialogue with Buddhists, *Can Humanity Change* (Shambhala Publications, 2003) 5

ONE

WHY MEDITATE?

Great Buddha Statue - Bodhgaya, India

A: So, what is your son doing nowadays?
B: He's practicing something called meditation. I'm not sure what it is, but at least he isn't sitting around and doing nothing.

Ba-dum-tshh! Although meditation is becoming more widely acknowledged, it is still mentioned with some derision in mainstream culture, characterized as a new-age, navel-gazing, hippie self-indulgence. Admittedly, meditation techniques can be often found in the repertoire of the self-absorbed navel-gazer, but in truth, most anyone can practice meditation, and quite simply, it can help a person develop an awareness of how the conditioned mind works so that one can live more mindfully, more honestly, less anxiously, less destructively, and it can even help a person to lose weight. Really. Why not meditate?

In our free time, we all engage in activities that are enjoyable and free us from the obligations and pressures of everyday life. It is quite acceptable to spend hours at the gym, exercising and developing an impressive physique. It is normal to go out for a night to watch a basketball game or to have a drink. It is customary to sit for several mind-numbing hours watching television or surfing the internet. But try to become a more centered, mindful, and kinder person by sitting and meditating, and: *What are you doing? You're wasting time! Doing nothing! You're just sitting there!*

Okay, it's true, you are sitting there, but not just. Meditation is far from a passive activity. Your mind is actively engaged, and you will find that "just" sitting is not all that easy. More likely, it will be a distinct challenge to your intellect and consciousness.

First introduced to a type of focus meditation when practicing Chinese kung fu as a teenager, I was taught how to sit, how to breathe, and how to focus on my dantián—a qì (or chi) point about three finger widths below the navel and two finger widths in—so that I could "clear my mind." Intent on becoming a proficient martial artist, I sat, diligently, concentrating, focusing, all the while distracted by constant, random thoughts prattling on in my head such as: *This is boring. What time is it? I need to go do this or that. Are we almost done yet?* Unable to grasp the point of the whole matter, I could only wonder, *Why am I sitting here focusing on—nothing?*

I did not understand why I was doing what I was doing, sitting there, with my eyes closed. Apparently, I was trying to cultivate what the Japanese call "mushin" (無心), the first word "mu" (no, none, without), and the second, "shin" (heart, mind, or feeling). The meaning can be translated as: without mind, without thought, without emotion, without ego.

What I did not realize was that I was practicing to liberate myself from the distraction of feelings, thoughts, and intentions. I would then, theoretically, be able to respond freely when engaged in a fight and would not be hampered by desire or fear or anger. I would be able to express totally and fluidly, with mental clarity and pure action, the full range of whatever fighting ability I had learned. A sense of presence would allow me to act upon and react to my opponent with spontaneity, focus, calmness, decisiveness, and fearlessness, with no concern for defeat nor desire for victory—egoless—pure being.

Well, I didn't get it. I had too many things to think about, like punching my opponent in the head and kicking him in the groin while simultaneously trying to avoid his smashing me in the face. I didn't understand the process of meditation and felt only boredom, restlessness, and distraction.

Years later, I was living in Taiwan and began practicing tai chi chuan (also tai chi or tàijíquán). I can't exactly recall why I wanted to learn, but it seemed like the thing to do since I regularly observed locals practicing in the parks. Even though I was able to pick up the tai chi postures and movements fairly quickly, a few months later I quit, indifferent and uninspired. The movements were done so leisurely that it drove me nuts! During practice, I had flashbacks to my previous experience with meditation: *This is boring. What time is it? I need to go do this or that. Are we almost done yet?* Still unable to understand the point, I could only think, *Moving so tediously during tai chi is about as stimulating as watching grass grow.*

Not until I was introduced to teachings of the Buddha, the Taoist philosophies of Lao-zi (also Lao-Tzu) and Zhuang-zi, and the insights of Indian philosopher Jiddu Krishnamurti did I became intrigued and inspired by the logic of and rationale for meditation. I then began to see how observing the nature of the mind could bring a person to realize: the true nature of the self, the true nature of our relationship to the external world, and the true nature of our existential reality, allowing one to live more boldly, more engaged, more genuine, more present, and, ultimately, more content.

Insight Meditation

I imagine every spiritual tradition has some form of mental discipline that could be termed meditative. It is quite simple to learn a meditation technique and to immediately start a meditation practice. Before starting, though, you should ask yourself why you are interested in meditation. What is your intent because your intent will influence the effect. Here are several reasons people give for how they think meditation can be useful:

- **Meditation as a form of therapy, self-hypnosis, or stress reliever.** Most people living in modern society suffer from stress and anxiety. They hope to become calmer and more relaxed, free of their frustrations and discontent.

- **Meditation to feel in control of your mind and emotions.** Some want to feel stronger, more confident, empowered, self-assured, emotionally stable, to be able to decisively face the challenges in their lives.

- **Meditation to overcome the fear and anxiousness of failure, defeat.** There are those who wish to cultivate mushin and function at a peak level, to improve their golf game, to fight in the martial arts, to become an accomplished performer, and so on.

- **Meditation used like a drug.** Looking to escape the mundanity of their lives, there are people searching for a natural sense of euphoria, a healthy way to "get high."

- **Meditation as a means to create the egoistic identity of a spiritual individual.** There are those who enjoy becoming self-absorbed in a world of esoteric thoughts, seeking to embody some ideal of cosmic enlightenment.

- **Meditation as a way to develop supernatural or psychic powers.** Some hope to perform preternatural tricks that impress others, in an attempt to satiate egoistic cravings for distinction, uniqueness, and celebrity.

It is understandable why people might have these motivations. Some are purely egoistic; others, although practical, fail to appreciate the greater potential benefit of a meditation practice.

Although meditation techniques can bring about moments of mental stillness, mental clarity, and a feeling of serenity, are you interested in only a temporary state of calm, whereupon when finished meditating, you revert to an anxious, distracted, impatient, discontented self, constantly reminding yourself to "be mindful" as you ruminate and obsess and un-mindfully react? Or do you hope to live more content, to transform how you perceive of and respond to life circumstances so that you can move throughout the day more composed and present?

To be content is to have awakened to truth and freed oneself from the mental conflict that arises suffering, i.e., the activity of the self. The meditation technique often called insight meditation is a practice that allows us to observe the nature of our minds, minds that have been conditioned to live in conflict: distracted, anxious, and craving; angry, bitter, and spiteful; prideful, vain, and arrogant; self-righteous, intolerant, and derisive; or, perhaps, fearful, self-conscious, self-loathing, and all the rest of it.

Before beginning a practice of meditation, consider first these two fundamental points:

1: Impermanence: In other words, material forms as well as mental formations—thoughts, perceptions, sensations, emotions, etc.—are never fixed, unchanging, and everlasting;

2: The Voice in Your Head: Your thoughts arise spontaneously, as a constant streaming narrative coursing through your mind.

1: Impermanence

The thought, "You cannot step twice into the same river; for other waters are ever flowing on to you," famously attributed to the ancient Greek philosopher Heraclitus, can be interpreted to mean that not only is the water forever changing from one moment to the next, but you are changing as well.

The world and our individual worlds in it are continuously in flux, impermanent and transitory. The physical world of material forms is constantly cycling from one state to another: dying and decaying, being retransformed and growing anew. Our mental states are never static either. Thought, perception, sensation, attention, and emotion are constantly active and interactive, adapting and changing from moment to moment and situation to situation.

Observe the evidence of impermanence around us: Flowers bloom with bursts of color; blossoms wither and fade. You fall intensely and euphorically in love; you fall intensely and sorrowfully out of love. You gain weight; you lose weight. You fall in love again. A relative passes away; a relative has a baby. You are an omnivore; you become a vegetarian. You crave eating meat and become a flexitarian . . . and so on.

To consider that all is impermanent can generate exhilarating feelings of hope and anticipation for progress and transformation, or, contrarily, anxiety and the fear of loss and the unknown. Regardless, once one acknowledges the truth of impermanence, accepts it with clarity and understanding, he or she will be able to live with a sense of fearlessness and freedom (while also feeling greater gratitude and appreciation for the advantages, privileges, and opportunities in one's current life) as one realizes that no matter the situation, change perpetually takes place. Nothing is static and permanent.

2: The Voice in Your Head

I once found myself sitting in a jazz bar in Taiwan, chatting with a young Taiwanese woman I had become acquainted with through my work as an English teacher. As we sat listening to music, we talked about her previous travels to the U.S., my life in Taiwan, and our past personal relationships. I was having a quite relaxing and enjoyable time when she, a bit abruptly, blurted out, "I hear a voice in my head. You don't think that's strange, do you?"

"Of course not. Everyone has a voice in their head," I replied with an awkward chuckle, as alarm bells clang and the voice in my own head sounded, *Red flag!*

Although admitting to having a voice in your head may not be the most effective getting-to-know-you topic, my companion's admission didn't really put me off. Maybe it was culturally acceptable here to talk about voices rattling around in your head. I had no idea, and as a visitor, I tried to keep an open mind. Besides, we all have a steady stream of thought, an ongoing internal dialogue, a narrative that runs on while processing events as they happen, as they have happened, or as they might happen, no?—a recitation of often random words, ideas, and images: *Does she like me?. . . I should lose some weight . . . Why did she say that? . . . I hate it when people do that . . . Who is he looking at? . . . I should have said this when she said that . . . Where are my keys? . . . I'm so busy . . . What time is it? . . . I shouldn't have done that . . . Everyone likes me . . . Everyone hates me . . .* and on and on, a constant stream of mental jibber-jabber.

Even now, as you read these words, the reading arises in your mind as a voice of thought, your internal narrative. Have you noticed? And every so often, you lose track of—*I need to do that today*—what you're reading—*Why didn't he/she call me?*—as unexpected,—*I should check my text messages*—random thoughts—*I hate it when he/she does that*—inexplicably arise.

Of course, there is nothing wrong with thinking. We certainly need thinking to arrange our lives, make effective decisions, solve problems, and learn new skills. It is not thinking but rather the steady stream of discursive, mundane, oftentimes obsessive, mental prattling that distracts us from being present and grateful for whatever good fortune, advantages, privileges, and comforts that

11

we do have in our lives, right now, as we sit here. The incessant flow of mental chatter keeps us ruminating about a past that no longer exists or anxious about a future that is perpetually yet to arrive. We live distracted, struggling to be present and appreciative in the here and now. This is no revelation; it is the activity of the ego-self. This mental process we can easily observe. But why does this happen, and can we do anything about it? Begin by understanding the activity of the self.

> "If you do not understand the activity of the self, then your meditation only leads to illusion, your meditation then only leads to self-deception, your meditation then will only lead to further self-distortion. So to understand what meditation is, you must understand the activity of the self."—Jiddu Krishnamurti[7]

[7] Jiddu Krishnamurti, *This Light in Oneself* (Krishnamurti Foundation Trust Ltd, 1999) 71

TWO

ACTIVITY OF THE SELF—FIVE DECEITS OF THE CONDITIONED MIND

Life is Suffering

A dentist friend told me of a new patient he had recently seen: a thirty-something woman who was so terrified of going to the dentist that when he approached her as she sat in the dental chair, she broke down and began to weep. This is not pain; this is suffering.

We are all familiar with physical pain. We have observed others or have had our own experience with the discomforts of physical injury, physical exertion, ill health, or aging. Physical discomfort and pain are certain and unavoidable aspects of living. Suffering, though, exists solely in our thoughts. Fear, anxiety, and the torment of suffering are created from the conversations we have with ourselves, occurring solely in our heads.

The answer to ending mental suffering can be found at the

source of mental suffering, that is, the activity of the self, the origins of the incessant mental prattling, the discursive internal narrative that keeps us disengaged, distracted, and anxious. What, exactly, is all our mental jibber-jabber about?

Activity of the Self

1. The Illusory Self
2. Social Status and the Conditioned Mind
3. Body Image
4. The Craving for Sensation
5. The Dualistic Worldview

1: The Illusory Self

I often came across the notion that the sense of self is an illusion, that the sense of identity and ego are illusory.

> "Attachment to the self is a fact, but the self that is the object of that attachment has no true existence; it exists nowhere and in no way as an autonomous and permanent entity."—Matthieu Ricard[8]

I didn't get it. How can this be? I know who I am and who I am is how I present myself to the world. Who I am is how people know me. Here I am. I have a history. You can see me, touch me. I exist. What does it mean, exactly, to claim that the "I" is illusory? Can this be defined, and then, how does an attachment to the illusory self inevitably result in conflict and suffering?

Who are you? Think about that, beginning with your birth, being named by your parents, and everything that you know, feel, have opinions on, have experienced, and are able to do. The image you describe may include information such as the following:

[8] Jean-Francois Revel & Matthieu Ricard, *The Monk and the Philosopher*, (Random House, 1998) 31

- Name and Age
- Place of Birth (Nationality)
- Physical Appearance (Ethnicity)
- Personality and Emotional Traits
- Academic History
- Profession and Professional History
- Personal and Professional Achievements
- Past Disappointments
- Past Emotional and Physical Traumas
- Unique Knowledge, Skills, and Hobbies
- Family Responsibilities and History
- Religion
- Health Status
- Immediate, Short-term, and Long-term Goals
- Location of Residence
- Possessions and Accumulated Wealth

This is your story—Mr. or Ms. XYZ—the image of your "self" and whatever you believe about yourself, your life, your relationships, your work, your possessions, your past, and your future. These are the words and images that make you *you*, a unique, autonomous identity distinct from others.

Most everything defining who you are resides in your memory. How could you know yourself if you lost all memory of past experiences? How would you describe yourself if you forgot all factual memory of your life? How much ability could you demonstrate if you could not remember how to perform the skills you have acquired over a lifetime?

If memory is necessary to define who you are, then let us consider what memory is.

Memories—Constructs of the Brain

Many believe that experiential memory is like a movie camera that accurately records episodes in time. It is not.[9] Can you be certain of the accuracy of memories? Studies suggest otherwise.

We have experiences and believe our perceptions and thoughts of events to be factual, but they are undoubtedly colored by our mental, emotional, and physical states at the time, our level of attention or inattention, our attitudes and prejudices. We have perceptions that are inexact, and after we interpret these dubious impressions, our brains may then construct and encode a memory. Experiential memories, though, are not normally encoded as a whole and complete account. Current research shows that only a general representation or individual features of an original event are stored in memory, and it is only later that we then add details to recreate, fabricate, and, finally, re-encode a fresh narrative of the memory *each time we recall it.*[10] In the here and now, when conjuring up a past occurrence, our minds elaborate on a scant recollection by filling in the gaps with what we expect should have taken place. We refer to familiarity, expectations, and whatever other inputs, suggestions, and influences we have received since the experience to complete the narrative. Although a memory is typically based on an actual event, comprehensive details are often lost; memories can be confused (e.g., a memory may be misidentified with an incorrect time, place, or participant); memories can be distorted (e.g., a memory or aspects of it may have been appropriated from something we read, heard from another person, or picked up from some other source)[11]; completely false memories can be created by a questioner's leading and suggestive enquiry[12], and so on. Memories are known to be malleable and impermanent, false, imagined, coerced, and, oftentimes, completely missing. Memory is far from infallible.

Memories—our thoughts and images of past experiences, our mental collection of facts, our ability to remember how to per-

[9] Leonard Mlodinow, *Subliminal, How Your Unconscious Mind Rules Your Behavior* (Pantheon Books, 2012) 58-59

[10] Mlodinow, *Subliminal, How Your Unconscious Mind Rules Your Behavior,* 66-78

[11] Daniel Schacter, *"The Sin of Misattribution"* in *The Seven Sins of Memory* (Houghton Mifflin Company, 2001) 88-111

[12] Schacter, *"The Sin of Suggestibility"* in *The Seven Sins of Memory,* 112-137

form acquired skills—are stored as patterns of structural connections between the neurons (nerve cells) of our brains. Though these networks of neural connections regularly break down and fragment, they are reconstructed when we attempt to recall an event; then, electrochemical signals, once again, occur between neurons, strengthening old or creating new connections.[13] This activity of memory twinkles within the vast cosmos of our brains, which are estimated to consist of from 86 to 100 billion neurons with over 100 trillion connections.[14][15] We have memories, yes, but they are impermanent, constantly organizing and reorganizing as patterns and networks of mutable neural connections.

In everyday life, though, our memory serves us practically enough. We remember where we left our keys; we remember how to get to the supermarket and where we parked the car; we remember to keep our appointments and how to use our electronic gadgets. Memory is quite necessary to function efficiently. It also allows us to maintain intimately connected to our world: recognizing the aroma of a home-cooked meal, bringing to mind an image of our joyous children, recalling the melody of a favorite song, and so on. And, of course, we need memory to accumulate knowledge so that we can protect ourselves, maintain our physical health, learn new skills, innovate, build, and create.

Memory is necessary to maintain order in our world. It keeps us connected to the familiar. It creates structure for our daily living and gives us a basis to improve upon, to move forward, and there is nothing adverse to recalling experiences that bring joy or insight or meaning to our lives. Life would be dull and confusing without memory.

[13] Schacter, *The Seven Sins of Memory*, 32-33

[14] Bradley Voytek, *Are There Really as Many Neurons in the Human Brain as Stars in the Milky Way?* (Nature Education, Nature Publishing Group, 05/20/13), http://www.nature.com/scitable/blog/brain-metrics/are_there_really_as_many (retrieved 05/28/2014)

[15] *Neuron*, Wikipedia, http://en.wikipedia.org/wiki/Neuron#cite_note-nervenet-28 (retrieved 05/28/2014)

The Illusion

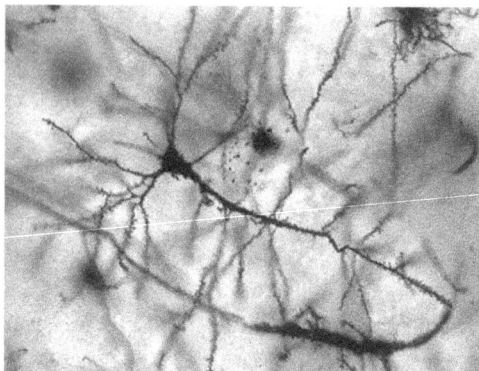

Neuron, 40 times magnification[16]

In addition to memory-like thoughts, most of what makes up the rest of our personal stories are thoughts about our: beliefs, plans for the future, valuation of possessions, and interpretations of the world. This is the foundation for the self, the mental construct of identity, the ego. We all have our stories, and the illusion is the belief that our stories, our identities, our egos, our selves—fabrications of memory and thought—are tangible, actual, and permanent. They are not.

Let us say I am a teacher in my professional life and I am sitting at a sunny café, drinking tea and reading this book. Who am I? I think, *I am Mr. XYZ, who graduated from the University of ABC with a degree in 123, and I am a teacher at the school of blah-blah-blah. I can juggle and play the accordion, and I have been recognized for this and that, and my childhood was happy or sad or mundane, and yap-yap-yap.* This would be the story in my mind of who I am based on memory-like thoughts. Perhaps I would add thoughts of an imagined fu-

[16] *Pyramidal hippocampal neuron 40x*, Creative Commons Attribution-Share Alike 2.5 Generic, http://commons.wikimedia.org/wiki/File:Pyramidal_hippocampal_neuron_40x.jpg (retrieved 04/16/2014)

ture, *I am Mr. XYZ, who also is going to get married next year and who has to go to the bank after leaving this café.*

Now perhaps you come in and sit at the next table and we become acquainted. I would introduce myself as Mr. XYZ, who graduated from the University of ABC with a degree in 123, and I am a teacher at the school of blah-blah-blah. I can juggle and play the accordion and yadda-yadda-yadda . . .

I am now facilitating the fabrication in your mind of my narrative, the who of the I am. When you think of me, Mr. XYZ, you reconstruct in your head this mental story, this collection of thoughts, twinkling patterns of neural connections that have been conveyed from my mind to be constructed as twinkling networks of neural connections in your mind. As I meet more people and more people get to know me, my individual ego story begins to develop into a larger collective illusion of who I am—my persona, my image, my social facade.

If it is suggested that my identity is an illusion, I might ask, "How can my being a teacher be an illusion? I AM a teacher!" Of course, but the basis for this statement is wholly dependent on memory-like thought, because at the moment, I am not teaching. I am sitting in a sunny café, chatting with you, a newly acquainted stranger. I have taught classes of students before and will, perhaps, teach once again. Possibly, but not necessarily so, because while the potential to teach again exists, potentiality is simply a likelihood, a possibility, a promise for the future. There is nothing realized about it. In fact, if I were to suffer a traumatic brain injury in the next moment—I spill my tea, jump back, trip over my chair and crack my head on the edge of your table—I may lose all ability to ever teach again.

Does my "story" constitute a definite reality, existing outside of thought? Do I exist here, in the present, as a teacher, or am I nothing more than a friendly stranger with a story? My relating to you who I am is no different from my reading a storybook out loud. You hear and imagine the tale, but it consists of only words, images, and ideas. Do not be fooled. The story is not happening;

there is nothing actual about it. The realness of what I am, my be-ing, is the activity that I am engaged in at the present—a teacher teaching, a parent parenting, a student studying, a traveler travel-ing, a passerby passing by. My being is not the past that does not exist nor the potential future that has yet to arrive. My being a teacher at this moment is illusory because be-ing is the present, which exists only in action. Right now . . . and now. Reality is the action of living. Being is energy and movement. Anything else is a thought-constructed story in my mind or the mind of others.

Okay then, so what? We all have our stories to tell when we need to present ourselves to the world. It is normal and necessary to relate our stories to others by way of introduction. What is wrong with having a story? Nothing. At all. It is not the story that causes anxiety and suffering. It is the voice of ego refusing to acknowledge that the stories we carry in our heads about our-selves are purely mental constructs. It is the voice of ego that is constantly fabricating a grander, more complex, more exclusive tale. It is the voice of ego that craves attention, approval, and recognition for a story that exists only in the mental projection of our imaginations. It is the egoistic chattering jibber-jabber of thought that causes us to believe that instead of just "be-ing," we are "some-thing"—an idea: unique, special, individual, which re-sults in comparing and separating oneself from others, with com-parison and separation invariably leading to conflict: "I" versus "other," creating pride, arrogance, self-righteousness, intolerance, jealousy, resentment, anger, sorrow, insecurity, self-pity, shame, self-doubt, self-loathing, and all the rest of it. Believing in and clinging to an intangible, mentally-constructed ego-story is futility, a source of mental torment.

The Collective Illusion

Besides having to contend with our own mental nattering, our minds are also preoccupied with the perceived chatter of others. We judge ourselves by how we imagine others see and judge us, which means the ego-story is supported and maintained and bolstered through the eyes of others (or, otherwise, threatened, damaged, and destroyed). There is an image that we assume others—friends, relatives, colleagues, neighbors, acquaintances, and so on—have privately fabricated about us in their minds. It is this construct of imagination that is often the topic with which our prattling voices of ego are occupied: *What do they think of me? They like me. They don't like me. What did she mean when she said that? She didn't say hello to me. She's mad at me. Why was he so rude to me? Why doesn't he like me? They're talking about me. Do they think I'm good? Talented? Admirable? Successful? Insignificant? Dull? A bore?*

We become neurotic over not only the personal but also the collective illusion of our ego-stories. Much of our discursive, egoistic mind chatter arises because the imagined realness of our ego-stories is reinforced and empowered by the collective illusion of who we are in the nattering minds of those around us. In essence, we have mind chatter about the mind chatter of others! And the greatest folly is believing that these others are so greatly concerned with our ego-stories when, in truth, they are singularly obsessed with their own ego-identity, their own ambitions, cravings, aversions, and fears, their own private mental universe.

2: Social Status and the Conditioned Mind

If it is a basic, egoistic human condition to crave attention, approval, and recognition from others, consider what the "others" respect, value, and desire. Let us examine Victor Lebow, a 20th century economist and retail analyst who had this take on the American way of life in 1955:

> "Our enormously productive economy demands that we make consumption our way of life, that we convert the buying and use of goods into rituals, that we seek our spiritual satisfactions, our ego satisfactions, in consumption. The measure of social status, of social acceptance, of prestige,

is now to be found in our consumptive patterns. The very meaning and significance of our lives today expressed in consumptive terms. The greater the pressures upon the individual to conform to safe and accepted social standards, the more does he tend to express his aspirations and his individuality in terms of what he wears, drives, eats—his home, his car, his pattern of food serving, his hobbies.

These commodities and services must be offered to the consumer with a special urgency . . . We need things consumed, burned up, worn out, replaced, and discarded at an ever increasing pace. We need to have people eat, drink, dress, ride, live, with ever more complicated and, therefore, constantly more expensive consumption."[17]

Shopping for Status and Recognition

There is something gratifying about the process of shopping, isn't there? Seeking out an object, considering the virtues of one choice over another, completing the transaction, and taking possession of the item. We gain a sense of satisfaction, accomplishment, and achievement through acquisition and ownership, especially so if the desired object is admired by others.

In some ways, shopping invents this purpose with which we can believe our life has meaning. For if we have the necessities of food, water, shelter, clothing, and healthcare, for what other motivation is working and accumulating additional wealth if nothing is ever purchased? Numbers of dollars piling up in a bank account have no practical significance.

Shopping is action. We aren't sitting at home just watching television; we're accomplishing something! Perhaps it fulfills some primal hunting-gathering urge to seek out and collect. Instead of returning with food, we display the spoils gathered from the shopping mall so that others can nod their approval, offering recognition of our originality, our style, our good judgment, our knowl-

[17] Victor Lebow, *Price Competition in 1955* (Journal of Retailing, Spring, 1955)

edge, our financial capabilities, and other ego-pleasing distinctions. We can construct and display our egoistic "I" story through the objects we possess and the lifestyles that the objects represent. We fulfill the egoistic craving for identity. We can become somebody unique, stylish, and individual, through what we buy. Is that it?

With pointed insight, the Bhutanese lama, filmmaker, and writer, Dzongsar Jamyang Khyentse Rinpoche, refers to the objects through which our material culture defines success and happiness as "grown-up baby rattles,"[18] playthings that captivate our attention as we purposefully distract ourselves from the true nature of our mundane existence.

Doesn't owning particular objects give you a sense of satisfaction, a sense of accomplishment, a sense of pride, a sense of importance? Isn't the mind chatter of your ego attached to the uniquely-yours possessions? It is quite reasonable, actually, for if your sense of self is based on a "story in your head" that is not tangible, what better way to make the story real than by fabricating an identity from an accumulation of physical objects? I am these things that can be seen and touched. I am the "insert famous brand or latest gadget here" guy or girl.

It does make one feel good, no? We feel smug, self-satisfied, proud that we have more or have something that is coveted by others (or, contrarily, inadequate because of what we lack). This is accompanied, once again, with separating and comparing—mine versus other's—leading to arrogance and greed, envy and resentment, to conflict and animosity, selfishness and loneliness, all expressed as discursive thought in the prattle of one's mind.

Can attachment to objects ever lead to true contentment, or can it result only in discontent? Can the voice of ego ever be content when the marketing and media machine constantly hound us with messages that our lack of the new this or that makes us unsuccessful and out of touch, a bore and a dullard, while those who

[18] Dzongsar Jamyang Khyentse Rinpoche, *What Makes You not a Buddhist* (Shambhala, 2007) 10

possess the latest brands and gadgets and styles are trendy and cool, fashionable and hip. We hear the message, and the chattering ego, conditioned by the marketing machine, constantly lives one product cycle removed from becoming insignificant.

Then there is the fear, obsessive and compulsive, when the truth of impermanence reveals objects and forms becoming old and damaged, decaying into nonexistence. We fear our possessions becoming dirty, stained, imperfect, broken down, outdated and obsolete. We become concerned with maintaining the physical perfection of our things with which we identify so as to prolong our personal illusion of permanence and immortality.

Ultimately, everything leads back to the jibber-jabber of ego. When Mr. Lebow asserts, "The measure of social status, of social acceptance, of prestige, is now to be found in our consumptive patterns," we can imagine the egoistic voice craving for recognition in the collective mental prattle of others.

Do you truly believe that what you possess represents who you are? You are the baby rattles that you own? This is some type of madness.

Regard the work of Edward Bernays, the "father of public relations," who combined the ideas of crowd psychology with the psychoanalytic ideas of his uncle, Sigmund Freud, to pioneer innovative public relations techniques used by both government and business to manipulate public opinion. A review of his book titles is revealing: Crystallizing Public Opinion (1923), Propaganda (1928), This Business of Propaganda (1928), Manipulating Public Opinion (1928), The Engineering of Consent (1955). In his 1928 book *Propaganda*, he writes:

> "The conscious and intelligent manipulation of the organized habits and opinions of the masses is an important element in democratic society. Those who manipulate this unseen mechanism of society constitute an invisible government which is the true ruling power of our country …

ACTIVITY OF THE SELF—FIVE DECEITS OF
THE CONDITIONED MIND

We are governed, our minds are molded, our tastes formed, our ideas suggested, largely by men we have never heard of.[19]

" … it remains a fact that in almost every act of our daily lives, whether in the sphere of politics or business, in our social conduct or our ethical thinking, we are dominated by the relatively small number of persons—a trifling fraction of our hundred and twenty million—who understand the mental processes and social patterns of the masses. It is they who pull the wires which control the public mind, who harness old social forces and contrive new ways to bind and guide the world."[20]

"If we understand the mechanism and motives of the group mind, is it not possible to control and regiment the masses according to our will without their knowing it?"[21]

A well-known example of Bernays' revolutionary marketing techniques is the "PR stunt," in which a business promotes a product by engineering an event targeted at the news media. The campaign that garnered him industry fame was devising for the cigarette industry a strategy to make women's smoking socially acceptable and to encourage more women to smoke.

During the 1920s, it was taboo (and in some places illegal) for a woman to smoke in public. Hired by the American Tobacco Company, Bernays arranged for fashion models masquerading as supporters of female emancipation and gender equality to march down Fifth Avenue in New York City during the 1929 Easter Parade. Upon his signal, the young women defiantly pulled out and lit their cigarettes, referring to them as their "Torches of Freedom." Bernays, of course, had sent a press release to the media in

[19] Edward Bernays, *Propaganda*, (1928) 9
[20] Bernays, *Propaganda*, (1928) 10
[21] Bernays, *Propaganda*, (1928) 47

advance so that they would be there to record the controversial "news" event. The campaign ignited national discussion, eventually leading to the increased acceptance of women's smoking in public, a greater number of women smokers, and great improvements in the profits of the tobacco industries (no such advance for women's health, I imagine).[22][23]

Why believe what you believe?

It is worthwhile to consider why you do the things you do, value the things you value, believe what you believe, and live the way you live. What is the rationale for all these ideas? Is your perspective your own, or have your thoughts been shrewdly manipulated, conditioned by social forces?

The cultural world of which we are a part has shaped and conditioned our mental make-up. Haven't you noticed? Psychology professor and author Ronald T. Kellogg points out that we "swim in culture in much the way fish swim in water. Culture surrounds us and we breathe it in as a kind of mental oxygen."[24] Thus, at some level, we all share conventional modes of behavior, rituals, customs, norms, and mores. These are the threads that interweave and create the cultural fabric of which we are a part: a common language, shared beliefs and thought processes, the manner in which we express ourselves, a historical and cultural narrative, preferences for food and fashion, ideals of success, love, and prosperity, attitudes toward politics and religion, opinions about the world, and so on. These are values, ideas, and beliefs that have been contrived by some other, values, ideas, and beliefs that we

[22] Allan M. Brandt, *Recruiting women smokers: the engineering of consent* (Journal of the American Medical Women's Association 51(1-2), 1996) 63-66, http://dash.harvard.edu/bitstream/handle/1/3372908/Brandt_Recruiting.pdf?sequence=1 (retrieved 05/05/2014)

[23] Amanda Amos, Margaretha Haglund, *From Social Taboo to "Torch of Freedom": the Marketing of Cigarettes to Women* (Tobacco Control 9.1, 2000), http://tobaccocontrol.bmj.com/content/9/1/3.full (retrieved 05/05/2014)

[24] Ronald T. Kellogg, *The Making of the Mind* (Prometheus Books, 2013) 58

have been conditioned to unquestioningly follow. We have been conditioned so readily that we have not at all noticed. Consider the account of this "experiment" popularized years ago in business and self-help books:

In the middle of a small room, a ladder is positioned beneath a bunch of bananas hanging from the ceiling. Five monkeys are placed in the room, and after a short time, one of the monkeys spots the bananas and scampers up the ladder to grab them. At that moment not only is this monkey blasted off the ladder with a jet of ice-cold water, but the rest of the monkeys are sprayed with ice-cold water as well. Bewildered, the monkeys screech and shake themselves dry.

Soon, another monkey makes its way toward the ladder to grab the bananas. The others are watching as, once again, blasts of ice-cold water knock the monkey off the ladder and also soak the others. This situation is repeated until the monkeys realize that reaching for the bananas offers the unpleasant and shivering prospect of an ice-cold shower of water.

Next, one of the monkeys is removed and replaced with a new monkey. After a short while, it notices the bananas hanging from the ceiling and makes its way to the ladder. The original four monkeys immediately shriek and attack the new monkey, dragging it away from the ladder. After several attempts followed by attacks from the others, the new monkey realizes that going up the ladder to retrieve the bananas is prohibited. This new monkey has now become wary of going up the ladder to retrieve the bananas.

Another of the original monkeys is removed and a second new monkey is introduced. Predictably, this new monkey eyes the bananas hanging from the ceiling and approaches the ladder. Once again, not only do the three remaining original monkeys attack the second new monkey, but the first new monkey also joins in the assault, attacking and dragging the second new monkey away from the ladder.

This scenario repeats itself as, one by one, the remaining three original monkeys are replaced by new monkeys until none of the original monkeys remain. In the end, there are five new monkeys in the room, none of whom have experienced the earlier blasts of cold water. Regardless, all five still refuse to climb the ladder to grab the bananas. They have been conditioned to behave in a counterintuitive way, and they live this way without having any experience of why.

This tale was used to depict the habituated workings of corporate and institutional culture but, apparently, was never proved to have actually taken place. Still, it can illustrate the notion of conditioned knowledge in human society and how the origin of traditions, rituals, values, and beliefs can be so far removed from one's present reality that a person can be ignorant to their rationale or original purpose, and, nevertheless, he or she blindly follows these modes of thinking and behavior that can be counterintuitive, nonsensical, and are simply not of one's own mind, not of one's own wisdom, not of one's own understanding of the truth.

Are your thoughts your own? Are your thoughts and values grounded in the truth, or are they the dogma of some other?

The Business of Perpetual Dissatisfaction

As the business industry utilizes marketing, media, and public relations models to "control and regiment the masses," we, the masses, become conditioned to living by the business industry paradigm of unlimited consumption. This is our modern material culture: "The measure of social status, of social acceptance, of prestige, is now to be found in our consumptive patterns. The very meaning and significance of our lives today expressed in consumptive terms . . . We need things consumed, burned up, worn out, replaced, and discarded at an ever increasing pace. We need to have people eat, drink, dress, ride, live, with ever more complicated and, therefore, constantly more expensive consumption."

ACTIVITY OF THE SELF—FIVE DECEITS OF
THE CONDITIONED MIND

If you are the average modern consumer, your home is stocked with a vast collection of possessions. You have rooms and shelves and closets and cabinets and drawers and garages and storage sheds to arrange, display, and stockpile your belongings. And still, there exists a tiny bit of dissatisfaction with what you have. Doesn't there? As if however much you have is not enough. As if you need only to purchase that next item from the catalog or the mall or the online store and life would be that much better. Then you do purchase that next thing and life IS better. Oh, for a few weeks, a few months perhaps, after you have acquired the new baby rattle to display and shake, yes, you feel a sense of excitement and satisfaction.

Imperceptibly, though, you sense a bit of regret, of discontent, of emptiness. The media and marketing machine begins again to insinuate itself into the ego chatter of pride and insecurity and dissatisfaction, because, of course, you must be kept perpetually dissatisfied so that you will continue to consume, your consumption fueling the economic machine. Look around your house. How much of what you own functionally improves your life? How much of what you own is attractive mainly because it boasts some social value, a social value fabricated and contrived by business, media, and marketers whose utopia is to have you spend your life forever dedicated to nurturing the economic machine?

How much stuff do you really need? I look at my bull terrier, Chubby, and he appears quite content to spend the day lying in the sun, running in the park, receiving the odd scratch here and there, and eating one nutritious and satisfying meal per day. Admittedly, he isn't especially productive, but neither does he demand much in resources. As with the other living creatures with whom we share this earth, the amount of resources he consumes for his survival is minimal. Contrast this with the average modern consumer, each needing a house, a car, furniture, appliances, a wardrobe, disposable electronic gadgets, more clothes, storage bins, three processed meals per day, more disposable electronic gadgets, processed snacks,

Chubby and the Goddess of Mercy

several more storage containers, a garage full of baby rattles, and so on. Every individual. Can we just regulate ourselves a bit, please? Beyond the essentials of food, water, shelter, clothing, and healthcare, the rest is extraneous—convenience, entertainment, and distraction. I am not suggesting we all become Luddites. Certain tools and technologies undeniably contribute to a more efficient and stimulating and enjoyable life, but can we not direct ourselves closer to a more moderate path? Humankind is over-consuming, depleting natural resources, and destroying the very environment necessary to sustain human life. Our behavior is counterintuitive to our survival, and yet, we compulsively march forward, searching for happiness and a tangible identity by means of a socioeconomic matrix designed to condition our egos into a state of perpetual dissatisfaction. It is madness.

So not only do we struggle against the endless blathering of our own ego-story and the collective illusion of what others imagine us to be, but we are also subject to a socioeconomic matrix that defines where we fit into society, our social status, a place characterized by our "consumptive patterns." This results in the further mental torment of insecurity and dissatisfaction as we have been conditioned to ceaselessly crave the accumulation and display of possessions.

Is it any wonder we suffer from so much anxiety? In a 2009 report, the National Institute of Mental Health, a component of the U.S. Department of Health and Human Services, states that "Anxiety Disorders affect about 40 million American adults age 18 years and older (about 18%) in a given year, causing them to be filled with fearfulness and uncertainty."[25]

3: Body Image: Attachment to the Physical

If we can fabricate a sense of identity from the things we own, what can be more natural than identifying with our physical bodies. We possess a sense of ownership of our bodies. We look in the mirror and there we are. We think "smile" and our faces smile back at us. We are bound within these physical bodies, objects of the world, with properties that can be experienced: size, color, scent, texture, and so on. Unlike thought, the body is tangible. Unlike possessions, my body *is* me. We are quite sure of it. It all seems so reasonable—until our bodily self-image is redirected into a rubber hand.

The Rubber Hand Illusion

You may be familiar with the rubber hand illusion. In this experiment, researchers discovered they could convince participants to feel that a fake rubber hand was the subject's own.[26] You can try this yourself with two small paintbrushes, a tabletop screen or partition, a towel or piece of cloth, a partner, and, of course, a rubber hand (a tissue-stuffed rubber glove may suffice). This is how it works:

Sit at a table and place your forearm and hand down in

[25] *Anxiety Disorders* (National Institute of Mental Health), http://www.nimh.nih.gov/health/topics/anxiety-disorders/index.shtml (retrieved 04/07/2014)

[26] Matthew Botvinick and Jonathan Cohen, *Rubber hands 'feel' touch that eyes see* (Nature, Nature Publishing Group, Vol. 391, Feb 19, 1998)

front of you. Move your hand slightly to the side, away from your body and place the rubber hand in its place. Set up the partition between the rubber hand and your real hand to block your view of your hand. You can now see only the rubber hand on the table. Drape the cloth from your shoulder to the rubber hand to act as a shirtsleeve-type covering as you do not want the rubber hand to be lying isolated on the table.

As you stare at the table, next to the rubber hand, your partner should brush the rubber hand and your real hand in the same way, simultaneously. The partner should brush different fingers and different parts of the hand, carefully keeping the motions identical and synchronized. Most people will soon experience an eerie shift in perception: they feel that the rubber hand is their own. If the rubber hand is threatened with a hammer or knife, participants will flinch in fear.

Have your partner continue to brush your hand and the rubber hand. Close your eyes and use your opposite hand to point at where you are being touched. You will point to the rubber hand! You know the hand is fake, but, still, you feel the rubber hand has become part of your body, part of you.

After the experiment, people say things like: "I really felt that my hand was transposed into that false hand." "I found myself looking at the fake hand thinking it was actually my own." "I felt like I could really move those fingers if I wanted to."

The effect is not only mental but physical as well: When participants felt the rubber hand becoming part of their own body, their real hand registered a drop in temperature, as if it were being "dis-owned."[27]

[27] Thakkar KN, Nichols HS, McIntosh LG, Park S, *Disturbances in Body Ownership in Schizophrenia: Evidence from the Rubber Hand Illusion and Case Study of a Spontaneous Out-of-Body Experience* (PLoS ONE 6(10): e27089. doi:10.1371/journal.pone.0027089, 2011), http://www.plosone.org/article/info%3Adoi%2F10.1371%2Fjournal.pone.0027089 (retrieved 04/07/2014)

The experiment can be repeated with an additional person, who places his or her hand on the table to replace the rubber hand. The original participant would then begin to feel as if the new person's hand were his or her own. The subject would feel as if he or she could move the other person's fingers if one wanted to.

A further experiment, called *The Body Swap Illusion*, showed that not only a hand, but a person's bodily sense of "self" could be similarly manipulated, fooling the participant into feeling that a mannequin and, finally, another person's body was one's own. The researchers state "how remarkably easy it is to 'move' a human centre of awareness from one body to another."[28][29]

It appears that perceptions of vision, touch, and proprioception (a sense of body position) are coordinated in our brains to create a sense of ownership of our bodies and that this impression of being embodied in a physical self is not fixed and permanent but rather a malleable projection of our minds.

Besides the sense of ownership of our bodies, there is also the sense that we dictate control over our bodies' behavior that leads us to believe, *This physical body is me*. But imagine you are driving on a long trip. The road is monotonous and seemingly unending as the sun's glare strains and exhausts your eyes. You have no radio. The sound of the wind and road noise drone on. Your eyes are heavy as you drift into stupor. Your mind alerts you, "Stay awake!" Nevertheless, "your" body requires sleep, ignores your mindful pleas, and eyelids, heavy with fatigue, gradually droop into unconsciousness. How much of your bodily action are you truly in command of? You are out of breath trudging up a hill, your eye twitches, you are nauseous and about to throw up, you have to urinate and can no longer hold it, you feel dizzy and faint, or, more soberly, you have a stroke or heart attack or other serious health condition.

[28] Petkova VI, Ehrsson HH, *If I Were You: Perceptual Illusion of Body Swapping* (PLoS ONE 3(12): e3832.doi:10.1371/journal.pone.0003832, 2008) http://www.plosone.org/article/info%3Adoi%2F10.1371%2Fjournal.pone.0003832 (retrieved 04/07/2014)

[29] Mo Costandi, *Your plastic self* (ThInk, April 7, 2013), http://thinkneuroscience.wordpress.com/2013/04/07/your-plastic-self (retrieved 04/07/2014)

Take a minute to think about it and notice that "your" body regularly takes action regardless of your conscious wishes or intentions.

Body-image and Identity

As with our ego-stories, our body-image identities are subject to the same individual and collective mental prattling. We judge our physical value based on society's arbitrary ideals of attractiveness. We adopt an attitude, a look, in order to display—*This is my style,* which once again returns us to "my story," the individual and collective illusion. Inevitably, this results in anxiety and conflict about how we compare to society's arbitrary, media-driven ideal, and the accompanying ego chatter: *I'm fat. I'm unattractive. I'm a geek.* Unless, of course, you are one of the "beautiful" people. Anxiety and conflict? None at all. Your mental gibberish sounds more like: *I'm thin! I'm beautiful! I'm cool! Others notice me! Admire me! Envy me!* You are undoubtedly fortunate. Well, except for the downside. That is, behind the strut of vanity lies the truth of impermanence, and eventually, the truth of impermanence can no longer be denied. You one day face the mirror, and the mental prattling of fear and anxiety arises: *My skin looks blotchy, loose, saggy. Can they inject something to puff up my face. How much is botox? Or a chemical peel? Laser surgery? Oh, a gray hair. My hair is thinning. Will I look younger if I dye my hair? My eyes look tired. I'm getting soft. My whole body is droopy. I'm losing muscle tone.*

No, it is not your appearance that causes anxiety and suffering. It is the voice of ego grasping at society's collective mental chatter regarding arbitrary ideals of attractiveness. It is the voice of ego refusing to accept the truth of impermanence. It is the voice of ego that is attached to and becomes consumed by the illusion of "my" body-image. It is the jibber-jabber of egoistic thought that causes you to believe that you are "some-thing"—a body image unique, special, individual—which results in comparing and separating yourself from others, with comparison and separation invariably leading to conflict: "I" versus "other," creating pride, arrogance, jealousy, resentment, anger, sorrow, insecurity, self-pity, shame, self-doubt, discontent. Attachment to the body-image is the source of mental torment, and it is torment because attaching to and identifying with impermanent conditions or an illusory image is futile. It is all so familiar. Is it not?

4: Craving Sensation

Attachment to the physical does not necessarily equate to vanity or body-image anxiety. It can also manifest itself as a craving for sensation: food, sex, exercise, and so on.

Craving arises when our senses are stimulated and we perceive an object or endeavour as providing pleasurable sensation, or when movement of thought involves grasping at memories of a pleasurable sensory experience—images, emotions, tastes, touch, sounds—along with the anticipation and longing that accompany the desire for satiation. Mental conflict arises when desire cannot be satisfied, and as the mental dissonance increases, the craving for satiation becomes focused and obsessive, accumulating tension and creating agitation. Our thoughts obsess on satiation, the means of satiation, the process of satiation.

Satiation then brings release. Release from the persistent compulsion of a preoccupied and chattering mind. Release from mental irritation and distraction, release from emotional and physical tension. Finally, satiated, the body and mind become still, languid, whole, temporarily, until the anxiety, the mental chattering of craving returns. To seek satiation means to constantly crave sensation. Craving undoubtedly returns. Contentment is fleeting.

This is not to suggest that physical sensory experience should be avoided. Of course not. There is nothing unnatural or unseemly about experiencing sensation, physical and emotional enjoyment and pleasure. Life would be less vibrant, dull and uninspired, without a variety of sensory experiences. No, it is not physical sensation that causes torment. It is the excessive mental chatter of craving that causes discontent; it is indulging the mental prattle of your craving while disregarding other aspects of your life that causes suffering; it is allowing a craving to result in physical or emotional harm to yourself or others that creates conflict and misery.

5: Perception—The Dualistic Mind—Non-duality

Perception is reality?

The first time I heard the expression *perception is reality*, it seemed to suggest that whatever you subjectively perceive to be or not to be exists as your reality and you are not constrained by the external world. I didn't quite get it. This thought came to mind while I was traveling by train through India, reading a local newspaper report describing a scenario that I imagine is becoming more common worldwide:

> On Saturday afternoon, an unidentified teenaged boy, who was using earphones to listen to music while texting, never heard the train coming. The teen had walked around the lowered crossing gates and into the path of a speeding train. The victim, rushed to a private hospital with severe head injuries and a severed leg, did not survive.
> "The train horn was blowing and people were shouting, warning him about the oncoming train, but he never noticed. It was too late," said a witness.

Apparently, this young man's perceptions of reality consisted of his music and the text he was typing. The train may not have existed in the teen's perception of reality, but it surely existed as an actual form in the external world.

A reality where your perceptions have no restrictions from an external world, and you are limited by only thought and imagination, is called a dream, or, perhaps, a delusion. Real life consists of your perceptions constrained by circumstances of the external world, and your survival, clearly, can be adversely affected by the external world of energy and material forms. Perception alone does not constitute reality, so as your mother would say, "Stop daydreaming! Look both ways before crossing the street!"

Perception IS reality. Sort of.

"There is no single face in nature because every eye that looks upon it, sees it from its own angle. So every man's spice box seasons his own food."—Zora Neale Hurston

It is true that we do not directly experience the external world, and it is our perceptions that make up our sense of reality. Our sense organs are stimulated by the various energies, forces, and chemicals in the external world around us and transmit this information as electrical nerve impulses to our brains. Our brains then interpret, organize, and define the information as phenomena and experience. We define light, a form of energy called electromagnetic radiation, as color when some object reflects (or emits) particular parts of the visible light spectrum and stimulates our eyes. The idea of color, however, does not exist in the energy of electromagnetic radiation. We hear music and sound, but the notion of music and sound does not exist in the mechanical energy of sound waves that vibrate our eardrums. We smell flowers or fresh-brewed coffee or rotting garbage, but the concept of pleasant and unpleasant fragrances does not exist in the chemical molecules that stimulate our noses. We taste sweet, sour, bitter, salty, and umami, but flavors do not exist in the chemical molecules that stimulate our sense of taste. We touch rough and smooth, feel pressure and vibration, but these definitions do not exist at the sensory receptors that are stimulated in our skin and muscles. Sensory information is transmitted by electrical impulses to our brains, where—depending on the state of our experience, knowledge, opinions, moods, and feelings—it is then defined as being one thing or another.

Our sense of reality, then, *is* a mental fabrication. We live inside worlds of perceptions that exist only in our minds, patterns of electrochemical activity in our brains. They are worlds constrained by the limitations of our sensory awareness and the degree of mindfulness we accord our perceptions. Zhuang-zi, the ancient Chinese Taoist philosopher, relates the story of a frog that lived in an old, dilapidated well:

井底之蛙

一口廢井裏住著一隻青蛙。有一天，青蛙在井邊碰上了一隻從海裏來的大龜。青蛙就對海龜誇口說：「你看，我住在這裏多快樂！有時高興了，就在井欄邊跳躍一陣；疲倦了，就回到井裏，睡在磚洞邊一回。或者只留出頭和嘴巴，安安靜靜地把全身泡在水裏；或者在軟綿綿的泥漿裏散一回步，也很舒適。看看那些蝦和蝌蝦，誰也比不上我。而且，我是這個井裏的主人，在這井裏極自由自在，你爲什麼不常到井裏來遊賞呢！」那海龜聽了青蛙的話，倒真想進去看看。但它的左腳還沒有整個伸進去，右腳就已經絆住了。它連忙後退了兩步，把大海的情形告訴青蛙說：「你看過海嗎？海的廣大，哪止千里；海的深度，哪只千來丈。古時候，十年有九年大水，海裏的水，並不漲了多少；後來，八年裏有七年大旱，海裏的水，也不見得淺了多少。可見大海是不受旱澇影響的。住在那樣的大海裏，才是真的快樂呢！」井蛙聽了海龜的一番話，吃驚地呆在那裏，再沒有話可說了。

A frog living in an old well met a large sea turtle that was one day passing by. The frog within the well boasted, "My life here is wonderful! I can hop out and jump along the railing of the well, or when I'm tired, I can hop back down and relax in the gap between the broken bricks. Whenever I please, I can splash down into the water and enjoy myself sinking into the soft, cool mud. If I look around, I see that the crabs and tadpoles down here are nothing compared to me. I am the master of this well and am free to do whatever I please. Wouldn't you like to come down and visit me?"

The sea turtle heard what the frog had to say and was curious to take a look. He stepped carefully into the well with his left foot, but his right leg became wedged in the limited space of the opening. As he stepped back out, he said, "Have you never seen the sea? A distance of one thousand Chinese miles cannot describe its width nor one thousand fathoms its depth. During ancient times, there was flooding nine years out of ten, but the sea's waters did not rise. Later, there were droughts for seven years out of eight, but the sea's waters did not recede. So, you can see, the sea remains constant and unaffected, no matter the conditions. Living in such a vast sea is true joy as well."

The frog of the dilapidated well, taken aback by realization of the the world's profound vastness, sat silent. Humbled and realizing his ignorance, he knew not what to say.

Our perception of reality, like the frog's, is quite limited. There is much more to the actual nature of the world than what the world of our perceptions reveals. At every moment the environment is vibrating with an array of energies and is being pervaded with various chemical stimuli. Our senses, however, allow us a perspective on only a tiny fragment of it. What we are not able to detect and be aware of is much greater than what we are able to.

Other species, of course, have sensory organs that are stimulated to form their own distinct worlds of perceptions. Ultraviolet light from sunlight is invisible to us but visible to a variety of animals and insects. We cannot see infrared light (the kind detected by certain night-vision goggles) or perceive the infrared thermal radiation that some snakes can sense.[30] Radio waves, microwaves, X-rays, and gamma rays also belong to the spectrum of electromagnetic radiation; we cannot see any of them. Ultrasonic frequencies are beyond the limit of human hearing, but bats, dogs, cats, mice, dolphins, and some insects have no problem recognizing them. Bats can echolocate to detect a tiny insect 18 feet away, in the dark. Some fish and sharks can locate prey or sense a nearby

[30] Janet Fang, *Snake infrared detection unravelled* (Nature, doi:10.1038/news.2010.122, March 14, 2010), http://www.nature.com/news/2010/100314/full/news.2010.122.html (retrieved 05/08/2014)

[31] *Black Bear Biology and Behavior* (NJ Division of Fish and Wildlife), http://www.state.nj.us/dep/fgw/bearfacts_biology.htm (retrieved 05/08/2014)

predator by detecting the electric fields of those creatures. Bears can detect the scent of food from miles away.[31] Birds and some insects are known to detect the earth's magnetic field to sense direction. Flies and butterflies have taste receptors on their feet and can taste what they land or walk on.[32]

Imagine if we could echolocate, hear ultrasound, see ultraviolet and infrared light, smell things from miles away, have an innate sense of direction, and taste things with our feet? What we call reality would become quite unlike the world we now know. Art, sports, music, food, technology, the infrastructure of our cities, and our shoes, certainly, would be radically different.

Our realities are constructed from the world of our perceptions, and since our worlds of perceptions exist only in our minds, minds that are conditioned by memory, fear, and desire, we are prone to misperceptions that often result in anxiety and discontent.

A Buddhist parable describes a man walking along a forest path at dusk. In the dim light, he is startled by a long, slender shape stretched out along the path a few steps in front of him—a cobra! Eyes wide, he gasps and freezes, trembling with fright. Petrified, heart racing, he begins to notice that the snake is motionless. Peering intently, he bends down and gingerly lifts up the object with a stick. Relieved and chuckling to himself, he discovers that the "cobra" is, in fact, an old piece of rope.

So was the snake real? Some might argue that in the reality of the man's perceived world, the "cobra" was as real as any live, writhing cobra. Perhaps if the man had immediately dashed away, raced home, and related to others that he had nearly stepped on a cobra, his perception, his story, his memory, would have forever remained his reality: the object would have remained a cobra.

In truth, however, the perception of a cobra and the subsequent fear arose from some memory of what a cobra appears to

[32] *Amazing Animal Senses* (Neuroscience for kids), http://faculty.washington.edu/chudler/amaze.html (retrieved 05/08/2014)

be. In truth, this object of the external world was not a cobra and did not possess the physical energy or material properties of a cobra. It was a piece of rope, with the physical energy and material properties of a piece of rope. For the man to maintain his illusion, he would have had to avoid being mindful of his perceptions from the external world. Once he observed the object deliberately, however, and picked it up, he recognized it as an old and harmless piece of rope, as it had originally and always been. His fear and anxiety had existed only in his mind and, at last, dissipated when he recognized the truth.

Physical realities are determined by how subjective minds perceive and define what their limited sensory organs can detect. The absolute physical reality of the natural world, then, consisting of various energies, forces, and chemical compositions, cannot be objectively defined. Similarly, a person with a dualistic mind-set subjectively characterizes one life situation to be desired while another is to be avoided. In truth, life is non-dualistic: good and bad, better and worse cannot be objectively defined because, well, they do not exist anywhere outside of our singular, private thoughts.

Most are familiar with the Taoist symbol tàijítú, commonly referred to as the "yin-yang symbol," made up of a circle intersected with a curving line that separates the circle into halves, one of which is the white yáng state, containing a small black dot. The other half is the black yin state, containing a small white dot. Note that as the white yáng state reaches its peak, a black yin dot appears, leading to the birth of the black yin state, which then develops to its culmination, where the white yáng dot appears, leading back to the birth of the white yáng state.

Although the two halves may appear to represent opposites, they are not in opposition. One cannot exist without the other. The yin state and the yáng state are complementary and interdependent, two halves of an absolute whole. One does not have more value, is not more essential, is not more desired or avoided than the other. This is non-duality.

As the yin state arises from the yáng state and the yáng state arises from the yin state, we can observe a cycle of continuous transition and flux, the impermanence and ever-changing transformation of compounded phenomena, energy perpetually shifting from potential to kinetic to potential to kinetic ad infinitum, constantly evolving toward a state of the absolute—natural, balanced, effortless, and whole.

Non-duality

In the non-dualistic view, there is nothing desirable or undesirable, better or worse. Consider creation and destruction, or birth and death. Which is desirable? Which is to be avoided? The dualistic mind is drawn to what is "good" or "positive"—creation and birth—but imagine a world where nothing since the beginning of existence was ever destroyed; nothing ever died. You cannot. It would be chaos, and madness.

The non-dualistic mind recognizes creation arising from destruction and destruction the culmination of creation, birth arising from death and death the culmination of birth, then back again. These events are complementary and interdependent, effortless and fluid, forever maintaining an equilibrium, a non-governing homeostasis in the totality of the natural world.

The following story is adapted from a well-known Taoist parable about a farmer and his horse (塞翁失馬，焉知非福):

Near the northern border of China, there lived a farmer who owned a magnificent mare, acclaimed throughout the region. Not only beautiful and fast, it also pulled the farmer's plow to till his fields.

One morning following a raging storm, the farmer went out to discover that the fence had been damaged and his prized mare had disappeared. His neighbor, always a bit envious of the farmer and his mare, heard the news and snickered. Quietly gratified, he dropped by to visit the farmer.

"I heard that your horse ran off," the neighbor called out. "What a shame."

To which the farmer replied, "Sure, I suppose so."

Puzzled, the neighbor walked off, *What do you mean you suppose so? It IS a shame that your horse ran off. Too bad for you.*

A few days later, the farmer looked out and spotted his mare back on the farm. Not only had his mare come home, but it had returned with three wild horses.

Upon hearing the news, the farmer's neighbor felt slightly irritated, *I can't believe it. He now has four horses.*

Once again, the neighbor went to pay the farmer a visit.

"I see your mare has returned and brought back with her three wild horses," he said to the farmer, adding with a note of insincerity, "That's great. You're the luckiest person in the village."

To which the farmer replied, "Sure, I suppose so."

Shaking his head, the neighbor returned home, muttering, "What do you mean you suppose so? You have the finest mare in the village and now three wild horses. I have one old, sick mare. You ARE lucky."

The next day the farmer's teen-aged son decided to train one of the wild horses. After choosing the most spirited of the three, he clambered atop, whereupon the untamed horse bucked and tossed the son into the air. Tumbling to the ground with an unsettling crack, the young man broke his leg.

The farmer's neighbor, predictably, returned to the farmer's house, "I'm so sorry to hear about your son. Now you'll have to do all your farm work by yourself. That's tough. I guess getting those three horses was bad luck after all."

To which the farmer replied, "Sure, I suppose so."

The neighbor could hardly disguise a smirk as he left, *You suppose so? You're nuts!*

Two weeks later war broke out with the country to the north. Military officials and soldiers soon arrived at the village and began forcibly conscripting young men into the army. They came to the house of the farmer's neighbor and took away his eldest son. The neighbor then led them to the house of the farmer and shouted, "War has broken out! Military officials want to talk with you!" The farmer came out of his house, with his son hobbling behind him. The officials, seeing that the young man's leg was broken, turned away, saying, "He's useless. Let's go."

The neighbor stared at the farmer in disbelief. The farmer, glancing back at his neighbor, shrugged his shoulders and stepped back into his house.

I was once relating this story to a friend when he exclaimed, "Yes! Who's to know?"

Curious, I asked, "Who's to know what?"

"Who's to know if something is good or bad? You never know what might happen next."

Well, yes, while it may be true that we never know what will happen at any following moment, my friend overlooked the essence of this Taoist story. That is, the tale of the farmer and his horse embodies the view of non-duality: perceptions of good and bad do not exist independently of our conditioned thoughts. This goes beyond the notion of who is to know whether an occurrence is good or not good, bad or not bad, for presupposing that there exists a good or bad condition, in itself, indicates a dualistic worldview.

In the perception of the dualistic mind, the concept of good is to be desired and bad is to be avoided. This results in comparing and judging and separating, which invariably leads to conflict, the conflict of craving versus aversion. The manifestation of conflict then gives rise to the mental prattling of a grasping and fearful or dissatisfied dualistic mind, as in: "When this happens, my life will be perfect (good). If that happens, my life will be a mess (bad). He/she wants to be with me (good). He/she wants to break up with me (bad). That's what I want! I got it (good). I can't believe I didn't get it (bad)." And so on.

Being successful, being unsuccessful; being fortunate, being unfortunate; being recognized, being unknown; being unique, being ordinary; being important, being insignificant; being noticed, being ignored, all are concepts manufactured by the dualistic mind to be craved or avoided. The dualistic, conditioned mind is, ultimately, a source of mental torment, conflicted with the discontent from unsatiated craving and the anxiety arising from aversion.

In the phenomena of the natural world (e.g., creation and destruction, birth and death) the characteristics of good and bad do not exist. In the non-dualistic mind, likewise, when something occurs, it is not perceived as this or that, not defined as good or bad. It simply is.

In the non-dualistic mind, there is only life, and living, dynamically, and in constant motion; living with events that are complementary and interdependent; living with the truth of impermanence and constant transformation. Living—without the sorrow and misery of memory and craving and aversion. Living—without the futile grasping of a chattering, prattling mind.

It matters not what we think of or how we feel about some circumstance. Conditions change. Constantly. We continue to live, and work, and learn, and be inspired, and create, and persevere. Another happening occurs, and regardless, we simply live, without defining and comparing and judging and separating and craving. Like a farmer and his horse.

Clinging to Ego: The Egotistical, the Insecure, the Self-loathing—and Everything Else

e • go • tis • ti • cal (adj.): to have an inflated opinion of oneself; to have an exaggerated sense of self-importance; to be self-absorbed, smug, and conceited

Finally, there is the common misconception that having a strong ego is akin to being egotistical. No, a strong ego-attachment can manifest as the narcissistic and arrogant as well as the insecure and self-loathing. The martyr, the victim, the self-conscious, etc. cling just as strongly to their private, mentally projected ego-identities, ego-identities fabricated from experiential memory, conditioned thoughts, and concerns for social recognition and validation.

The self-pitying individual whose inner voice claims *I have suffered these torments; I have denied myself these joys; I am the self-sacrificing one, the giving one, the compassionate one, the virtuous one* has no less an attachment to ego-identity than the egotistical, vain, and bloated. Both suffer the incessant mental prattle of an excessively strong, egoistic attachment to a mental construct of the self.

Our "stories" based on memory and thought, our identification with possessions, our aspirations for social status and recognition, our identification with our bodies and body-image, these distinctions make up the mental construct of the self. It is not, however, the idea of self that causes our mental distress, it is the activity of the self: attachment to, constant aggrandizement of, and struggle to maintain the mental construct of the self, along with physical and emotional craving and a dualistic world-view—that constitutes much of what the voice in our head is incessantly and neurotically prattling on about.

THREE

NON-ATTACHMENT—A STILL MIND—THE ART OF FIGHTING WITHOUT FIGHTING

Sunrise on the Ganges River - Varanasi, India

Release from the Origins of Suffering

"The practice of developing or cultivating equanimity involves a form of detachment, but it is important to understand what detachment means. Sometimes when people hear about the Buddhist practice of detachment, they think that Buddhism is advocating indifference toward all things, but that is not the case."—His Holiness the 14th Dalai Lama[33]

---

[33] His Holiness the 14th Dalai Lama, *Training the Mind: Verse 2*, http://www.dalailama.com/teachings/training-the-mind/verse-2 (retrieved 05/09/2014)

There are frequent and rather cynical misconceptions about the concept of detachment. Some think it suggests a person should escape ordinary life by walking away from one's family and employment so that he or she can live in a cave and meditate. No, that is excessive and impractical. There are others who hear "detachment" and assume it is equivalent to being detached from feeling, indifferent to the world, emotionally dead. No. Such a morose and dour view of life, who would feel inspired to live like that?

Detachment does not refer to either of these scenarios. In fact, the term detachment itself is rather misleading, a more appropriate term is non-attachment. Non-attachment refers to being non-attached to the incessant mind chatter of the self as well as the fabricated story of self. Non-attachment means to be non-attached to an internal egoistic voice that is constantly prattling on over attachment to and craving for the five conditioned deceits of one's mind:

- The Illusory Self
- Social Status and the Conditioned Mind
- Body Image
- The Craving for Sensation
- The Dualistic World-view

Non-attachment to the ego-story does not mean detachment from life experience or detachment from others or the nature around you. Quite the contrary, non-attachment from the idea of the self dissolves the illusion that you are a separate, autonomous being; non-attachment from the idea of the self allows you to clearly observe the interrelationship and interdependence between you and others and everything in nature.

Non-attachment does not mean to be devoid of passion and emotion but rather not to cling to and pine for a transient moment or feeling or experience. Life is a continuum of transformation and flux, with no situations, conditions, or states being fixed, permanent, and unchanging.

Non-attachment does not imply passivity or disinterest. In fact, non-attachment from the voice of ego allows you to live with more spontaneity and less apprehension, greater possibilities and fewer fears.

The Chatterbox of Ego

Once when I was engaged in snarky banter with my brash, sarcastic, and typically absurd teen-aged niece about what I had observed was her apparently irrepressible and excessive mind chatter, she cheekily responded, "Well, what if I like the voice in my head?"

Ah, yes, what insight. We, most of us, surely, are enthralled with the voice of ego in our heads. It is the voice of ego that tells us we are unique, distinctive, original. It is the voice of ego that wants to own and cling to the story, the identity, the social facade. It is the self-admiring voice of ego that takes such pride and satisfaction in I, me, mine. It is the voice of ego that pats us on the back, rubs us on the head, and applauds, "Good job!"

Well, fabulous. If your voice of ego is joyful and carefree and fulfilling, then, congratulations. If, however, you suffer because the conflict that is created by the individualistic voice of pride and vanity and indulgence leads to feelings of uncertainty, anxiousness, dissatisfaction, anger, fear, self-doubt, sorrow, boredom, or discontent, non-attachment to the chatterbox of ego may be a potentiality to consider embracing.

Waking to Stillness

On the morning of December 10, 1996, neuroanatomist Dr. Jill Bolte Taylor suffered a debilitating stroke when a blood vessel in her brain burst. While distressed by her weakening physical condition, as a brain scientist, she was also fascinated to witness various functions of her brain beginning to deteriorate, including the area of her brain responsible for language. Most notable was that her internal voice of discursive mental chatter was fragmenting. The stream of prattling thoughts, no longer flowing, had become erratic, sporadically interrupted by gaps of silence. As the mental jibber-jabber faded to absolute stillness, she describes being overcome by "a sense of peacefulness". . . "euphoria."

She recalls that though she maintained conscious awareness, she had lost all capacity for language. She could no longer speak nor comprehend the spoken words of others. Lacking the linguistic ability to define and compare and separate, the usual incessant chattering of the self had wholly dissipated, and within that dissipation was her story of identity, her ego-story. She recounts the cessation of memory-like thoughts and the cessation of her attachment to her history and self-identity: the achievements, the mistakes, the expectations, the stress, the "emotional baggage," the anger, her beliefs and opinions. All was dissipating to nothingness as the mind chatter of ego became silent. And concurrent with this silence, she experienced "relief" and "joy."

Still "conscious and constantly present," her concept and sense of time ceased. While she was aware of what she was experiencing from moment to moment, a continuum of past, present, and future no longer existed. Memories of the past and notions of the future, with whatever sorrows and anxieties were associated with them, had faded away. She experienced freedom, freedom from the conditioning of what she describes as "the insignificant affairs of society."

Physically, she encountered another profound occurrence: as her mind became empty of the jibber-jabber of ego, her body-image perception of being a distinct individual, separate from the external world dissolved. Beginning to feel more "fluid" than "solid," she observed the boundaries of her physical self shifting to blur with the energies and forces of the external world, "the atoms and the molecules of my arm blended with the atoms and molecules of the wall, and all I could detect was this energy." She described that she no longer felt confined to the boundaries of her physical body and experienced a communion with the universe, "I felt enormous and expansive. I felt at one with all the energy that was, and it was beautiful there."[34]

After surgery and an eight-year recovery, Dr. Taylor writes in her book, *My Stroke of Insight,* that the Jill Bolte Taylor she had been for 37 years "died" that morning of the stroke. A shift in her perceptions and awareness had occurred, and she had transformed into a quite different person: one who felt more interconnected than independent and isolated, more expansive than small and limited, more at peace than angry, more enthusiastic than critical, and more inspired to be than to do.[35]

Finding this story to be rather compelling, I shared it with a Taiwanese Buddhist friend, and she asked, "So, is that it? We just need to have a stroke and become enlightened?"

Well, not exactly.

We suffer because the incessant chattering of ego holds our minds hostage, keeping us disengaged from the only life we can truly know and experience—the action of living, our life in the present.

It is no great insight to state that the discursive mental nattering of thoughts distracts us from being present and mindful and connected to the world around us. It seems apparent, then, that the path to living a more engaging and joyful life is to cultivate the ability to rein in and control the torrent of indiscriminate and neurotic mental jibber-jabber, yes? (Well, actually, no, but we're getting to that.) This concept has been popularized in a profusion of self-help books that encourage and instruct a person to tame or modify the chattering mind so that one can be more confident, more optimistic, more empowered, more successful, and more everything else. Many techniques are meant to neutralize "negative self-talk" with "positive self-talk" (or some ethereal "positive" energy) in order to feel upbeat about the idea of ourselves, while underlying it all is the anxious desire to acquire: success, love, power, wealth,

[34] Dr. Jill Bolte Taylor, *My Stroke of Insight* (TED talk, February 2008), http://www.ted.com/talks/jill_bolte_taylor_s_powerful_stroke_of_insight#t-5065 (retrieved 05/09/2014)
[35] Dr. Jill Bolte Taylor, *My Stroke of Insight* (Viking, 2006)

status, possessions, and so on. Amidst this campaign of positivity fabricated to ease the dissatisfaction brought about by unmet cravings, we are cheered on by catchy expressions like: Every cloud has a silver lining. Is the glass half empty or half full? Everything happens for a reason. And, When fate hands you a lemon, make lemonade.

Optimism and a cheerful attitude can be uplifting for a moment, yes, but the irony of "positive self-talk" is that any "self-talk" is purely additional mental chatter, the mental nattering of a dualistic mind that is conflicted with an unrelenting craving and thirst for one outcome and an aversion and fear to another. Any self-talk from the voice of ego leads, inevitably, to a struggle against conflict and anxiety.

To break the spell of a streaming, discursive narrative that clings to the fabrication of ego is not a matter of controlling the mind, nor empowering the mind, nor taming the mind; the practice is to focus conscious attention to the jibber-jabber of your egoistic voice and to observe the truth of your thoughts: They are nothing more than the projections of a mentally fabricated ego-self, an ego-self tormented by the deceptions of a conditioned mind, and these thoughts exist nowhere other than in your imagination. They endure only in your head. Observe the thoughts, the mental chatter, the self-talk, as they are, without defining and judging and grasping and avoiding. Just observe them—and observe them—until they fade—and dissipate—into absolute stillness.

Stillness—In the Flow

Over coffee one day, a musician acquaintance confessed, "But I need the anxiety to drive me, motivate me, push me to get better. If I didn't have the fear of others being better than me, or if I were satisfied with where I'm at, I would never improve. I wouldn't be able to reach the level of success that I want."

When I was younger, practicing martial arts, I had similar thoughts of adapting emotion to serve as a motivator. Since anyone practicing martial arts faces the fear of defeat or injury, my strategy was to use fear as the energy to drive me to improve my skills and to instill a sense of courage when I fought. I used "self-talk" to manipulate my fear into anger, because, contrary to the instinct to flee when one is afraid, anger emboldened me to stand and fight. I focused the intensity of hatred at my opponent for inducing in me the sensation of fear. It was a twisted mental game of chattering self-talk. Effective in making me a more aggressive and capable fighter, it also caused me to become an individual with a hostile and ill-tempered mind-set and influenced my attitude toward all aspects of life. My egoistic chattering of self-talk created a malcontent who was always competing and comparing, always ready to fight, always wanted to win, always needed to be right—not a pleasant way to live.

The simple truth is that if you want to develop a particular ability, you need only spend sustained and concentrated effort, hours and hours of repetition and correct technical training, and you will, undoubtedly, improve. Can this be done without the conflict of a chattering, anxious, antagonistic mind, with only the joy and exhilaration of learning and developing as motivation? Surely. And when the doing, creating, and performing surpass mere physical and mental discipline, when movement and awareness merge to become solely presence and being, effortless action and flow can be transcendent. In the martial arts, this is the essence of mushin. Sports psychology refers to this as being "in the zone" or "in the flow"—acting without mind, without thought, without emotion, without ego; acting with mental clarity and pure action, without desire or fear or anger or anxiety—fluid, focused, calm, and fearless—pure presence, pure being.

In his autobiography *Second Wind: The Memoirs of an Opinionated Man*, NBA legend Bill Russell of the Boston Celtics describes an experience of mushin, or being in the flow. He describes that a game would sometimes become so intense that it went beyond a physical or even mental experience, and became "magical." In this state, with both teams fueled by a fierce and relentless aggression, he did not feel competitive, at all. Instead, he experienced the odd sensation of the game being played in slow motion, saying, "I could almost sense how the next play would develop and where the next shot would be taken." Before the competition could inbound the ball, he was so certain how the play would take place he wanted to alert his teammates with a shout, "It's coming there!" But he did not, because he knew that if he had "everything would change," the spell of being in the flow would have been broken. Russell goes on to describe that his instincts were "consistently" spot-on and that not only could he intuit the intentions of his teammates and the opposing players but he felt they all were just as in tune with him. At those times, when this state of being was maintained to the end of the game, he was present purely in the moment, and the idea of winning and losing lost all meaning: "I literally did not care who had won. If we lost, I'd still be as free and high as a sky hawk."[36]

Sounds of Stillness

"Good music should touch the heart and bring spiritual elevation . . . The best result can be achieved with the purest heart one can keep. That is, one must free the mind, and be humble such that the performer becomes the instrument."—Liu-fang[37]

The pípá: a four-stringed Chinese lute.

A performance by internationally acclaimed Chinese pípá virtuoso Liu-fang is more than an experience of sound; it is akin to musical theater, wherein you witness the musician transformed into an expression of music itself, her being and movement fusing to be-

[36] William F. Russell and Taylor Branch, *Second Wind: The Memoirs of an Opinionated Man* (Random House, 1979) 156

[37] Paula E. Kirman, *Traditional Chinese Music is in Her Heart and Soul* (Inside World Music, June 24, 2001), http://www.insideworldmusic.com/library/weekly/aa062201a.htm (retrieved 05/12/2014)

come lyrical energy.[38]

Riveting, emotionally intense, spiritual, delicate, poetic, and dazzling are expressions reviewers have used to describe her live performances. Madame Lorraine Chalifoux, producer of Radio-Canada, says this: "I've rarely seen someone so focused and absorbed when she plays her instrument. It consumes her entirety, and music flows out of her fingers, out of her pores."[39]

When performing live in a crowded concert hall, Liu-fang describes feeling moved by the "spiritual and emotional vibration of the atmosphere." Sensing the energy and sentiment of her listeners, she is inspired to interact with them through her instrument, "Sometimes I answer to them . . . sometimes I bring them to my musical world. Sometimes I push them to another corner."[40] Characterizing her state of mind when she plays, she says, "When I play pípá, I feel like I'm singing, or dancing . . . or I'm simply in nature. I don't have any sense of playing pípá . . . in my mind there is no music, no pípá, nothing at all. My mind is empty."[41]

She also relates, "When I'm playing a tune, I am singing in my heart. When I'm playing a sad tune, I am crying in my heart. I often hear from listeners that they hear singing in my music . . . In particular, I am very moved when somebody comes to me with tears in their eyes, telling me how much they enjoyed my music . . . Comparatively, I don't like talking with people as much because it is too easy to have misunderstandings because of language. By making music, I feel the freedom and joy that I can never have by talking."[42]

[38] Liu Fang, *Dance of the Yi Tribe*, http://www.youtube.com/watch?v=yY-xPla0aJU (retrieved 05/12/2014)

[39] *The charm of ancient traditional music of China*, http://www.youtube.com/watch?v=6k_4DsiM9-g (retrieved 05/12/2014)

[40] *Liu Fang Interview & Live 2*, http://www.youtube.com/watch?v=wNcs6ZqCy9U (retrieved 05/09/2014)

[41] *Pipa Soloist Liu Fang*, http://www.youtube.com/watch?v=vD8XsQ8R7o8 (retrieved 05/12/2014)

[42] *Liu Fang Interview*, http://www.youtube.com/watch?v=lpIyL02dV-g (retrieved 05/12/2014)

The Art of Fighting without Fighting

Contrary to what some believe, non-attachment to the chattering voice of ego does not mean to be self-absorbed in your own world of peaceful bliss, unconcerned with the realities of the world. It does not mean to be indifferent to the welfare of others, nor to become a grinning, timid, tambourine-tapping, zombie-like punching bag to be abused by others. Some have the impression that by following an egoless path, you will react to life situations with passivity and apathy. If you are threatened, if you are physically or verbally attacked, if a lunatic is attacking your family in front of you, you will capitulate or comply, submissively. Not, at all, true.

The 1970s martial arts icon Bruce Lee was not only a brilliant and innovative martial artist but also a keen student of philosophy. Throughout much of his television and film work, Lee strove to convey the spirit of his philosophical thoughts, which were influenced by the ideas of Taoism, Buddhism, and, in particular, Jiddu Krishnamurti.[43]

In the seminal martial arts film *Enter the Dragon*, Bruce plays the role of an exceptionally skilled kung fu practitioner from Hong Kong who finds himself on a ship with several other accomplished fighters. They are headed to compete in an international combat tournament on a nearby Hong Kong island. One of the foreign combatants, a bullying thug, roams the ship amusing himself by terrorizing the Chinese crewmen. With leisurely indifference, he arbitrarily knocks a basket of oranges out of the grasp of a deckhand and kicks the startled man to the ground. He stalks across the deck as the other crew members cower; then he approaches Lee from behind. As he throws punches of intimidation into the air toward the side of Lee's head, Lee quietly turns, looks him up and down, and with a glance of disregard, gazes back out toward the sea and ignores him.

[43] Documentary film by John Little, *Bruce Lee: A Warrior's Journey*, 2000

"What's your style?" the grinning thug asks.

"My style?" Lee asks. Then, with a shrug, he adds, "You can call it the art of fighting without fighting."

When the bully sneers and demands that Lee demonstrate his technique for him, Lee ignores him and turns to leave. With a menacing glower, the thug thrusts out his hand and blocks Lee's path. "All right," Lee complies nonchalantly, "Don't you think we need more room?"

The thug looks around the cluttered ship and asks, "Where else?"

Lee points toward a distant island and suggests the beach, "We can take this boat," as he gestures to a small rowboat tied to the back of the ship.

The bully looks down skeptically but is obliged to agree. He descends, and as soon as he steps into the small dinghy, Lee, instead of following him in, steps back and plays out the tow rope, letting the rowboat drift away and trail the ship at a distance.

"Hey, what the hell are you doing?" the thug yells, staggering to balance himself on the bobbing and lurching dinghy while the ship's crew cheers and laughs in the background.

Although Lee's character has the fighting skills to crush his opponents, in this instance, he leaves the bullying thug vanquished but unharmed, humbled and no longer a threat to the others on the boat—the art of fighting without fighting.

The path of non-attachment to the ego-story and the accompanying chatter of ego is the path of mushin. Absent the vanity of the ego, with a mind that is silent, there is no consideration for threats, insults, or provocation. It means responding dispassionately to neutralize an antagonistic situation with the minimum force necessary. Sometimes the response can be as simple as a sincere, "I'm sorry about that," or "You're right," or "Sure, we'll do it your way" (and, by all means, whenever possible, allow your opposition a face-saving retreat).

Of course, when absolute force is necessary, it is applied decisively, without ego or emotion, without pride or vengeance or animosity—focused, calm, and emotionless. It simply means to live, to act, to work, to communicate, to take care of your business with equanimity and presence, detached from the arrogance, self-righteousness, anger, conceit, and conflict of an egoistic chattering mind.

Still Mind

"Empty your mind. Be formless, shapeless, like water. Now, you put water into a cup, it becomes the cup. You put water into a bottle, it becomes the bottle. You put it into a teapot, it becomes the teapot. Now, water can flow, or it can crash. Be water, my friend."—Bruce Lee[44]

It is certainly no simple task to still the persistently churning mental prattling of ego and to live each day present and mindful. How can it be done, or can it be done? Try a few simple exercises:

#1: Note where you are right now. Are you at home? At the beach? In a hotel room? Stop reading. Look up for a moment, quietly and deliberately observe the environment around you while taking two slow, deep, easy breaths. Do not strain. Go ahead.

Now look around and find any random object you had not taken notice of before. Your cup of coffee there, perhaps. Do not regard its shape or color; do not identify it as anything in particular. Simply focus your gaze intently upon it and concentrate. Notice how light is reflected from it and creates shadows. Focus intently while taking three slow, deep, easy breaths.

Next, maintain your gaze upon the object but relax your focus. Use your peripheral vision to direct your concentration to the background area that surrounds the object. Again, take three slow, deep, easy breaths.

How was that? Feeling a bit enlightened now? Try the next exercise.

#2: Look across at something a slight distance from you, perhaps the opposite wall ten feet away. Your eyes are focused clearly on the wall, yes? Now, shift your focus midway, so that your gaze is about five feet in front of you. There is nothing there, of course, so imagine that you are looking at the air, at a two foot square sheet of air suspended five feet away. (You might imagine a sheet of crystal clear glass instead). This may seem a bit odd and difficult at first, but concentrate your attention at the sheet of air or imagined glass. At the same time, note any sounds that you had not noticed before: birds chirping, the rustle of leaves in the breeze, the hum of traffic and street noise, the ticking of a clock, the whirring of a fan, the barking of a distant dog. Again, take three slow, deep, easy breaths.

#3: Combine exercises #1 and #2 by focusing on an object while concentrating on the background sounds around you.

What did you experience? These simple focus techniques may have caused you to feel a slight shift in your perceptions. Did the object you were focusing on, the object that you would have normally disregarded, appear more vivid? Did the sounds that constantly surround you, but which you hardly notice during your daily life, become more vibrant? If you were genuinely focused, the mind chatter of your ego likely fell silent, and you inadvertently experienced a sense of stillness, if only for a few moments.

Being mindful means to be less self-absorbed and distracted by the endless prattle of an egoistic mind, whether one is active or at rest. Being mindful means to be consciously engaged with the energies and stimuli present around you, whether you are crossing the street, driving a car, speaking with others, walking in the park, or eating a meal. Being mindful means to live more engaged with the life and energy that is perpetually around you, and it can be quite refreshing, if not exhilarating.

FOUR

MEDITATION

Mountain Sunset - Taiwan

I once believed that after learning concepts and acknowledging things to be true (e.g., the self is a mental fabrication, attachment to the ego-self and craving causes suffering, one is not his or her thoughts, and so on), I could use this knowledge as a guide to living. I could not. Knowing is not being.

Studying, discussing, gathering knowledge and learning philosophical concepts simply led to the accumulation of thoughts, ideas, and pretension, further prattle for my mind. It did not lead to Truth. I remained captive to a lifetime of conditioning which dictated how I perceived and responded to others and life events, a lifetime of conditioning which manifested itself as instant and spontaneous reaction, thoughtless and egoistic. I felt I understood the idea of mindfulness and what it meant to "live in the moment," but my chattering thoughts would, invariably, display themselves in "the moment" long before any mindfulness could catch up.

> "Meditation in daily life is the transformation of the mind, a psychological revolution so that we live a daily life—not in theory, not as an ideal, but in every movement of that life—in which there is compassion, love, and the energy to transcend all the pettiness, the narrowness, the shallowness."—Jiddu Krishnamurti[45]

After the fact, at the end of the day, I would recognize the day's mental chatter and remind myself about when: I had not been present; I had reacted without being mindful; I had let my egoistic voice create thoughts of ill-will, anger, conceit, or craving, and all the rest of it. The irony is that reflecting upon being mindful or not being mindful, or how to be mindful, simply became a further nattering discourse in my mind. I understood the idea of mindfulness, but I could not live it.

A Raft Parable

> "To see the truth, the mind must be free from all knowledge."—Walpola Rahula[46]

> "Meditation is freedom from the known . . . And in that meditation, there is absolute silence."—Jiddu Krishnamurti[47]

One of the most well-known parables attributed to the Buddha is the *Parable of the Raft*. Since there already exist various versions

[45] Jiddu Krishnamurti, *This Light in Oneself* (Krishnamurti Foundation Trust Ltd., 1999) 8
[46] Jiddu Krishnamurti in Dialogue with Buddhists, *Can Humanity Change*, (Shambhala Publications, 2003), 8
[47] Jiddu Krishnamurti, *This Light in Oneself*, 26

and interpretations, one more is unnecessary; instead, I offer a somewhat related tale of my own:

> A traveler is searching for a Path to the Truth and comes upon an expanse of water. The Path can be found on the further shore, but this person has available neither boat nor bridge, nor can this individual swim. Undeterred, the traveler gathers the appropriate materials—logs, branches, and vines—and fashions a suitable raft. After safely crossing the river, this seeker of Truth arrives on the opposite side and acknowledges the "path." It is a large circle with neither beginning nor end, a path without destination. Leaving the raft behind, the traveler takes to the path and continues on.

There is an obstacle before the path to the truth, and it is a river, a river of ignorance. Gather what is necessary to surmount this river—the knowledge, the concepts, the rationale—and once you have crossed over and come to the path, abandon the raft; it is no longer necessary. Conditioned thought (in fact, all movement of thought) is a hindrance to the truth. Abandon the raft, that is, all accumulated knowledge.

The path, if we can call it that, might be meditation and mindfulness. More distinctly, it is freedom from the known, freedom from conditioned and accumulated knowledge. When one has the space, the "absolute silence," to realize truth, there is no thought, there is no knowing. There is simply being.

Mindfulness is not something to contemplate, nor something about which you need remind yourself; it is a way of being, and a practice of it is meditation. Understanding what it means to meditate is not unlike learning to speak a foreign language, to play a musical instrument, or to perform a new sport or exercise, let us say: swimming. You cannot have an understanding of swimming by only reading books, discussing with instructors, and knowing correct swimming techniques. No, you develop the sense and understanding of swimming when you step into the water, flail about, practice, struggle, and make mistakes. Then you practice more until you can apply your knowledge of correct technique, and you are eventually able to swim and swim well, with less and less effort, until finally, swimming has become second nature.

To deconstruct a lifetime of conditioning takes a considerable amount of intention and practice. Our lives have been lived with a mind full of discursive thoughts constantly prattling about in our heads. So habitual and regular are they that you may not even be aware that they are there. When you take the time to sit and meditate, you are focusing deliberate attention to the endless jibber-jabber of your mind.

Meditation is solely a technique. There is nothing mystical or esoteric about it. You are simply observing your thoughts without defining or judging or grasping or avoiding (which certainly is no simple thing to do). Observe your thoughts, the mental chatter, the self-talk, and recognize that through dispassionate observation, you can maintain space from the movement of thoughts and images, and allow them to dissipate . . . to stillness.

Preparation and Posture

Place – It is helpful to create and maintain a regular place to meditate. Find a quiet, comfortable space where you will not be interrupted or disturbed. Avoid a place where you will feel as if you are on display.

Time – Any time is suitable, but the early morning quiet is ideal. Wake up earlier and reserve the time for meditation only. Evenings are usually a convenient time to meditate, but avoid meditating if you are sleepy.

To begin, meditating for 10-15 minutes in the morning and the evening is suggested. Frequent, short periods of time are more effective than longer periods at an infrequent rate.

Do not eat a full meal for at least an hour or two before meditating; otherwise, you may feel drowsy and lethargic.

Stretch – A few simple stretching exercises helps to relax your body and focus your mind.

Sitting – The most important thing is to sit in a comfortable position that will keep your spine straight. You can sit on the ground cross-legged, in half lotus, or full lotus. For extended periods of meditation, it is comfortable to sit on a thick raised cushion. Sit near the edge of the cushion with your crossed legs resting on the floor. If you are not used to sitting on the ground, you can sit on a chair with a firm seat, feet comfortably flat on the floor. Do not choose a chair with a soft seat into which you will sink.

Sit with your spine straight, shoulders pulled gently back and down (do not hunch); keep your chin slightly lowered. Experiment a bit to feel comfortable and settle into this position. Relax while keeping your spine straight but not stiff.

Hand Position – There are a variety of hand positions you can use. Two common variations are: (1) Rest both hands on the knees, palms down, or (2) Rest the left hand on the lap, palm up, and place the right hand, palm up, on top of the left. Let the tips of the thumbs touch.

You might also slightly flare your elbows out, away from the body, so that your arms are not hanging down completely relaxed.

Eyes – Keep your eyes slightly open, gazing downward past your nose to a point about five feet (one and a half metres) in front of you. Do not focus on or stare at anything in particular.

Some prefer to meditate with eyes shut, which may more easily bring about a feeling of serenity or shift in perceptions, but there is also a greater tendency to (1) become unconsciously absorbed into a narrative of thought, (2) be consumed by a mental image, or (3) enter into a dream-like state. All things to avoid.

If you find yourself too easily distracted and drifting from conscious awareness, it is best to keep your eyes half open.

Mouth – Keep the mouth closed; do not clench the teeth. Touch the tip of the tongue to the top of your mouth, behind the front teeth.

Abdominal Breathing – Most people inhale by expanding their ribs and inflating their chests. Practice breathing from the abdomen, which will allow you to breathe smoothly and with less tension. Although expanding your abdomen may feel a bit unusual at first, abdominal breathing allows greater use of your lung capacity. Inhale easily and naturally through your nose and let your belly expand, protruding slightly. Allow your lungs to fill from the bottom up. Do not strain. As you exhale slowly, relax your shoulders and feel the contracting of your chest naturally release the tension in the shoulders, pulling them slightly back and down. Do not hold your breath between inhaling and exhaling, a slight pause is fine but consider the tàijítú (the yin-yang symbol) and imagine gradually, nearly imperceptibly, fusing where the inhalations and exhalations meet so that your breathing is more akin to one continuous, flowing movement. Breathe comfortably and rhythmically.

Meditation One

When first observing your mind, you may be surprised at how unconsciously and indiscriminately thoughts and mental images stream forth. It happens so naturally that you may have never before noticed how overwhelming the constant movement of thought can be. This first exercise helps to cultivate focused concentration that allows you to step away from and objectively observe your stream of mental activity, the cascading flow of thoughts and images.

1) You do not want to feel distracted by an uncomfortable sitting posture that causes you to constantly shift and adjust your legs and hips; therefore, take a few moments to establish a suitable position, settle into the position, and generally maintain this position throughout your meditation.

2) You also do not want to feel so comfortable and relaxed that you doze off. If you begin to feel drowsy, you will find your shoulders starting to slump down as your head and body fall forward. Imagine a string attached to the top of your head, pulling and elongating your spine straight. By consciously maintaining this posture and gently pulling your shoulders back and down, you will be able to retain a state of quiet, concentrated attentiveness, not total relaxation.

3) You are now sitting comfortably, spine straight and shoulders not hunched, eyes slightly open and chin a bit lowered, mouth closed and the tip of your tongue touching the top of your mouth behind the front teeth. Develop concentration by counting the number of breaths you take. As you slowly inhale count, "In-ha-a-a-a-a-ale," then, slowly, "ex-ha-a-a-a-a-ale—one . . . in-ha-a-a-a-a-ale, ex-ha-a-a-a-a-ale—two," and so on. Remember not to hold your breath between inhaling and exhaling. Count up to ten and repeat, beginning again at one, for a total of 20-30 breaths.

4) Focus on the rise of your belly and the sensation of air flowing into your nose. Notice how the shoulders relax as you slowly exhale. If you feel any muscle tension—in your legs, in your neck, in your back—relax and let it dissipate into your body as you breathe easily. Note any sounds in the environment around you. Do not identify them as anything in particular, just note that they are there.

5) At some point you may find your mind wandering off on a stray thought. This is quite natural and to be expected. Do not struggle with it. Do not try to suppress it. Notice the thought, observe it, and then quietly return to focusing on the sensation of breathing. Continue counting.

6) After 20-30 breaths, sit quietly for a minute or two. Now rub your hands briskly together for a few seconds to create warmth, cover your face with the palms of both hands and inhale fully. Breathe in slowly through your nose and let your belly extend a bit, allow the ribcage to open as the lungs begin to expand and fill with air, exhale into the palms of your hands and repeat three times. Open the eyes slowly, lower your hands, and gradually become aware of your surroundings.

Continue this practice a few times a day for several days until you are comfortably able to use the breath as a means to focus your attention and concentrate. This technique helps you habituate using the breath as a reference point to which your attention can return when your mind becomes distracted with a random thought or image.

Practicing meditation is not unlike practicing to learn any other skill. The ease of performing the action well or the degree of skill acquired depends on how regular the practice is. If you practice swimming every day, you will be able to maintain a constant level of proficiency and gradually improve. If you practice sporadically, your progress will likewise be erratic and doubtful. It is much more effective to practice regularly each day for a short period of time rather than to practice once every few days for several hours. Consistent and regular practice will more easily transform into a habitual routine, a way of living and being.

A Word of Caution

"Although Vipassana (or Insight) meditation is beneficial

for most people, it is not a substitute for medical or psychiatric treatment and we do not recommend it for people with serious psychiatric disorders."[48]

For those interested in meditation, be cautioned that it may provoke mental or emotional affliction, and one, therefore, must be closely attentive to the meditation experience. When there is an intense identification with mental activity as the sense of self, and there is difficulty recognizing that "you are not your thoughts," a person might experience a disturbing sensation of detachment from the external world or "detachment from the self."[49][50]

This may lead one to feel that the observing self is detached from the participatory self of existential reality, and after meditation, the result is a sense that life is distant and unreal, numb, dream-like, as if one were living in a movie—dissociation.[51][52]

If you have ever suffered from dissociative disorders, heard voices in your head that seem to be the real voices of others, become overwhelmed by memories and emotions, or are taking anti-anxiety or anti-depressant medication, you may find the practice of meditation disconcerting or distressing. In this case, the assistance of an experienced meditation teacher or a therapist with knowledge of meditation practices should first be sought before starting any meditation practice. If you experience mental or emotional discomfort or unease of any kind, stop your meditation practice and consult a mental health professional.

[48] *Persons With Serious Mental Disorders in Introduction to the Technique* (Vipassana Meditation As Taught By S.N. Goenka), http://www2.dhamma.org/en/code.shtml (retrieved 05/25/2014)

[49] *What is dissociation?* (The International Society for the Study of Trauma and Dissociation), http://www.isst-d.org/default.asp?contentID=76#diss (retrieved 05/25/2014)

[50] *Diseases and Conditions: Depersonalization disorder,* http://www.mayoclinic.org/diseases-conditions/depersonalization/basics/definition/con-20033401 (retrieved 05/25/2014)

[51] Castillo RJ, *Depersonalization and meditation* (Psychiatry, 1990 May;53(2):158-68), https://www.ncbi.nlm.nih.gov/pubmed/2191357 (retrieved 05/25/2014)

[52] Sandy Brundage, *Bad Vibes, Warning: Meditating may be hazardous to your health* (SF Weekly News, 28 Aug 2002), http://www.sfweekly.com/2002-08-28/news/bad-vibes/full/ (retrieved 05/25/2014)

Meditation Two

After you are able to use the breath as a means to focus, you can meditate without counting. Use a timer or small alarm clock set for 10-20 minutes.

Continue your meditation practice as in Meditation One, using your breathing as a means to focus your attention and concentrate, but now, do not count your breaths.

Do not expect to experience anything in particular, nothing especially dramatic or enlightening or profound. You may experience a pulsing or tingling, maybe a buzzing sensation. These feelings are not important. They are simply sensory experiences that become more pronounced when you begin to quiet the distraction of your mental chatter. You may feel a lightness, a peacefulness, a trance-like contentment, perhaps spontaneous joy or clarity. Do not crave or become attached to these sensations. You may feel a bit relaxed, you may feel a slight shift in perceptions or, perhaps, nothing but a bit of boredom or restlessness or annoyance. Keep in mind that feeling any particular sensation is not the purpose of meditation. You are meditating merely to observe the random and spontaneous nature in which the thoughts and images of your conditioned mind arise.

Invariably, your focus will wander off on a stray thought. Do not feel frustrated. This is good. This is what allows you to practice. The practice is not to try and stop the arising of thoughts; you cannot. The practice is to observe your thoughts and refrain from clinging to them and chattering out a narrative. This happens so naturally that not until halfway through some aimless discourse do you realize, "Hey, my mind has drifted off chattering about that for a while. Get back here! Pay attention! Focus on the breath!" Ironically, this realization is nothing more than additional mental activity. Note this as well and do not be discouraged. Do not judge yourself harshly. These mental ramblings are an utterly natural habit of your conditioned mind. Simply recognize the thoughts and images, observe their truth as simply intangible mental fabrications, and then quietly return to focus on the sensation of breathing.

To create space from the thought, you might simply observe the thought as it is: *Hmm, an old memory-like thought*, or *Oh, a craving-sensation thought*, or *Yes, a distracted, anxious-about-a-future-event thought.* Do not cling to or be critical of any thought or image. Observe it, step back from it, and let it pass on. Another thought may immediately arise or there may be a slight gap before the next thought arises. Regardless, let the thoughts come, observe them, and let them go. You will soon realize that thoughts, like all conditions, like your inhalations and exhalations, are transitory and impermanent.

The truth is that as you are sitting there meditating, thoughts that arise are wholly unnecessary. Life goes on around you, and your thinking of any particular thing makes absolutely no difference. Of course, when you are in the midst of trying to solve a problem or are in the moment of arranging your schedule or getting your kids to school or being on time for an appointment, you must be focused and attentive. In moments of sitting meditation practice, however, your extraneous thoughts are solely discursive mental chatter. Observe them and understand that they are simply mental fabrications that randomly appear and will just as naturally fade away, provided that you do not cling to and cultivate them.

It is instructive to realize that people everywhere, the people around you, the people whom you know along with the countless anonymous passersby, the other billions inhabiting the earth, whether they seem brooding and cynical or patient and good-natured, are not unlike you, that is: living in a private world of discursive mental activity over a wholly mentally-fabricated ego-story, or feeling the anxiety and apprehension that arises from the mental ruminations of imagined future events. We all face the same struggles of piercing through the deceptions of a conditioned mind; it is our shared human condition.

Meditation in Motion

Tai chi (tàijíquán) is an ancient Chinese martial art sometimes performed for competition and often studied for exercise, stress-relief, and other purported health benefits. Less commonly, tai chi can be practiced as a form of what a Buddhist might describe as doing satipatthana (mindfulness) practice or what sports psychologists describe as achieving "flow"—the merging of awareness with action to experience the moment-to-moment continuum of motion and being. Practicing tai chi with this approach is not performed for show nor performed to impress others. There is no event. There is no drama.

What is it like to notice the passing of clouds in the sky? The flowing of water down a stream? The rustling of tall grass in the breeze? To observe someone in the mindful practice of tai chi is to observe something similar; that is: nothing in particular. There is merely an unfettered and tranquil flow of energy, movement that is not processed, nor contrived, nor purposeful, nor embellished with the dramatic flourishes of ego.

If you have the opportunity to learn and practice tai chi, I recommend it as an effective way to develop the mental concentration necessary for meditation. Tai chi offers several advantages to the beginning meditator: (1) the physical movement is less tedious than continued sitting, (2) the slow-moving shift in positions can be used as a reference to which the practitioner's focus can return when discursive thoughts arise, and (3) unlike focusing on only the breath (where your mind can sometimes meander off into daydreaming or extended discursive thought), practicing tai chi is much less forgiving.

Practicing a variation of the slow Yang-style long form demands focusing attention over a period of 30 to 40 minutes. The repetitive sequence of movements necessitates constant concentrated awareness. If you are distracted by mental chatter, you will confuse the sequence of postures and hesitate, conspicuously breaking your rhythm of movement. Immediately, your attention returns to the present moment where you can recognize, *Ah, I just got distracted by the random thought of this or that.* You can then bring your focus back to practicing the tai chi movements as you observe and release the egoistic chatterings of your mind.

Training in tai chi offers benefits similar to the previous meditation exercises by helping to develop focused concentration that allows one to become mindful of discursive thought and then to step back from its constant and relentless streaming.

Meditation Three

Keep in mind that you are not trying to control or tame your mind; you are not trying to build up a strength of willpower that can overcome physical pain; you are not trying to experience flashing colors and lights, nor trying to induce a dream-like or trance-like state. You are not trying to achieve anything. Do not crave the attainment of "spiritual enlightenment," profound wisdom, mystical powers, joyful bliss, and so on. This is all utter nonsense. Give up the ego fantasy of being or becoming anything. Meditation is the renunciation of all egoistic fairy-tales and illusions. You are practicing merely to observe the truth that the movement of egoistic thought is purely mental fabrication. The ego-story is imagined, intangible, and transitory.

1) Set a timer for 20-30 minutes and settle into a comfortable sitting position.

2) Begin by observing and counting five breaths.

3) Discontinue counting, but continue to breathe comfortably and easily, maintaining a natural rhythm. Now, refrain from focusing any attention on your breathing at all. In this meditation, solely observe whatever thoughts and images arise in your mind, observe them and let them dissipate. If there is a gap of no-thought, simply be present in the stillness.

• Under normal daily circumstances, our consciousness is unknowingly swept along with the mind-stream of thoughts and images. During meditation, we can step outside the stream and merely observe it. It is now not necessary to label an arising thought or image as anything in particular. Simply observe them. You might imagine them as dandelion seeds drifting up and away on a gentle current of air. It matters not whether the thoughts and images are pleasant or unpleasant. Be solely an observer, observing that all thoughts and images are nothing more than movements of the mind, imaginary and transitory.

• If you are struggling with a thought or image, focus on the view from your half-opened eyes as you let the thought or image dissipate. If necessary, focus on your breathing just until you regain your concentration. Then, once again, disregard your breathing and simply observe whatever thoughts and images arise. Observe them and let them dissipate. Do not cling to them and create a narrative.

• Be wholly aware of the energy around you: the warmth of the sun, the brush of air across your face, the chirping of a bird, the sound of trickling water, the cool scent of the morning air. Do not identify these things as anything in particular; simply note that they are there as they pass through your awareness and then fade away.

• Keep your spine straight, shoulders pulled gently back and down. If you feel sleepy or enter a trance-like or dream-like state, stop and take a break. Stand up and stretch. Take a nap or take a short walk. You do not want to feel sluggish or drowsy. Meditation requires a lucid and alert state of awareness.

• You may feel frustrated or aggravated that discursive thoughts arise and you cannot control them: *Why am I thinking about that again? It's not important. That's a disturbing mental image. Stop! Why can't I concentrate? I shouldn't be thinking about that. I can't do this! This is boring.*

Relax. You cannot control your thoughts and the desire to do so, the craving for a "proper" result, merely produces further mental prattling of the egoistic mind. Do not try to "become" or to "succeed in" anything. Observe the thoughts of frustration and aggravation. Simply observe them as movement of thought, and then let them drift off, along with all transient thought.

• As you become more accustomed to meditating, gradually increase the period of time you sit, but remember that short periods of time at regular intervals are much more meaningful than long periods of time at infrequent intervals. A half hour to an hour every morning and evening is reasonable practice for the average individual.

• You may become more aware of your bodily sensations— an itch here, a twitch there. As you sit for longer periods of time, you will likely experience some discomfort or numbness in your legs. What happens when you feel a bothersome sensation? Your mind identifies "discomfort" and acts to immediately alleviate it: *Move the leg! Scratch the itch! Rub the eye!* Instead of immediately reacting to the thought and moving to seek absolute comfort, take a moment and create space between your conscious awareness and the thought of discomfort. Focus your attention on the actual sensation of discomfort. Is it truly pain or merely discomfort being projected as pain? Resistance to a sensation creates mental conflict and anxiety, a heightened sensitivity leading to fear that translates into a lower tolerance for unpleasant stimuli.

Throughout a normal day we have impulsive, egoistic responses to random or reactionary thoughts and feelings that arise. We hear someone's comments, we arise a memory, we experience accomplishments or difficulties in our work, and we then spontaneously feel annoyed, angry, embarrassed, proud, anxious, fearful, conceited, envious, sarcastic, derisive, snarky, and all the rest. A significant benefit of meditation is the practice of creating space between your conscious awareness and reactionary thoughts. Instead of mindlessly reacting, we can learn to dispassionately observe our thoughts and feelings. It is a focused non-reaction to the movement of thought. During meditation, accept bodily sensation without defining it as "pain." Create a moment of space from the sensation and your instinctive reaction that arises a thought of discomfort. Merely observe it. How does the feeling arise? When does discomfort truly become unbearable? How does your mind decide when discomfort becomes defined as intolerable? Is the unpleasant sensation truly causing you physical harm, or is it simply the neurotic chattering of your mind that is causing you to feel anxiety and suffering? Is not your level of pain tolerance, or intolerance, primarily defined by the past experiences of your conditioned mind, memory-like thought? Recall the earlier story of the young woman sobbing in the dental chair before any dental work had begun.

When you observe unpleasant sensation long enough, absent the activity of thought, discomfort will become less intense, oftentimes fading away. Of course, if the feeling becomes severe, do not consider it a test to prove your level of willpower: *I don't care how painful it is. I'm going to stick it out. I'm not going to give up or give in to the pain. No pain, no gain!* No, this is merely additional mental discourse of the egoistic mind, further construction of the ego-story when you prevail and push past the pain. There is no difference whether the mind chatter arises from the craving for comfort or the craving to overcome discomfort and to "become" or to "succeed in" something. Know that there is no success or failure in meditation. There is only sitting and observing the truth of your egoistic, prattling mind.

If it is truly necessary to modify your position, do not instinctively react and move. Observe the discomfort, observe the activity of thought, and move only when you are no longer clinging to and struggling with the anxious thoughts of a conditioned mind. Move slowly, quietly, and mindfully. Observe the change in physical sensation as your body changes position. Observe any movement of thought.

Perhaps there will be none. It matters not.

After meditation practice, it is beneficial to reflect on your experience of what the nature of your mind is like: Your mind clings to an arising thought, which leads to fabrication of an escalating narrative and mind-story as you begin to ponder and brood over the idea. This single thought can eventually result in an emotional response that stimulates your nervous system and leaves you with an acutely real, visceral sensation of stress, anxiety, self-doubt, craving, or, in contrast, self-satisfaction, pride, conceit, and so on.

Contemplate your discursive thoughts and consider how they originate from the deceptions of a conditioned mind which may be ruminating about the past or speculating on and having expectations of future events. This is the private, imaginary world of your mental jibber-jabber, where a past occurrence is an imaginary memory-like thought, a craving is a discontented grasping at transient sensations, and expectations about the future are projected outcomes based on dualistic perspectives. Meditation is simply the practice of non-clinging to these discursive, imaginary ideas.

Modified Diaphragmatic Breathing

If you have become accustomed to abdominal breathing, you can practice a different breathing technique called diaphragmatic breathing. This method takes getting used to, but diaphragmatic breathing has a stronger, deeper, and more calming and engaging effect for meditation. It can more readily bring you to a point of stillness.

The thoracic diaphragm is an internal, relatively dome-shaped sheet of muscle and tendon that extends across the bottom of the ribcage, separating the upper thoracic cavity (lungs, heart, and ribs) from the lower abdominal cavity, which includes a variety of organs: stomach, liver, gallbladder, spleen, pancreas, adrenal glands, kidneys, small intestine, and large intestine. In the abdominal breathing you have been practicing, you relax your abdominal muscles so that when you inhale, the diaphragm contracts, pulls downward, and pushes on the fluid and organs of the abdominal cavity, which causes the abdomen to protrude as the thoracic cavity becomes deeper. Meanwhile, the lungs are pulled down and lengthen, allowing them to expand and fill with air. When you exhale, the diaphragm relaxes and returns to its original position, pushing against the lungs and forcing air out.

In diaphragmatic breathing, neither the abdomen nor upper chest expand. On inhalation, the lower abdominal muscles are engaged, lightly tensed so that the abdomen is not allowed to protrude. As the diaphragm contracts downward, the force, instead of pushing down and expanding the abdominal cavity, is exerted against the lower ribcage, which spreads outward, causing the thoracic cavity to widen as it deepens. You should feel the lower ribs stretching outward from side to side and front to back. The lungs widen and deepen as well, expanding and filling with air on inhalation. As the diaphragm relaxes, it forces air out of the lungs as it returns to its resting state in the process of exhalation.

There should be no movement in the upper chest. In the uppermost abdomen, near the area of the diaphragm, slight movement may be noticeable, but avoid movement in the abdomen below that point.

Breathe comfortably and deeply. Do not strain or exaggerate the depth of inhalation. Feel the lower ribs stretching outward from side to side and front to back as the diaphragm expands outwards in width. As you exhale slowly, feel tension release from your shoulders and neck. Breathe smoothly. Do not hold your breath between inhaling and exhaling.

In the beginning, it may be helpful to stand sideways in front of a mirror to observe and maintain the stillness of your upper chest and abdomen. Remain calm and relaxed. If your breathing becomes shallow and focused in the upper chest, try to release tension around your lower ribcage while maintaining slight tension in your abdominals. Try to feel the lower ribs stretching and expanding. If your breathing becomes irregular or unsteady, or you have trouble finding a rhythm, it may be best to stop, rest, and resume practicing at a later time.

Practice diaphragmatic breathing first as a breathing technique. Once you can maintain this breathing method comfortably, you can then incorporate a modified version into your meditation practice. When meditating, allow the lower ribcage to spread outward as the diaphragm expands but do not be concerned with undue movement in the abdomen. Leave it relaxed, not tensed. Slight abdominal movement and expansion is okay. Breathing should be natural, smooth, rhythmic, and calming to a point of stillness.

A Healthy Body and A Healthy Mind

We know it is healthful to have regular physical exercise and to eat a variety of fresh, wholesome, unprocessed foods, yes? Consider if we religiously worked out at the gym for a few months and then quit, or ate fresh, natural, nutritious foods occasionally but infrequently, how beneficial would these practices be to our overall health? Not very. Meditation is not unlike any other aspect of healthful living. If you practice for a while and quit, if you complete a multi-day meditation retreat and do not continue practicing regularly, if you practice but practice infrequently, meditation will be of limited benefit for a healthful life.

Some are doubtful about the particular benefits of meditation and believe that sitting quietly and relaxing is just as meaningful as meditating. There is nothing wrong with sitting in moments of silence, and, in fact, there reportedly are a myriad of health benefits to be had from the practice. My question is this: The next time you are stuck in traffic, or your flight is delayed, or somebody is rude or insulting to you, or you are brooding over some past event, or you are anxious about a future event, will sitting quietly for a period of time previously be of benefit to you now, as you are experiencing anxiety and discontent in your present life?

The unique benefit of regular meditation practice is that you are practicing to observe the truth of your imaginary and transitory mind chatter so that as you are living your life from moment to moment, you are not constantly deceived and distracted and tormented by the discursive, imaginary thoughts that habitually arise in your mind.

An individual who tries meditation to relieve stress but does not make it a regular part of his or her life is not unlike a person who diets solely to lose weight. When dieting, if the intention is to restrict food intake only until some arbitrary ideal goal weight can be reached, it is probable that bad dietary habits will later return and the individual will continue to struggle with a diet-binge cycle of eating. If, however, the intent is to live more healthfully and habits are arranged to include a natural, nutritious, and healthful balanced diet along with regular exercise, a way of life can be cultivated so that a healthy weight is naturally maintained.

Practicing meditation with the intention of seeking to alleviate stress may provide temporary relief and a sense of calm, but this seldom leads to a regular practice of meditation. Like wanting to lose weight and yo-yo dieting, an individual who meditates but does not cultivate a regular practice of meditation will eventually return to the same life habits that originally caused their stress to arise. If, on the other hand, the intent of meditation practice is to develop a more mindful and healthful way of life, meditation will be habituated into a way of living that leads to cultivating a mindset and perspective that is less anxious and disturbed by discursive thought and is more present and engaged with the moment of living.

Meditation and the Distraction of Technology

It is quite normal to expend time, effort, and resources working out at the gym and creating or arranging specialized diets for a healthful lifestyle. Why not commit similar efforts to your mental and emotional wellbeing? If we can afford several hours each day watching inane television programming or becoming engrossed by the flashing screen of some electronic virtual-reality gadget, there is ample time for a regular meditation practice. Of course, it is much easier to sit passively and have our minds distracted by flickering electronic lights and images than to sit in active observation of our minds. It is quite understandable, really, that we are so attracted to television, video, and film media, because with no effort of our own, not even the mental effort of creativity or visualization, our minds are impregnated with fanciful, invented narratives and ideas, or contrived and calculated dramas. Our attention is thus effectively (albeit temporarily) distracted from the anxious and uneasy restlessness of our private thoughts. Without our distractions, we would be left wholly alone to silently confront the discursive ruminations of our minds, minds which are in perpetual conflict over egoistic deceptions to which they have been conditioned. And who wants to face the illusions, self-doubts, fears, and outright uninspired boredom of their ego?

That we are so consumed by the operation of personal electronic devices and social media is not at all surprising. The profusion of electronic gadgetry is the infrastructure through which the banality of social media arrives, seducing us with instant gratification for our egoistic impulses. We invent virtual ego-worlds in which we can fantasize that our random, discursive, nattering thoughts and opinions are meaningful and substantial. We communally tap, click, publish, and text in a desperate attempt to bring recognition to I, me, my, and mine. We become immersed in a self-absorbed virtual-reality mental playground, contrived for egoistic minds that are so yearning to give life to their vacuous, puerile jibber-jabber, egoistic minds so yearning to become "something" tangible, real, and permanent, egoistic minds so desperately eager to construct and reinforce the individual and collective illusion of self as, all the while, our presence to life experience mindlessly twitters away.

Contrast this with the practice of meditation, where individual self-deceptions and the matrix of collective illusion are purposefully stripped away. A person is left to simply observe the truth of the transient, impermanent, and imaginary nature of his or her thoughts and ego-story, freeing oneself from the limitations and fears and anxieties that arise from the mental agitations of discursive and conditioned thought.

Admittedly, at first glance, indulging in technology-based entertainment as a stimulating distraction appears a bit more enjoyable than practicing meditation. The truth, though, is that the yáng of mental stimulation is complemented by the yin of non-stimulation. That is, stimulation is accompanied with a state of boredom.

As the constant craving for noise, mental distraction, and the virtual ego-stroke becomes habituated, one struggles against boredom and anxiousness whenever he or she is removed from the electronic fantasy-world of virtual stimulation. The result is a prattling, craving, distracted mind persistently drawing a person away from the joy of being physically and consciously present, engaged and alive.

Meditation, in contrast, offers the unfettered understanding of: the true nature of impermanence and non-duality, the true nature of our interconnectedness, and the true nature of the illusory self. Meditation can bring about a fuller participation and interest in life experience, leading to the nonexistence of boredom, as having a heightened engagement with the existing, external world of energy and stimuli makes the activity of living a richer and more fulfilling one. The natural world that surrounds you at every moment becomes clearly apparent on a conscious level and is available for you to sense, take joy in, and appreciate. There is no boredom and no need for stimulation beyond solely being aware, present, and in union with the action of living—mindfulness.

Meditation Four: Mindfulness

Sitting meditation is a practice, but you are not practicing to become a professional meditator. You are practicing to observe the true nature of your mind so that you can live with not the preoccupation of your imagination but with awareness and presence.

Mindfulness is bringing the practice of meditation into daily life. Which means what, exactly? It does not mean that when you are driving your car you are thinking, *I am driving my car . . . Look at all the traffic . . . My hands are on the steering wheel . . . I am turning . . . There is a red light . . . Now, I am stopping.* Mindfulness does not mean that when you are washing the dishes you are thinking, *My hands feel wet . . . There is the water, swirling around . . . The plate is greasy . . . I am washing the grease off of the greasy plate . . . The plate is now clean.*

No, mindfulness does not mean that you begin to mentally babble on about everything you observe in the present moment. Mindfulness means that you are active without the thought of action. There is no mental chatter at all. The practice of mindfulness is not unlike the practice of mushin or being "in the flow," where action and awareness merge to become solely presence and being. There is no mind chatter distracting you from the action of living. You are simply living while present to the energy and movement of the moment in which you exist.

Become more conscious of the external world, without the distraction of a chattering mind, and you may begin to see things that you had not observed before, hear sounds that you had not noticed before, smell fragrances that you had not perceived before, taste flavors that you had not distinguished before, and feel sensations that you had not recognized before. You do not attain extrasensory abilities but rather become attentive to the energies and stimuli that have always existed and will continue to exist around you, the energies and stimuli whose presence has gone unnoticed because one's mind is normally preoccupied and distracted by the chattering internal thoughts of ego.

Living and Present

Where does the present moment exist but in movement and activity. The present is the action that one is engaged in at any particular moment: eating, walking, talking, traveling, working, exercising, and so on. Living in the moment means to live in action.

As you go about your day, stop yourself every so often, interrupt the train of discursive thought for a few moments, look up and notice where you are. Notice the world of objects and energies around you and be mindful of what you are doing and where you are doing it—right now.

Note: You may consider some of the following exercises venturing worryingly toward navel-gazing, tambourine-rattling nonsense. Rest assured there is nothing mystical, or mysterious, or supernatural about them. No need to put on airs or pretensions. They are merely ordinary exercises that one can practice at his or her convenience throughout the day. The intent is to occasionally break the spell of one's conscious awareness being swept off with the unrelenting and unmindful current of discursive, rambling mental noise. You are not your thoughts. Step away from the constant burbling babble of thought and simply be present in whatever you are doing, be "in the flow,"—mushin.

Eating:

Regrettably, we often consume food not especially present to the experience of eating. When driven only by the craving for satiation, we chew and swallow mindlessly, not fully appreciating the experience that eating can be. Heaping food into our mouths, we busily and distractedly click and tap on electronic gadgets, chat with others, watch TV, read, and so on. At least occasionally, take the time to fully appreciate such a complete sensory experience as consuming a good meal.

Regardless of where you are eating, whether it is at home or in a restaurant, stop for a moment and simply observe. Look about. Take a breath. Listen to and quietly observe the environment around you. Feel your forearms resting upon the table. Now, simply note the appearance of your food, its shape, color, texture, and the light reflected upon it. Look at your hand holding the fork or holding the food. Take in the aroma. Do not create a discourse in your head about what you are observing, merely experience your perceptions and sensations. As when meditating, if discursive mental chattering arises (e.g., *This is goofy, navel-gazing nonsense!*) simply observe it, and let it pass on. Return your concentration to the experience of eating. Take a bite of food and chew leisurely. Observe the various flavors, juices, and textures, shifting, blending, and transforming. Focus your attention and you will be able to hear the sounds of your chewing as the food is crunched on, crushed, and mashed. Before you take another mouthful, swallow and follow the movement of food as it works its way down your throat.

As you become more mindful to the experience of eating, your actions will likely slow, but deliberate, slow movement and self-conscious thought about what you are doing is not the intent. Simply live in the activity of eating, absent any movement of thought. Be conscious of the experience as it naturally unfolds.

Hiking or Taking a Walk:

Step easily and leisurely, with a posture and approach similar to sitting meditation: spine straight, shoulders slightly back and down, touch the tip of your tongue to the top of your mouth behind the front teeth, breathe comfortably from the abdomen or diaphragm. Note the movement of your legs and feet as your heel touches the ground, and your foot rolls forward and pushes off from the ball of your foot and your toes. Feel the shift in body balance as you move. Look and observe the objects surrounding you. See the shapes and forms of things passing around you and by you as you focus on the sensation of your physical movement through space. Look down, look ahead, look around. Look up at the sky. Moving through space, hear the sound of your footsteps, the rustling of the leaves in the trees. Feel the warmth of sun on your face, the momentary breeze. Smell the air, the trees, the grass. Perhaps you will begin to sense changes in temperature as you make your way through sunlight and shade. Observe without defining or contemplating. Simply note your observations.

Study the plants and grasses. Initially, they may appear stationary and seemingly inanimate. Watch quietly and you will begin to see movement, everywhere: a slight sway, a rustle, creatures crawling, hopping, buzzing, slithering. Life, energy, and movement is all around you. Walk on. If discursive mental chatter arises, observe it, let it pass, and return your awareness to the sensory experience of your movement. If you are in a safe place free of obstacles or moving hazards, try the previous focus technique of concentrating your gaze on a sheet of air at some midpoint in front of you as you walk.

Walking outdoors is pleasant on a nice day, but this practice can be done anywhere, at any time. Throughout the day, decide to take a moment and be mindful of your movement—inside your house, at the market, in your office, anywhere—and you may experience a shift in your perceptions that changes the way you view your relationship to space, time, and the external world.

Communicating:

Speaking mindfully is no easy task when the voice of ego is eager to assert itself and be acknowledged. Do you recognize the following manifestations of the chattering, egoistic mind?

• Speaking with an uncontrollable compulsion, expelling mental chatter to discharge the agitation brought about by the conflict of emotion—anger, fear, self-doubt, or pride, conceit, vanity, and all the rest of it.

• Simply talking. Jabbering. Pointedly talking over others, oblivious or indifferent to what others are saying.

• Forcefully stating opinions and ideas to feel recognized, eager to be proved that one is right.

• Self-consciously anxious to be approved of and applauded for what one says. Scrutinizing the comments and expressions of others for evidence of their attention, confirmation, or agreement.

• Smug silence. Sitting with a mind that is quietly nattering out dismissive, judgmental, and derisive commentary about others while finding satisfaction in one's own private, ego-tistical, smirking self-approval.

To be a mindful speaker is first to be a mindful listener. Is your mind attentive, open, non-judgmental and quietly non-chattering when someone is speaking to you? Or are you privately jabbering out opinions, judgments, and criticisms in your head, or, conversely, are you preoccupied with anxious thoughts of self-consciousness and self-doubt? Are you engaged with the speaker and the ideas being expressed, or are you distractedly looking at or listening to others nearby? Is your mind continuously occupied with its own internal prattle as you merely wait for the speaker to just ... stop ... talking so that you can state your own opinion?

To begin with, do not listen to others through memories of the past. When we live through the mind-stories in our heads, we con-sider our relations, friends, and acquaintances through the assess-ments, emotions, and expectations of our past experiences with them. We cannot see them as they truly are in the present but view them through our memory-like thoughts. To whomever you are speaking, regard the person before you without judgment, without criticism, without preconceptions. Approach the person simply as the individual before you and listen, without the prejudice derived from history. Listen not only to a person's words but seek to un-derstand the person's feelings, the person's intent, the person's de-sires, the person's fears. Do not assume you know when you do not know. Do not make up stories in your head. When you are uncertain, enquire for clarification, with patience and humility. Lis-ten with understanding, and presence.

When you are listening to someone speak, be mindful of the egoistic nattering in your mind. Whatever it might be comprised of—images, feelings, criticisms, judgments, prejudices, random thoughts, and so on—do not take hold of these thoughts and cre-ate a narrative in your head. Recognize them and let them go. Let them dissipate and return your attention to what the person whom you are with is saying.

Speaking mindfully means to communicate and respond to others with thoughtfulness and consideration, which means that mindfulness does not take place when you are speaking but when you are pondering what to say. One of the most useful suggestions I have received for communicating mindfully is: Don't say anything!

Don't say anything!

Years ago, in a typically adequate but pedestrian Chinese hotel room, my elderly father and I, with my younger sister as witness to it all, were having an increasingly heated debate over what to do with the significant pile of local currency before us.

We had met in Southern China, arriving from three separate countries—my dad from the U.S., my sister from Thailand, and I from Taiwan, and we had been traveling together and visiting relatives for the previous two weeks. Also on our itinerary was a family business transaction, which we had just finalized. Now due to depart in another week and go our separate ways, we had first to determine what to do with the stack of money on the table.

I suggested, "Why don't we leave it here with a relative or let them invest in a piece of property for us? Or we can open a bank account and leave it here so we'll have some cash whenever we come back to visit. The Chinese economy is really growing now, and the renminbi (Chinese currency) is getting stronger."

My father, forever distrustful of the Chinese political and financial system, felt otherwise, "No, I want to take it with me."

I understood his apprehension, but already stressed by the responsibility to look out for his health and safety while traveling in a foreign country, I didn't want to be troubled by carrying around and having to be watchful over a sack of currency.

"Everyone says that investing in China is the thing to do now. The economy is on the verge of booming."

"No, the banks here aren't safe."

"But, then we'll have to drag the money around with us for another week. And we won't want to leave it in hotel rooms. What? Do you want to walk around with all this cash stuffed into our pockets?"

"That's okay. I'll carry it," he insisted as I thought, *Sure, that's a great idea.*

"So, if someone wants to rob us, you're going to stop them, right? Come on, you don't even need the money over there in the States. And what about when we leave the country? You're not allowed to take that much cash out. If you get stopped going through customs, then what?"

I know this is going to end up being trouble, I kept thinking as I was feeling progressively more impatient that my father and I were having one of our debates, which typically pitted my "rationality" against his "irrationality."

Obstinate, my dad countered, "They won't catch me. I'll hide it in my luggage."

In those days I was prone to speaking fast, loud, and belligerently (nowadays, mostly just loud), my voice of ego often spewing faster than my mouth could jabber. With thoughts of *Are you kidding?* and a feeling of annoyance twisting me up, I sensed my face flush, my eyes narrow, and pressure throb in the vein of my forehead. I was about to respond yet again when I heard my sister interject, "Don't say anything."

And I didn't.

My acknowledging her advice somehow took me out of my own head, and I immediately felt at ease. I mentally stepped back from the conversation with my father and instead became an observer to my own chatter and the emotion that was developing from it.

"What? Nothing to say?" my father asked, in what I perceived as a condescending manner that would normally have aggravated me.

I paused, deliberatively, "No . . . Do what you think is best." I felt no frustration or annoyance, nothing. At that moment, I had stopped caring about making the point or trying to be right, and it was a relief not to be caught up in my head.

"Whatever happens happens. We'll just deal with whatever comes up."

And that was that.

When you sense that you are about to get caught up in some inconsequential verbal confrontation, remind yourself, *Don't say anything!* and then observe the egoistic mental chatter of wanting to be right or needing to assert your opinion slip away. Eventually, the not saying anything becomes the response, without the mental reminder, absent any movement of thought. You have become the being of it and can chuckle to yourself about the silliness of it all.

Speaking mindfully:

• Listen attentively. Be present by not letting extraneous mental chatter distract you. Observe your discursive thoughts and let them pass, bringing your attention back to the speaker. Observe him or her, their presence and physicalness, their expressions and mannerisms. Do not project your feelings, prejudices, or mind-stories upon the person. Simply listen to the tone and intent of their voice.

• Forgo the need to be right. In fact, forgo the need to be heard. If you are not being listened to, let it go unless it is truly, crucially urgent. What, really, demands to be said right now? What, really, demands to be heard by some other? When others are speaking out with aggression, impatience, anxiety, fear, anger, conceit, and all the rest, let them speak. *Don't say anything!* This can be a trying test and an ideal opportunity to observe the chatter of your egoistic mind. Wait, mindfully, observant of any movement of thought; focus on your breathing. It is possible you may not have the moment to voice your ideas at all, and so what? If you begin to feel sullen or defensive or irritated, note your reactive, egoistic thoughts that cause these feelings to arise. Observe the thoughts and let them go, fade away as if they were simply discursive, egoistic prattle, because that is, indeed, what they are.

• Take the opportunity to express yourself only when someone is willing to listen to you. Speak slowly and thoughtfully. Pause to gather your thoughts so that you speak clearly and concisely.

• Be mindful of your tone of voice. Do not speak with anger, derision, judgment, or condescension, but with patience and equanimity.

• Avoid speaking meaningless mental chatter. A majority of everyday conversation is comprised of frivolous nonsense: complaining, gossiping, constructing mind-stories about others, bickering about who is right, and so on. Be mindful of talk that is arrogant, egotistical, self-righteous, judgmental, belittling, mean-spirited, or divisive.

When you become more mindful in communication, you will find that you speak less but more thoughtfully. You will listen more, with greater insight, understanding, and consideration.

Being Present in the Mundane:

I had just finished another afternoon grappling with a small gas-powered cultivator, tilling the muddy glop of a Taiwanese rice-paddy field when Richard, a young, recently arrived farm volunteer who had been watching me asked, "You ever feel bored, all day mixing the dirt?"

Ah, yes, boredom: the chattering mind distracted by the desire to be doing something else.

I had become acquainted with a local farmer and agreed to help him at his small organic farm in the mountains of Taiwan. Arriving several weeks earlier, I was prepared to approach the mundane, tedious farm labor as a form of mindfulness practice.

That is, focus my awareness solely on the action I was engaged in and the environment in which I was present. When I began to feel hot and fatigued, I observed these sensations arising from the movement of thought, mental grumblings about and aversion to ordinary discomfort even as my body was nowhere near its physical limit. When my mind drifted off with some rambling, extraneous chatter, I would return my focus to the physical movement in which I was involved, in this instance: taming the six and a half horsepower cultivator stubbornly bucking its own way through clods of clay and viscous mud and making sure my limbs stayed clear of its churning, haphazard path. I also simply observed my perceptions and sensations of the natural environment: the warm and intensifying sunshine, a random breeze, the grit of clay sludge oozing up around my bare feet, the fresh and humid mountain air, the cool of sloshing muddy water, frogs darting frantically from the whirling claws of the cultivator, the distant view of the hazy cityscape, and so on. From time to time, sweaty and splattered with mud, I would sit, heartily gulping down the chill spring water, a simple and refreshing joy. By being present to my actions and environment and not constantly distracted by a narrative of random, chattering thoughts, I felt quite content and high-spirited, a

Flooding the rice paddies – Mountains of Taiwan

sense of, as the French would say, joie de vivre, and a feeling of boredom never arose. I would not go so far as to describe my experiences to be (as Bill Russel might say) "magical," but I did find that the mundanity of everyday routine had become much less mundane. And then, my farmer friend handed me a chain saw.

"You can cut down those trees? They block sun. You before use chain saw?"

I looked up to the dense row of tall, slender trees growing along a slope covered with decaying vegetation. In my private imagination of apprehensive jibber-jabber, the first image that arose was the chainsaw's bouncing off a knot in the wood and my watching the spinning chain kick back and lop off my lower leg, my foot still in its boot. I was certain I'd read stories like that before. The next image I had was of my slipping on the moist, unsettled surface of the hill. Grasping out for balance, I see the whirling chain saw whack my wrist, and I then watch as my detached hand tumbles inertly to the ground.

Mental gibberish. I mused over how suddenly random thoughts can appear.

"Uh, no. I haven't ever used a chain saw before," I replied, handing it back to him and still contemplating whether the narratives in my head were merely unreasonable anxiety.

"Easy. You watch."

He repeatedly yanked the cord of the chain saw, causing nothing more than a reluctant spluttering. Another optimistic jerk and the chain buzzed eagerly, displaying an air of menace as it spewed smoke and a spray of oil flicked from the chain. He easily sliced through two trees standing nearby, then quickly sectioned them into more manageable pieces.

It didn't look so difficult. I figured staying wary of the mutilating capabilities possessed by the whirring chain was enough to keep me mindful and focused.

"Your turn," said the farmer as he handed me the saw.

I gripped the handle carefully as the motor coughed and died. Up I trudged to the top of the slope and roughly yanked at the cord, making sure to hold the whizzing chain away from my legs. The trigger of the saw was defective and had to be held in a particular position to remain functional. I felt a little aggravated. Random thoughts of gruesome work accidents I'd read about—falling into an industrial meat grinder or getting pulled into a wood chipper, to name a few—appeared and passed through my mental narrative as I remained particularly mindful of my actions: the firmness of my stance, the position of my body, the direction of the cut, the position of the tool in relation to the direction that the tree would fall, and so on. Of course, nothing disastrous occurred, but I was necessarily more focused and mindful handling the chain saw than I had been when cultivating the soil.

Being aware and present can be quite enjoyable in the mundane, but as the stress level of a situation rises, it is no simple task to remain mindful, e.g., when you are dealing with a classroom full of bored and truculent junior high school kids, or handling the hostility of an arrogant co-worker, or rushing to meet a deadline, or wielding a chain saw halfway up a hill. If you are able to cultivate the ability to step back and observe your mental chatter before it gets caught up in the madness of the moment, however, you will be more able to maintain a sense of equanimity and experience some measure of liberation from the stress of a difficult situation.

After the rice fields were tilled and the farm was organized, I visited an old friend back in the U.S. He was a good-hearted individual but a person wholly self-absorbed, living in his head as a hostage to his memory. Although he had the resources to live a comfortable and relatively carefree life, he would spend his days ruminating about the past, his regrets and failures, as he drank himself into a morose and hopeless stupor. In one infrequent moment of lucidity, he commented to me, "Oh, so you use meditation techniques to distract your mind."

No, quite the contrary.

For him, the reality and truth of life were grounded in his mental jibber-jabber: his ego-story and egoistic attachment to memory, the dualistic beliefs of his conditioned mind, and his non-acceptance of impermanence. In fact, it was exactly this: his mental prattling, that was his distraction. It was his constant mental discourse that kept him distracted from the joy of being present and engaged with the reality of the external world, distracted from being mindful of his actions and present to the energy and stimuli of his environment and the community of people around him. Mindfulness does not distract you from your mind. Mindfulness dissolves the distraction of your nattering ego so that you can live with an awareness and connectedness to the reality of the world around you.

Throughout the day, there are countless opportunities to practice mindfulness. Regardless of what you are doing—waiting for an appointment, washing the car, playing music, gardening, exercising, taking a shower, and so on—simply disengage your attention from the prattling discourse in your head and be present to the action you are living. Do not let your attention get drawn away by the mental activity of discursive thought. Do not ruminate about the past or obsess over a future event. As thoughts arise, let them pass on, one by one, noting that the movement of thought is merely mental fabrication. Do not become absorbed into an imagined narrative. Observe your sensory perceptions engaged with the environment in which you are present and return your awareness to the action you are performing, without undue mental chatter. The simple joys of experiential existence are available always. You are immersed in and move through them at every moment.

Lastly, do not let mindfulness become yet another egoistic pursuit. Do not become attached to and inspired by the attending to of simple sensory experience; otherwise, you may end up spending your days staring at your navel. The point is not to feel otherworldly by practicing mindfulness and becoming more aware of the moment-to-moment reality. No, the point is to use these exercises so that you can observe the nature of your mind, and you can then live life grounded in the truth: your ego-story and memory are illusory mental constructs; duality exists only in your mind; all compounded phenomena are impermanent, and we exist interconnected to the world around us.

FIVE

FEAR AND ANXIETY

Menjangan Island - Bali, Indonesia[53]

Is there a single word that describes both wonder and terror? The thought occurred to me as I drifted silently beyond the edge of the serene and brilliantly shimmering coral reef beneath me. Peering below, I watched as the underwater precipice sheared off into abrupt emptiness. My stomach flinched: the Abyss, inhabited, certainly, with some predatory creature whose indifferent, primal attention would be alerted to my graceless thrashing. In my limbic brain, visceral alerts were being triggered; I was an object to be consumed.

When I was visiting my youngest sister in Bali a few years back, she suggested taking an excursion, "How about we go snorkeling at Menjangan Island?"

97

My sister had been working and living in Bali, Indonesia, raising her daughter, Olivia, a spirited, adventurous child whose four young years had been spent in and around the sea. Olivia's eyes brightened when she heard her mother's offer, "Really, Mama? When?" I was a bit less enthusiastic. I had never gone snorkeling before and, honestly, would have rather stayed on land, where, with the earth beneath my feet, I could more clearly see or sense the approach of unfamiliar hazards. If necessary, I could (or imagined I could anyway) evade or fight, and, at the very least, knew how to instinctively run like hell. Besides, I have always suffocated in the water. Not drown, suffocate, as if when the water envelops me, it compresses and constricts my lungs. Immersed in water, I feel as if I'm unable to expand my lungs and breathe. I can never get a good, healthy lungful of oxygen until, finally, gasping, I'm back on dry land. I didn't grow up around the water and never felt the need to jump into it. Why would I want to do that? This is an especially pertinent question considering that I don't easily float. Lean and somewhat wiry, I sink, like a rock. Since laboring through dreaded swimming lessons those few childhood summers long ago, I have maintained a distinct image of my thrashing about, suffocating, and inevitably finding myself breathless, exhausted, and clinging to the safety of the pool's edge. Somehow I learned how to swim, sort of, but I had never felt especially comfortable in the water and considered myself an uncertain swimmer. I was perfectly content being a land-dweller, and while I watched with some envy others who could splash into the sea without a care, the thought of swimming in the ocean had never been particularly appealing.

Peering down at Olivia, eager and enthusiastic, I thought to myself, *Well, it really is all mental—right?* Maybe now was the opportunity to face my apprehension to swimming and being in the open water. Besides, a lot of people snorkel: younger, older, in-shape and out-of-shape, swimmers good and not-so-good. I would face my unease with mindfulness, simply see my discomfort for the mental chatter that it was. Normally, I would have easily declined an offer to jump off a boat and into open water, but, what the hell, why not test my mental focus?

"Yeah, sure. It sounds like fun," I lied.

Menjangan, meaning "deer" in the indigenous language, is a small island situated to the north-west of Bali. The name is said to have originated from local islanders who observed that every spring, wild deer herds could be seen swimming the approximately one kilometer distance to the island. A short 40-minute ride on a simple charter boat would deliver us there.

A few days later we were leaving Bali island on a sunny boat ride toward Menjangan. I let my sister attend to the banal chit-chat with fellow travelers while I silently enjoyed the cooling ocean spray and recalled an incident a Taiwanese friend, a biology academic, had had previously that year.

My friend, the Professor (as I called him) and I were spending the afternoon at a mountainside teahouse as he was describing to me his upcoming plans. He was about to embark on a two-week long backpacking trip to southern Malaysia before heading on a work-travel trip to Australia.

"Do you have a job set up? How long will you be in Australia?" I asked him.

"I'm not sure. It depends on what kind of job I get and how much I like to live there. After backpacking in Malaysia, I'll travel in Australia for a few weeks, then look for a job. Then I'll see what happens."

He was young and adventurous, carefree and eager for novel and foreign experiences. I continued my enquiry, "Do you have any friends there? How easy is it to find work?"

"I heard it isn't so hard to find some kind of work. Online, I've met Taiwanese people already there working, and they share information about where to find the jobs. I'm not so worried. Oh, and this girl just asked if she could join me for backpacking to Malaysia. She's between jobs and wants to take a vacation."

"How convenient. So, what do you mean, exactly, by 'this girl'? What, you met her walking down the street?"

"No, she's my friend's friend. I met her a few times, but I don't really know her so well. She seems friendly, and cute too."

He sipped his tea with a self-satisfied grin, quite pleased with himself. Who could blame him? He was a twenty-something young man, free of worry and responsibilities, cheerful and enthusiastic, and more than happy to have a young, female traveling companion. I couldn't help but smile with him. The days were sunny, warm, and easy. Life was good. I wished him luck and fun times working in Australia, and off he and his female acquaintance went on their Malaysian adventure.

Less than a week later, I ran into the Professor's mother and asked how my friend was doing on his trip. She looked at me and quickly looked away, "He's coming home in a few days."

"Coming home? What about Australia? What happened?"

She averted eye contact and seemed distressed. Appearing to be on the verge of tears, she shook her head. "I can't talk," and she walked off.

Huh? What was that about? I imagined a relative or family friend or childhood classmate had suffered some misfortune, and my friend would have to return to Taiwan for a hospital visit. Or funeral, perhaps? Asian people are funny that way. They avoid openly talking about tragedy and death in the fear that bad juju may somehow set foot at their door.

My friend's younger brother was standing nearby, so I approached him, "How's your brother? Is he okay? What happened?"

Blankly, he replied, "I don't know. You can talk to him when he gets back."

Huh? What? Ominous signs, for sure. "Oh, okay. Tell him to contact me."

Several days later, I was sitting on a bus heading back up the mountain to meet the Professor. I saw him standing in front of the teahouse, waiting for me. He spotted me as I walked up, so I gave him a wave, "Professor, long time no see. You look fine. Are you okay?"

"Yes, I'm fine. How are you?"

"Good. What happened? Did a relative pass away?"

"No, nothing like that. I'll tell you about it inside."

After sitting down and preparing our tea-making set-up, he started to explain, "Well, this girl and I were traveling in Malaysia, right. We were having fun and spent a few days at a beach in the south, but then we wanted to look for something different to do and saw a flyer for a three-day trip to a resort on a smaller island, off the coast. We took a small charter boat over there and checked into the room and everything. And the next day, we went snorkeling. A storm had passed through, so the water was a little dirty, but it wasn't too bad."

"So you two were getting along okay? You like her?"

"Yeah, she was fun. She always was ready to do something new. We got along really well. She was funny, a little goofy. Did I tell you she was cute?"

"Yes, I heard about that." (Eye roll.) "And then what?"

"Well, after snorkeling for a while, we were resting on the beach, just hanging around. We decided to get lunch, but I wanted to go out one more time before we went back. I asked her if she wanted to go with me, but she told me that she was tired and would wait for me there, on the beach, so I went back out for a short time. When I was finished, I was coming out of the water and saw several people charging past me, running into the ocean. I turned around to look where they're running and saw a body floating on the water . . . I knew it was her."

"What? What do you mean? Your friend went back out there? Why'd she do that?"

"I don't know. She said she didn't want to go back out, but she did anyway, after I went out. They pulled her out of the water and did CPR, then they took her away. I had to stay and talk to the police. When I finished, they told me she died."

"What? Oh, I'm sorry to hear that."

"Then I went back to the hotel and packed up her and my stuff. The next morning, I woke up and it was kind of like a dream. I was looking around, and I saw our bags there, hers and mine, next to each other. She wasn't in the room, and . . . I don't know. Later,

I took the small charter boat back to the mainland. She was in a body bag lying next to me, on the same bench seat we were sitting on when we arrived a couple days before. I felt very strange."

"Are you feeling okay about everything? That sounds pretty awful."

"I'm okay."

I studied the Professor's face as he poured me another cup of tea. He was expressionless and didn't appear especially disturbed by any of it. He must have been a Taoist. I found the whole affair slightly unsettling.

"It's kind of weird. Why'd she go back out there?"

He filled his own cup, "I don't know."

Wondering if it might relieve my friend of any guilt, although he seemed quite unaffected, I offered, "Maybe she was depressed and wanted to commit suicide. You know, because she had lost her job and all."

"No, I don't think so. In Singapore, she had a job interview that she was pretty excited about."

"Oh, okay, maybe not. And then you brought her body back to Taiwan?"

"No, then I had to call her family. They live in a different city and didn't know she went traveling with me, or that she quit her job. They thought she was still working at her old job in Taipei, and they had no idea who I was because, well, I was only an acquaintance. When I called her parents, they didn't believe me and hung up on me. I called several times, and then I talked to her older brother. Finally, I convinced him that I wasn't trying to con them. I waited in Malaysia for her mother and aunt to come and get the body. Then they had a cremation. After that, we all came back together. It was pretty terrible."

We were about there; it had been a quick boat ride. I was heading to my own snorkeling adventure at Menjangan Island. Thinking about the Professor's snorkeling incident wasn't so comforting. I wondered how I would feel, swimming in the open sea, and I was curious to see how trying to be mindful and observant of my mental chatter might inhibit the arising of emotion—fear, anxiety, apprehension, and whatever else.

Fear

We need fear. Fear looks out for our personal welfare. Fear prompts us to assess possible danger and to make rational decisions to avoid injury, or worse. Fear kicks us in the backside—*Watch out!*—to instinctively jump out of the way when a car comes speeding our way. Fear is our primal guardian angel.

All animals have a fear response, naturally; it is the necessary ability to detect and respond to threatening stimuli for protection and survival. Fear is our friend. Unless, that is, it paralyzes us. Unless we become so paralyzed with fear that we cannot take appropriate action to neutralize or escape a threat. Fear can shut down rational thought so that we act in wholly irrational ways. Fear can, sometimes, be our worst enemy.

When we experience fear, numerous regions of the brain are involved in processes and interactions that happen instantly, simultaneously, and continuously, a storm of neural activity. Although a thorough explanation of our fear response is complex, the basic picture looks like this: Sensory input—spotting a cobra on the trail ahead, for instance—is transmitted to an older (evolution-wise) region of the brain, the amygdala. The amygdala, which handles major emotions and many of the more primitive processes of the brain, is linked to long-term memory processing and the identification of known threats. As sensory information—*See cobra on trail!*—is received, threat associations are subconsciously identified: *cobra = danger!* Instinctively and immediately, signals are then sent to the hypothalamus, which triggers a torrent of biochemistry that surges through our bodies and prepares our bodies with the fight-or-flight response. Our hearts pound and blood pressure rises, increasing blood supply to our muscles. Breathing becomes rapid as oxygen intake is increased. To conserve energy, nonessential immune and digestive systems temporarily shut down. Our mouths go dry. Our stomachs knot up. Muscles tense. Pupils dilate. Sound fades. We become hyper-alert. This instinctive fear response occurs in a subconscious flash, and before we are aware of what has happened, we are prepared to fight to the death, or run like hell.

Of course, if this were all there were to it, we would be nervous wrecks, jumpy and jittery, freezing with a deer-in-the-headlights stare or striking out or scattering at the slightest provocation. Most of us are much more composed, thankfully, and for this we can be grateful for a more recent (evolution-wise) development of our brains: the neo-cortex, or more specifically, the frontal lobe of the neo-cortex. The frontal cortex is associated with more advanced mental functions: complex language processing, rational thinking, strategic planning, and so on. The frontal cortex receives sensory information as well—*See cobra on trail!*—but instead of instinctively reacting like the amygdala, the frontal cortex will more slowly (relatively) and deliberately analyze detail and context: *object not moving, no distinct head or tail, coloring unlike cobra, looks like rope.* As the frontal cortex assesses the threat, it is having ongoing interaction and communication with the amygdala. Meanwhile, the amygdala has already gotten us physically wound tight, poised to take immediate action. If, a moment later, the frontal cortex determines there is no danger, it tells the amygdala, *Calm down. It is not a threat*—and the amygdala then signals the hypothalamus to shut down the fight-or-flight response. We can breathe easy now and chuckle to ourselves, *It is only a piece of rope.*

Our fear response system serves us well, as long as it remains judiciously balanced between the rational and the primal. Occasionally, however, extreme sensory input and a desperate sense of imminent destruction may be so acute that the amygdala response overwhelms any process of rational thinking, and the brain becomes paralyzed. In a war zone, a plane crash, a burning building, the mind can go blank. Vision narrows, hearing mutes, and the result is panic. We are mentally frozen; we cannot think straight; we lose the ability to take decisive, strategic, and effective action;

we struggle not to run away, screaming. In fact, we may act wholly counterintuitive for our safety and survival. Fear can be friend or foe.[54][55]

Anxiety to Fear

Fear is derived from physical reality. Anxiety is derived from imagination.

When we are flush with the sensation of fear, it is because external stimuli has been identified as a threat. The threat may not be real—a piece of rope mistaken for a cobra, for example—but the perceived menacing encounter, a true physical situation, exists.

Although anxiety might feel similar to fear, it is vague and diffuse, less acute, arising without the presence of a physical threat, fabricated wholly in our minds. We create anxiety with thoughts and images, chattering and discursive ruminations of dire consequences and future catastrophe. This mental activity then gives rise to emotions, based on nothing more than imagined situations which may or may not occur, or imagined situations that are irrational and non-existent. This leads to feelings of apprehension, dread, and distress.

If we are walking in the woods and spot a cobra-like object on the trail ahead, an alert fear response is desirable. If we feel anxious and apprehensive upon visiting the dentist, this is anxiety, our imaginations in distress.

The boat stopped about 50 yards offshore, and everyone put on their worn and ill-fitting rental gear—mask, snorkel, and flippers. *No flotation vest?* Of course, I wasn't about to convince myself to do something foolish and drown, just to prove a point to myself. I

[54] Jeff Wise, *Extreme Fear: The Science of Your Mind in Danger* (Palgrave MacMillan, 2009) 15-22

[55] *Understanding the stress response* (Harvard Health Publications, March, 2011), http://www.health.harvard.edu/newsletters/Harvard_Mental_Health_Letter/2011/March/understanding-the-stress-response (retrieved 05/15/2014)

began assessing the risk. The water was calm and clear, coral and marine life easily visible ten to fifteen feet below. Not scary deep, but more than deep enough to drown. The local snorkeling guide announced, "We drop you off here. Swim that direction. We pick you up in one hour."

"Have you snorkeled before?" my sister asked.

Now, you ask me. "No, where do I go if I want to take a break?"

"Swim in about thirty yards. It's shallower there and you can probably stand up, but make sure you step on sand, not coral. If you step on coral, you'll kill it."

Thirty yards to safety. It sounded reasonable. She and Olivia dropped into the water. I followed, soon wondering why I had to kick so much more to stay afloat while they seemed to be casually drifting about. I began to feel not so comfortable and looked at the shore, so inviting and tranquil, and safe—the pool's edge.

"Just put your face in the water and float. You don't have to kick so much. Relax and breathe through the snorkeling tube." This was my sister's five-second snorkeling lesson.

Using the snorkeling tube and breathing through my mouth with my face underwater seemed disquietingly odd and unnatural, and left me feeling oxygen-deprived. I tried to relax and breathe easily, but seawater somehow began flooding the tube. A neural alarm alerted: *Water in tube! Suffocation!* Spitting free the mouthpiece and a mouthful of seawater, I raised my head and took a sharp, gratifying lungful of air.

My sister and Olivia looked up, "Mama, what's Uncle Bob doing?"

"I don't know. I think he's drowning. Hey, are you okay over there?"

I think he's drowning. Ha-ha, very funny. I AM drowning! "Yeah, what's with this snorkeling tube?! It keeps filling up with water."

"You have to exhale really hard to blow out all the water before you inhale," my sister belatedly informed me.

I once again immersed my face underwater and tried inhaling (and occasionally expelling forcefully all water from the breathing tube). Sometimes, it seemed to work well, other times, not so much. I continued, practicing to overcome the uneasy anticipation of inhaling a mouthful of seawater, until, finally, I was able to become sufficiently accustomed to it, sort of, not really.

We snorkeled together for a while before floating off into different directions. I drifted aimlessly, conscientious and conscious of my distance from shore and purposefully getting used to breathing through a tube with my face submerged in sea water.

Snorkeling is otherworldly and wondrous for those drawn to the phenomena of the natural world, and not unlike meditation, your thoughts and sensory perceptions are somehow heightened by the solitude of it all. It was mesmerizing and quite enjoyable, albeit tempered with a whisper of apprehension.

"How're you doing over there? Are you okay?" my sister yelled out from a distance farther out.

I had unknowingly, perhaps subconsciously, maneuvered myself closer to shore. Ready to rest for a minute and return to solid footing, I found a sandy spot, stood up cheerfully relieved and casually drew in lungs-full of air.

"I'm fine. Just taking a break."

"Come out here! Olivia just saw a huge parrotfish."

After a short rest and feeling a confidence that accompanies familiarity, I pushed off and kicked over to where my sister and Olivia had spotted the parrotfish. They had long since moved on, and I now found myself floating further seaward, noticing the end of the coral cliff defining a distinct boundary at the threshold of the abyss. Apprehension arose, and for a moment, I considered turning back. Curiosity and the mental challenge, however, compelled me across the divide. I kicked my feet to cross the edge of the reef and looked down—a stark drop into emptiness. Taken slightly aback, it felt as if I had stepped off a high-rise building and were floating in space, noiselessly suspended over a vast and bottomless void. Hundreds of feet deep, or more? How could I know? It was an intensifying murkiness, diminishing downward to nothing but darkening, alien desolation. *There must be things lurking down there, somewhere.* I felt tingling at the nape of my neck. While the circumstances were not at all unexpected, and, in fact, anticipated, my body still tensed. Feeling both fascination and a creeping sense of unease, I was somehow drawn to the sound of my breathing, and it felt as if I weren't getting enough oxygen. My breathing became shallow as the snorkeling gear became more of an annoyance. I kicked harder with my fins to raise my head above water while attempting to drain the mask. Exhaling a forceful burst through the snorkel, I felt exasperated that I still had a mouthful of seawater. A thought flickered, *I wonder if this is what she felt, the Professor's friend in Malaysia,* and another, *Wow, you can drown pretty easily—and quickly.* Ripples of anxiety turned more fearful, discomfort not from foreboding as to what might arise from the sea's depths but of losing control of my mental processes as I thought of drowning. Feeling uneasy, I was determined to focus attention on my breathing and not get overwhelmed by anxious thought. Even so, the feeling of discomfort escalated, and it took a concentrated moment to calm myself, and my amygdala: *Exhale forcefully and slowly, swallow a bit of seawater. Inhale slowly, deeply. Focus on the sensation of breathing.* I stifled a reflexive gag as I took a gulp of saltwater and began to relax my movements, breathing more deliberately, more deeply, returning to a state of relative composure. Starting to feel okay, and floating more easily again, I retreated to the comfort of the coral reef as my sister shouted out from another direction, "Hey, over here! Olivia just saw a barracuda!"

Unprepared for Fear

To experience fear on occasion is a normal and necessary part of life. Although we no longer live in the wild, our modern urban environment presents its own unique hazards, uncertainties, and predatory threats. We want not and need not to live fearfully, but this requires readiness and knowledge on our part, including recognition that the sensation of fear cannot be entirely avoided. No matter how we might prepare, the fear response initiated by the amygdala occurs at a subconscious level: We feel afraid before we are conscious of the fear. And unlike the movie-star hero or non-hero, it is not prudent to fearlessly charge headlong into a dangerous situation nor attempt to immediately run from and escape a threatening situation, absent of any rational thought. The challenge is that while, ideally, we are able to maintain a judicious balance between our rational and primal impulses, our minds do not always cooperate.

If sensory input escalates to a distressing intensity, and we are convinced that disaster is imminent, our sense of being in control begins slipping completely away from us, and at this moment, we panic. I am not referring to a clichéd screaming and running down the street in your underwear kind of panic, but a more subtle and stealthy kind of fear that takes control of and overwhelms your rational mind, even as you watch. I experienced a moment like this once, when I was abandoned in a burning building.

Panic

It was the summer of 1997, and I had been teaching English to junior high students at a language center in the capital city of Taipei, Taiwan. As was typical with private learning institutions there, the school occupied one floor of a high-rise building, the sixth. From the classroom, I enjoyed a pleasant view of the sky and surrounding mountains, a soothing escape from the madness of motorscooters, buses, and cars below. The job itself, however, of encouraging and, basically, entertaining with a foreign language, rooms-full of disinterested, disengaged, and overworked junior-high schoolers was an aggravating task. Though I strove to accomplish the job using creativity and humor, I was hardly successful. The students were simply tired, irritated, and bored, and would rather have been out goofing around with their friends. Compounding the atmosphere of unpleasantness was the female half of the middle-aged couple who owned and managed the enterprise. Two retired Taiwanese English teachers, they were kind and supportive

Taipei City, Taiwan

enough, but the wife, Mrs. Li, who also acted as the receptionist-office manager, was a nervous and neurotic wreck. I felt badly for her as I imagined the stress of running a business could only affect her in an unhealthful way, but it seemed the more light-hearted and cheery my demeanor, the more anxious she became. Perhaps if I had approached the job with a grave and determined attitude, she would have been reassured. I doubt it. Wearing a perpetual expression of doom while wringing her hands dry, she constantly fretted and scampered about, behaving as if the business were about to implode at any moment.

One day I was ending another late afternoon of teaching grammar to a class of droopy-eyed and listless preteen students, whose only linguistic effort was to utter in Mandarin: "Wú-liáo! Wú-liáo!" (Boring! Boring!) as they referred to another of my creative attempts at encouraging their verbal participation. After an hour and twenty minutes of practicing past and present perfect verb tenses, I pronounced four words that would reanimate the dead, "Okay, class is over." The students sprang to life and practiced their favorite English phrase, "Bye-bye, teacher!" as they trooped toward the back and cheerily filed out of the classroom. The last student swung the door behind him, clicking it shut and leaving me in solitude to sit back in relief and to ponder the tranquility of the distant mountainside. Fifteen minutes of filling out paperwork later, I gathered my things to head home. Flipping off the light switch, I opened the classroom door and stepped into the hallway.

That's odd. It's so quiet. Where is everybody? I looked up and down the hall. Empty. I then walked through the deserted study area. Nobody anywhere, not a single student, nor were there any other teachers in sight. Usually, one or two Taiwanese teachers would be milling around at this time, but there were none. *Okay, well, I'm sure Mrs. Li is at the reception counter.* Further down the hallway, I turned the corner and approached the front entrance. I could see that the reception area had been abandoned. *Hmm, what's going on?* I looked around and called out, "Hello? Is anyone here?" Silence. *Weird. Is today some kind of holiday?* I was used to all manner of strange customs in my travels. Was this one of them? I had no energy to contemplate it. I was calling it a day and heading home. When I began to pass the reception counter, I saw the haze. *What's that?*

Outside the glass doors of the front entrance I could see a dark gray mass of smoke near the ceiling, swirling lazily as it rose to the top, then circulating down a bit before rising back up. I walked toward the doors. The area of smoke was becoming denser and thicker and beginning to fill the space from the ceiling downwards. *What the hell?* My first thought was to check all the classrooms to notify everyone. I rushed back down the hall, running from classroom to classroom, flinging open all the doors; the rooms, I found, were all empty. Apparently, everyone had run off and left me there. *Come on, people, you couldn't knock on the door and let me know the place was on fire?*

I wasn't feeling especially nervous, not yet anyway. I was staying calm, figuring out what to do. Stepping out and into the foyer, I watched with concern the volume of smoke flowing and twisting, accumulating near the ceiling. It was dark and toxic-smelling. *No fire alarm?* I held my breath. People usually don't burn to death in a fire, most die from smoke inhalation. *Okay, I need to get out of here.* I was standing near the elevator. *Don't take the elevator. Take the stairs.* I turned toward the stairs and trotted over. Smoke was billowing up from the stairwell. *Great.* I ran back into the school, which was beginning to fill with smoke. I closed the door. *No emergency exits or fire escapes? No sprinkler system? Christ, what the hell?* I stepped over to the windows; the mountains beyond now appeared especially blissful. *Well, I'm not going out this way.* I looked down at the traffic. It didn't look so chaotic and annoying anymore. I noticed the quietness. *No sirens? Damn, Mrs. Li, could I bother you to call the fire department? . . . Yes, call 911.* I grabbed the phone at the front counter and punched in 9-1-1 . . . dial tone (I was later informed that the number for an emergency is 119). Starting to feel anxious, I returned to the reception area. *Okay, have to get out of here. Not upstairs. Have to go down.* I went back out to the foyer. Smoke was more than a third of the way down from the ceiling. Stooping, I hurried back over to the stairs. Smoke from the stairwell was now heavier. *How do I get out of here?* Returning to the foyer once again, I found myself standing in front of the elevator. This was the moment—*Don't take the elevator*—I panicked.

I knew the advice, regularly recommended by fire safety experts, that you should not use an elevator during a fire. Smoke may draft up the elevator shaft, exposing you to toxic gases, or the elevator may stop on the floor where the fire is burning, or the elevator may suddenly malfunction, trapping you in the building. I was aware of all that, and yet, there I was, pressing the elevator's down button. The floor lights lit up, and the elevator rumbled. *Don't take the elevator.* There was no hysterical screaming, but I am quite certain I was panicking. Even as my frontal cortex was reminding me not to take the elevator and my rational mind told me to stop, my amygdala was muting those messages with, *Get the hell out of here, now!* The elevator doors opened and I stepped inside. Acting against rational thought, I pressed the first floor button— click. Nothing happened. I paused and pressed again, twice. Click. Click. Nothing. It was a strange moment. I felt kind of relieved.

Okay . . . get out! I didn't consider for a moment going back to the school, closing the door, sealing it with wet towels, and waiting for help. Maybe I should have, but my brain was now hard-wired to my amygdala. With an increasing urgency, I went directly to the stair landing and looked down the stairwell; the smoke was still flowing thick and dark. I held my breath and charged down. Pivoting at the between-floors landing, I came down upon a number of people huddled outside the doorway of the fifth floor, frozen and staring down the stairwell at the source of the fire: building debris and carpeting from apparent remodeling work was piled high along the sides of the stairway between the fourth and the fifth floors. On the fifth floor landing, numerous ten gallon cans of paint or solvent or some other construction chemicals labeled with a Flammable! icon sat beneath the rubbish. Not good. I hesitated for an instant. The fire itself was not yet out of control, but it was intense, throwing up a plume of toxic smoke and growing larger as it worked its way up the mound of construction waste, headed, inevitability, toward the metal containers of volatile chemicals. *Go! Now!*

"Duì-bù-qi, bù-hao-yì-si, jiè-guò, jiè-guò," (Excuse me. I'm sorry. Passing by. Passing by.) I said as I rushed by the people immobilized there. I continued down the stairs, quickly past the heat and smoke of the fire and away from the spreading flames.

A few steps past the bottom of the debris pile, I swiftly regained my composure. My frontal cortex had, apparently, come back online, and I felt calm enough to turn around and think, *I'm safe below fire. Fire will worsen. People still there. Drag away flaming bottom of waste pile to stop spread.* I began yanking pieces of burning wood scraps and various building materials away, separating the fire from the still unlit mound. Several moments later, noticing movement above me, I looked up into the exhaust end of a fire extinguisher and got blasted in the face with fire retardant. I turned away, coughing and stumbling down the steps. Someone on the fifth floor had finally snapped out of their brain-frozen stupor and dragged out a fire extinguisher.

Later, when thinking about proper procedures for using, or not using, an elevator during a fire, I wondered, *Why did I react that way?* I was irritated with myself because although I felt quite aware of what I was doing, and I knew even as I was in the elevator that I should not be taking the elevator, I still found myself standing in there, pressing the button to go down. Not a major blunder, I suppose. Not like I jumped out the window or dashed out and abandoned everyone else . . . Mrs. Li? I never felt completely unnerved throughout the event, not really, but still, I realized that a single lapse could have ended in misfortune. Although it was not reassuring, my reaction, it turns out, was quite normal.

Preparing for Fear

Odd things happen to our brains in the midst of panic. Although we would like to believe that we are in control and can maintain our composure, it is remarkable how easily one can lose their head. We all reach a tipping point, and along the way, our brains are in conflict with themselves, a struggle between rationality and primal terror, the frontal cortex and the amygdala battling for influence. Once our bodies are tense with the biochemistry of the fight-or-flight response and danger is increasingly perceived as imminent annihilation, our frontal cortices reach the point of no return. They finally become so overwhelmed from the biochemical response that they short out, our rational minds go blank. Our amygdala has prevailed, and we are now running on mere primal instinct—freeze, fight, or flight—for better or worse.

Of course, nobody wants to panic, becoming ineffective and inept or paralyzed with fear, because the result is, usually, for the worse. What can be done? People whose work often puts them in intense conditions—soldiers, police, firefighters, first responders, airline pilots, and so on—practice certain strategies to prepare for the effects of the fear response, and these strategies, coincidentally, are similar to those practiced by martial artists: training and habituation, complemented with mindful breathing techniques.

Training to Respond: Correctly train the required skills, the fundamentals, repeatedly, and then some more, rote drills, until the movements become instinctive. Proper motor control eventually becomes embedded in the subconscious, and conscious thought is no longer necessary for precise execution. When the frontal cortex has been shut down by the instinctive fear response, performance can remain efficient and effective, even as our minds have gone blank. We are "in the flow."

Habituation: Familiarize fear response to the threat by simulating the particular stress-inducing conditions. Frequent and regular exposure and training under simulated conditions can somewhat desensitize the mind to fear of the perceived danger. In the martial arts, this is accomplished through light-contact and heavy-contact sparring, as well as simulated confrontations. In behavioral therapy, a treatment with similar strategies, called "exposure therapy," is effectively used to neutralize the fear of such things as spiders, snakes, germs, and so on.[56]

People whose occupations involve stressful situations can simulate conditions in which to train, which helps prepare them to perform, under adversity, specific tasks that they might expect to carry out in their work. For the rest of us, though, life is much less predictable. We cannot prepare ourselves for every random threat and can hope only that we will respond well to our fear response in general. Our preparation, then, as much as there can be, is to practice techniques that help to keep the rational mind engaged so that we remain calm enough to continually assess a perilous situation as it is evolving, taking the most prudent and effective course of action available.

Abdominal Breathing: Breathing is a unique process in that it is normally controlled through subconscious, invol-

[56] Johanna S. Kaplan, PhD and David F. Tolin, PhD, *Exposure Therapy for Anxiety Disorders* (Psychiatric Times, September 06, 2011), http://www.psychiatrictimes.com/anxiety/exposure-therapy-anxiety-disorders (retrieved 06/02/2014)

untary action (of the autonomic nervous system) but can be quite easily modulated with conscious, voluntary action. When this is done, when the unconscious, quickened, shallow breath of anxiety and fear is moderated by the practice of purposeful, slower, and deeper inhalations and exhalations, the physical sensations of agitation and tension bought on by the fear response can be blunted, as breathing and heart rate settles.

Law enforcement and military personnel are now often taught a form of abdominal breathing called "tactical breathing" or "combat breathing."[57] Recommended to be used during high-stress situations, its purpose is to slow heart rate and lower blood pressure so that the individual can remain composed and clear-headed under adverse conditions.

Tactical Breathing

Using abdominal or diaphragmatic breathing, follow this sequence:

1) Inhale steadily and calmly through the nose for a count of four, letting the abdomen/diaphragm expand (inhale-two-three-four);

2) Hold the breath for a count of four (hold-two-three-four);

3) Exhale slowly and smoothly for a count of four (exhale-two-three-four);

4) Wait for a count of four (wait-two-three-four);

5) Repeat the sequence four or five times, or more.

[57] Jeff Wise, *Extreme Fear: The Science of Your Mind in Danger* (Palgrave MacMillan, 2009), 178-179

You should not feel light-headed nor tense in the upper chest. You can also modify the breathing pattern to whatever feels comfortable and natural. Here is a variation that provides a calmer, more continuous flow of diaphragmatic movement and breath:

1) Inhale steadily and calmly through the nose, letting the abdomen/diaphragm expand (inhale-two-three-four);

2) Relaxed pause, which allows slight but continued diaphragmatic movement (five-six-seven-eight);

3) Exhale slowly and smoothly through pursed lips for a longer count (exhale-two-three-four-five-six);

4) Unpurse lips, relax mouth, release remaining air in lungs with light "h-a-a-a-a-a" sound (seven-eight);

5) Stay relaxed and repeat the sequence four or five times, or more.

Practice breathing techniques throughout the day, while driving, during exercise, when involved in interpersonal conflict, or any time your heart rate and blood pressure are in a heightened state of arousal. Use them whenever you feel stressed, irritated, angry, or anxious.

Anxiety

While fear might cause us momentary acute stress, anxiety, which triggers the same physiological fight-or-flight response as fear, can cause us constant, unrelenting stress, degrading our long-term health, our general wellbeing, and our ability to accomplish everyday tasks.[58]

Unlike fear, anxiety is not the result of an existing, external threat but rather our imaginings of harmful, painful events based on past memory or projections of future difficulties and harm.

Some believe that feeling anxiety before a demanding event—taking a test, having an interview, making a speech—is a useful motivator when preparing for a challenging situation: the anxiety of failing and making mistakes will push one to spend the time and effort necessary to ready oneself. Perhaps, but is this type of anxiety truly necessary, or desirable? Will anxiety not make one more tentative and self-doubting? Is anxiety not simply the worrying mental chatter and ruminations over an undesired outcome? Can one not be determined and motivated to prepare as well as possible simply to perform to the best of his or her abilities, without the stressful physical effects of uncertainty and the nervousness of the fight-or-flight response? Is it possible for one to recognize the mental chatter as merely discursive thought, the simple ruminations of uncertainty, and then act confidently without any particular expectation? Can one interpret life not as a series of specific goals and destinations but as of a continuum, an ever-flowing, evolving, and non-dualistic process? Is it not true that without the nattering voice of ego, anxiety would hardly exist? (Of course, it is much easier to understand, acknowledge, and discuss philosophical truths than to live them. Knowing is not being after all.)

Other common anxieties are associated with the fear of physical danger, with imagining the physical threat of an activity in which you will be involved, e.g., you have to take a flight, you have to drive over a bridge, you have to have a medical procedure, you have to travel alone at night, and so on. These anxieties can be eased with training, familiarity, habituation, preparedness, and mindfulness. If these anxieties are debilitating, you may need to see your local behavioral psychologist.

---

[58] *Anxiety and physical illness* (Harvard Health Publications, July, 2008), http://www.health.harvard.edu/newsletters/Harvard_Womens_Health_Watch/2008/July/Anxiety_and_physical_illness (retrieved 05/15/2014)

Mindfulness

Fear (and, likewise, anxiety) does not exist out there in the ether somewhere; fear exists solely in our heads, and the seeds of that fear are memory and interpretation. While it is true that the fear response is activated subconsciously by the amygdala and the memory of known threats, it is the way we interpret the "threat" that defines our reaction to it. While most may feel terror encountering a cobra on a trail, a snake collector may spot the cobra and feel a thrill of anticipation and excitement as the snake, while still a deadly threat, is regarded as a challenge to capture. An object of fear to one becomes an exhilarating challenge to another.

After understanding how the fear response affects our physiology, we can respond to the instinctive sensation of fear with purposeful action, abdominal breathing for instance, along with mindful awareness of our reactive thoughts. We can strive to keep our frontal cortices engaged so that we are not overwhelmed by primal emotion as we reinterpret an object of fear into a challenge to overcome, and we accurately assess and effectively respond to the threat. The emotion of fear can be moderated so that we are not so quickly incapacitated or prone to panic.

Additionally, maintaining a healthy lifestyle so that one is physically confident and vigorous can mitigate the adverse effects of anxiety. Have regular exercise, a simple, nutritious, balanced, and natural diet, adequate rest, and avoid excessive caffeine, tobacco, and alcohol. Maintaining these habits are also opportunities to practice mindfulness as you live pro-actively and rationally, not as a mere hostage to your thoughts and impulses.

Continue to go about your day like any other. Organize your time and know what tasks need to be done. Accomplish what you need to accomplish. At the same time, while taking care of your daily business, practice breathing techniques regularly. Recognize your constant mental chatter and create space between the arising of thought and your conscious awareness of it so that you are less impulsive and reactive. Be mindful and stay non-attached to your ego-story, impulsive cravings, and mental fabrications.

It certainly takes persistence as thoughts constantly arise, and the presence of your mind is repeatedly swept into the discursive torrent of that voice of ego, but the way you live is your choice. You can live differently—less distracted, more present, less anxious—at any moment you decide. Awareness. Breath. Mindfulness. Living mindfully is a way of being.

SIX

ANGER

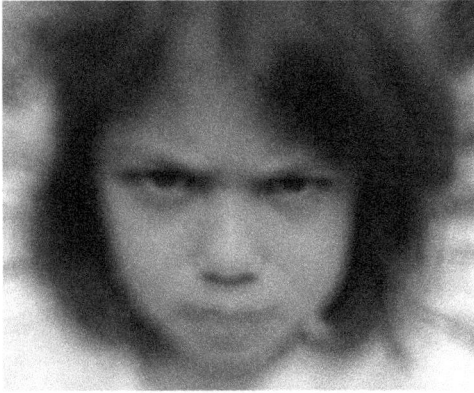

In a fight, anger is as good as courage.—Welsh proverb

While our frontal cortices, our rational minds, will struggle for influence against the primal fear response of the amygdala, other major emotions for which the amygdala is responsible can more readily compete with fear. Simply put, anger can override fear.[59]

When I was younger, I cultivated the belligerent and surly demeanor of an antisocial malcontent. I felt angry and enjoyed it. Waking up some days full of hostility, I felt energized and empowered. If I felt disrespected, I would curse people with contempt. If I didn't like the way somebody looked at me—*What are you looking at?*—I would return a glare in challenge. I wasn't one to bully others into a fight, but I was prepared to engage with someone who

[59] Jeff Wise, *Extreme Fear: The Science of Your Mind in Danger* (Palgrave MacMillan, 2009), 176-177

was willing. There were times when I simply did not care about consequences. Before SUVs and road rage became so commonplace, I would drive with aggression and an ill-tempered attitude: tailgating and pursuing drivers I determined to be jerks, shouting abuse and flipping off "incompetent" motorists, visualizing ramming the cars of idiots. Yes, I know, I was that obnoxious jerk. Eventually, I began to drive with a loaded Glock handgun in my car. At some point I thought, *Either I'm going to shoot somebody and end up in jail or somebody is going to kill me. For what? I'm not sure. This is no way to live.* I knew that I did not like the person I had become and I had to do something about it. Soon thereafter, presented with an opportunity to leave the U.S., I sold all my things, packed a few bags, and moved to Asia in search of another way, still not certain what that might be.

Years later I was reading a news story about two men who had had an encounter near where I had grown up—Sacramento, the capital city of California—on streets with which I was familiar. By then, I had found much more contentment not being that volatile person who I had been so many years before, and as I read the article, I thought, *I remember those roads and being more like these men.*

A Day of Rage, A Day of Lament

Donald R. Bell, married, a 52-year-old construction worker with a teen-aged son, sat next to the small pile of rocks and paper flowers that had been arranged on the side of the road. It was a makeshift memorial that had been left for a person whose memory now gave Bell torment, gave Mr. Donald R. Bell reason for suicidal thoughts.

Two weeks previously was the first Sunday of May, 2001. Metropolitan Sacramento was typically warm and sunny. Timothy Mann, a 53-year-old lineman for the local power company, his wife Nancie, and their adult son were just heading away from Sacramento, east on Highway 50, returning home after having just celebrated Nancie's birthday with a pleasant Sunday brunch. Though Nancie had lost her job at IBM a few weeks earlier, she and her husband were still planning their second cruise vacation in the fall. Their first cruise ever was taken the year before, in celebration of their 30th wedding anniversary. Timothy had asked Nancie to marry him again, a second proposal, a second wedding. A second cruise, naturally, was in order, job or no job.

Donald R. Bell was also out that morning, with his 15-year-old son. They were in Mr. Bell's white pickup truck, trying to locate a hobby shop where they planned to purchase parts to repair the teenager's motorized scooter. After realizing he had exited the freeway a little too soon, Donald Bell headed back to Highway 50 East to continue to the next exit.

Back on the freeway, Nancie Mann recalls that a white pickup truck entering Highway 50 suddenly cut in front of them, forcing her husband to brake—hard. "We slammed on our brakes, but didn't hit him. Then he slammed on his brakes in front of us, so my husband slammed on his even harder."

Donald Bell would later claim that as he was entering the freeway, the Mann's sedan had sped up and nearly rear-ended him. The particulars, however, make no difference, no damage to either vehicle had occurred. There was no mishap—yet.

Both cars continued east and ended up traveling next to each other. Timothy Mann and Donald Bell eyed one another and had a heated exchange. They traded sharp words and hostile hand gestures, then Mann sped away. Once again, everything could have been forgotten. But it was not. At the next off-ramp, Hazel Avenue, the Manns exited. Bell followed, later claiming that he and his son were still looking for that hobby shop. When Timothy Mann stopped at the stoplight, Donald Bell stopped his truck a couple of car lengths behind. Prepared for confrontation and intent on compelling Mann to back down before him, Bell exited his vehicle armed with a handgun.

Still seething, Timothy Mann saw Bell's truck stopped behind him. He, too, was ready to act. Nancie and her adult son pleaded with him to stay in the car, but Mann could not be reasoned with;

his amygdala had taken command. He swung open the door and stepped out, his body coursing with a biochemistry quite similar to that of the fear response, inciting more "fight," however, than freeze or flight.

Donald Bell's 15-year-old son watched helplessly from the truck as his father raised his weapon and aimed it at Mann. Witnesses say Bell shouted: "Get back in your car! Get back in your car!"

Timothy Mann did not yield. He was not afraid. He was not rational. He was enraged. Disregarding the handgun pointed at his chest, Timothy Mann walked up to Donald Bell and threw a punch. The gun went off.

Mann dropped to the asphalt—dead. Bell had shot him in the face.

The paramedics arrived first, then the sheriff's deputies. Bell maintained that it was self-defense, an accident.

"He hit me harder than a mule kick. That's what caused the gun to go off."

Nancie Mann and her adult son were stunned and distraught. Donald Bell was arrested for investigation of voluntary manslaughter and released on bail the next day.

Exactly two weeks later, Bell returned to the scene of the incident. There, someone had arranged the mound of river rocks and paper flowers in remembrance of Timothy Mann. Mr. Bell walked over to the memorial and sat down. He had just ended a cell phone call with a 911 dispatcher in which he stated, among other things: "I am so sorry for everything that has happened . . . I have brought such terrible misery . . . I acted in self-defense . . . I just ask God for his forgiveness."

It was a little after 10 a.m. and the morning was already heating up. The third Sunday of May was going to be another hot, dry Sacramento day. Donald Rodger Bell, sitting on the warming asphalt, next to a forlorn pile of stones at the Hazel Avenue exit-ramp, put a gun to his head and killed himself.[60][61]

Despite anger sometimes evolving into tragedy, it is generally recognized that anger is a natural and instinctive reaction that is not altogether unhealthy. As a basic element of our defense mechanism, it is a survival response that can override fear and our urge to freeze or flee. Anger can fuel our drive to take action, confront a threat, and fight.

If anger can steel our spirit to fight, can it not push us to meaningful action on other occasions? Motivated by anger, can we not transcend our malaise and anxiety with a confident and intense drive to compete and succeed? Driven by anger, do the powerless not become inflamed to protest? Filled with outrage, do we not overcome timidity and complacency to challenge injustice, manipulation, and domination by others? Is there not a thrill, a rush, a passion when we are filled with a spirit of fury? Yes, of course, because as anger summons the adrenaline (epinephrine), noradrenaline (norepinephrine), cortisol, and various other chemicals to surge through our bodies, we experience intense physical sensation. While "pleasurable" may not accurately describe the physical feeling of anger, exhilarating, passionate, empowering, and fear-conquering, along with occasional lunacy seem fitting descriptors. As with love, anger can enhance life experience with intensity, vibrancy, drama, and a bit of madness, can it not? Is the person who is forever calm, easygoing, and in control not a bit of a dullard? Life would be less colorful and eventful without the occasional fire of indignation and discontent, no?

His Holiness the Dalai Lama appears to disagree. He has reportedly said that although anger might have some positive effects in terms of survival or moral outrage, he did not accept anger of any kind as a virtuous emotion nor aggression as constructive behavior.[62]

[60] Peter H. King, *A Moment of Road Rage Changes Lives Forever* (Los Angeles Times, May 27, 2001), http://articles.latimes.com/2001/may/27/local/me-3290 (retrieved 4/30/2014)

[61] David Wright, *Road Rage Leads to Shooting, Suicide* (ABC News, June 19, 2001), http://abcnews.go.com/US/story?id=93070&page=1&singlePage=true (retrieved 4/30/2014)

[62] Lama Surya Das, *Transforming Anger #2* (05/03/2011), http://www.surya.org/transforming-anger-2/ (retrieved 06/02/2014)

The unappealing aspect of anger, besides the possibility that it can lead to the poor decision making and irrational behavior that results in hostility, aggression, and violence, is that it creates an atmosphere of discord, oppressiveness, and stress for everyone in close proximity to the raging malcontent. Not so pleasant. And not so pleasant, also, for the ill-tempered individual is that a life lived in constant anger and hostility is a life lived ruminating on the sources of one's irritations, frustrations, indignations, disappointments, oppressions, pains, and fears, as well as on the past interactions with individuals who have annoyed, offended, and provoked one. A life lived directing energies to the things that elicit anger is bound to be a joyless, discontent, and sullen existence. Why would one choose to live like that? And yes, it is definitely a choice.

> "I don't want to have a breath of hate, jealousy, anxiety or fear in me. I want to live completely at peace. Which doesn't mean that I want to die. I want to live on this marvelous earth, so full, so rich, so beautiful. I want to look at the trees, flowers, rivers, meadows, women, boys and girls, and at the same time live completely at peace with myself and the world."—Jiddu Krishnamurti[63]

Is Anger Necessary?

There is no doubt that anger can be somewhat useful as a defense mechanism when we are confronted with an existing threat. It can compel us to take action when we might otherwise be fearfully incapacitated. As with the fear response, however, anger can drive our minds past the tipping point of reason. If this happens, irrational and reckless behavior fueled by pure rage may result in tragedy, as the altercation between Donald Bell and Timothy Mann demonstrates.

His Holiness the Dalai Lama and Jiddu Krishnamurti suggest

[63] Jiddu Krishnamurti, *Freedom from the Known* (Rider Books, 2010) 48

that anger is not necessary, and we would be better off without it. Can we confront injustice, be inspired and driven to accomplishment, overcome our frustrations, pains, and fears, and handle antagonistic individuals, free from thoughts of anger, fear, or ego?

The highly-trained traditional martial artist would say that living without anger, fear, or ego will result not in passivity and weakness but rather clarity of awareness and a fluid spontaneity of movement. Mentioned previously, the Japanese term for this state is 無心の心 (mushin no shin), meaning "mind without mind," commonly shortened to "mushin," or "without mind." A more precise description would be: mind without movement of thought.

As noted earlier, physical preparation for the traditional martial artist includes rote training and habituation exercises. Martial arts movements and techniques are repeated endlessly until they can be performed instinctively during practice and then in sparring. What the traditional martial artists had recognized was that when one was facing a genuine physical threat, emotions of fear and anger could cause distraction and hesitancy, or overreaction and recklessness. This limited one's ability to perform authoritatively and effectively the techniques that he or she had mastered. The insight was to recognize that fear and anger arose from an egoistic mind of self-deceit, delusion, and craving, and that movement of egoistic thought restricted one's ability to perform spontaneously and dynamically. The purest and most effortless execution of martial arts expression was realized when action was solely governed by the egoless awareness of energy and egoless mastery of technique that is buried in the subconscious.

This state of mind (or more precisely, no mind) is a state of awareness without movement of thought, where fear, anger, anxiety, pride, self-consciousness, desires, passions, expectations, and intentions do not exist because they are simply not an aspect of the egoless, thought-free mental state. In this mental stillness, no distinction exists between awareness and movement; one becomes merely energy moving through space and time—motion, presence, and being.

"When the swordsman stands against his opponent, he is not to think of the opponent, nor of himself, nor of his enemy's sword movements. He just stands there with his sword which, forgetful of all technique, is ready only to follow the dictates of the subconscious. The man has effaced himself as the wielder of the sword. When he strikes, it is not the man but the sword in the hand of the man's subconscious that strikes."—Takuan Soho[64]

Since the traditional martial artist learns the way of combat that includes understanding the nature of the mind, practicing the art of mindfulness in daily life becomes part of the habituation of mushin. Do not be mistaken and think that stillness of mind means passivity and non-action. No, in fact, the mind of no thought is most necessary when one is in the midst of activity and motion. To further this notion, mushin is applied to the cultivation of any craft: playing music, writing calligraphy, performing a tea ceremony, woodworking, farming, painting, engaging in athletics, dancing—any physical engagement.

The following adaptation originates from the well-known Chinese tale of *The Butcher*, found in the classical Taoist text, the Zhuangzi. This story plainly illustrates the principal of mushin, acting free of egoistic intent and self-consciousness.

The Butcher

庖丁為文惠君殺牛，不論是用什麼方法，都立刻使皮骨分離，並且發出的聲音有如「桑林」與「經首」美妙的音樂，文惠君就問他說：「你真是太厲害了，你的刀法怎麼會如此高明呢？」庖丁說：「我所喜歡的是事物的道理，遠遠超過技巧這階段上，開始學殺牛時，不懂得牛的結構，一整頭牛往往不知從何下刀，經過三年的磨練之後，眼前所見的已經不是一頭全牛了，而是心神領會，停止一切感官知覺的活動，順著牛的生理結構，切開筋骨的縫隙，刀子悠

[64] Takuan Soho, translated by William Scott Wilson, *The Unfettered Mind* (Tokyo: Kodansha International Ltd., 1986)

游於骨節間，經絡相連和筋骨盤結的地方碰都每碰一下，何況是大骨呢？」技術高明的廚師，每年只要換一把刀就可以，因為他們是用刀來切肉，反之，一般笨拙的廚師，每個月都需要換新刀，因為他們是用刀來砍肉，而現在我這把刀已經用了十九年，所殺的牛也有幾千頭，但刀刃還像剛磨過刀一樣鋒利。是因為牛的骨節有縫隙的，而刀刃卻是沒有厚度，以沒有厚度的刀遊走在有縫隙的骨節間，自然是可以得心應手。」文惠君聽完之後便說：「說的很對，你的一番話，使我領悟到了養生之道！」

A cook named Ding was carving an ox for Lord Wen-hui. As the Lord looked on, the cook handled his cleaver with fluid precision and a melodic rhythm. With every deft touch, rise of his shoulder, step and shift of his balance, it was as if Ding were performing the Dance of the Mulberry Grove, the sound of the blades work moving in time to some classical tune.

"Yes, incredible!" exclaimed Lord Wen-hui. "You are a master of this craft?"

Ding set aside his cleaver and replied, "What I know is the Tao, which is beyond mastery of any skill. When I first began, I viewed the ox carcass as a whole and butchered it into pieces. After three years I no longer saw the body as a whole, and now I do not see it at all. Now I perform with my spirit. Perception and knowledge become silent as my spirit wields the blade. The natural structure of the carcass informs my awareness as I strike the major joints and the knife slips through large gaps. Following the form, the cleaver flows unimpeded, avoiding blood vessels, tendons, and ligaments, to say nothing of bone.

A good cook replaces his blade once a year, because he cuts. A mediocre cook replaces his blade once a month, as he chops. I have used this cleaver for nineteen years and have carved thousands of oxen. Yet the blade is as sharp as if it had just been lifted from the grindstone. You see, there are gaps between the joints, and the blade edge has no thickness. A blade with no thickness can glide freely through the empty space, with plenty of room to pass. Thus, after nineteen years of use, the blade is as sharp as it ever was.

Nonetheless, I sometimes encounter a more demanding area to work on, and, conscious of the difficulties, I slow my hand. Focusing my attention and moving with deliberation, I manipulate the blade with great subtlety until—splat!, the flesh separates, like a clod of earth crumbling apart upon the ground. Lifting my knife away, I thoroughly review my work. When I am completely satisfied, I clean the blade and carefully store it away."

"Excellent!" responds Lord Wen-hui, "I have listened to the words of Cook Ding, and I now understand how to live life."

Is Thought Necessary?

Of course, the rational mind must sometimes be engaged, and this is during the state of non-action: planning, reasoning, contemplating, strategizing, organizing, and so on, before action is initiated. Later, during the physically active state, action and technique are performed decisively and instinctively, without movement of thought, "mind of no mind"—mushin.

The occasional challenge is when we face a random threat for which we are unprepared. If a precarious situation is dynamic and fluid, our rational minds must remain calm and engaged, continually assessing the situation as it is evolving, before taking decisive action.

Root of Anger

The root of anger is the egoism of the self, responding to the perception that pain has been or will be inflicted upon it.

When we sense a physical threat, anger can naturally arise as part of the fear response, driving us past the paralysis of fear so that we actively respond to protect ourselves or others. Anger also arises from the perception of an egoistic threat, an attack that causes egoistic suffering: not being respected, not being acknowledged, not being heard, not being supported, not being appreciated, not being recognized that we are right, and so on. These are sleights, challenges, confrontations to the legitimacy of our mentally fabricated ego-stories. This anger arises out of pure egoistic conceit. Finally, there is the anger in response to circumstances not conforming to our expectations and desires, when we are faced with the reality that forces and objects (including people) in the external world, indeed, are not under our control.

As noted earlier, anger as part of the fear response can be relatively helpful as an instinctual, untrained reaction when we are confronted with physical danger. Anger originating from the perception of an egoistic attack, however, is simply the uncontrolled spewing of egoistic energy arising from an attachment to a delusion. The delusion, of course, is believing that the ego-story is in any way a real, tangible thing. Attachment to this illusory ego-story, this identity and the pridefulness that accompanies it is wholly irrational because this identity, this ego-story of who I am, Mr. or Ms. XYZ, is a pure mental fabrication, a deceit of the mind. What is it that responds with anger if not the illusory ego itself, indignant in its offended and haughty or pride-damaged and poor-me mental blathering. When our mentally constructed ego-fabrications are dinged, we are incensed by and intolerant of the perceived injury.

When Donald Bell and Timothy Mann had their road rage altercation on Highway 50, an initial surge of anger as a result of the fear response to a physical danger was instinctual, but the subsequent display of hostility and aggression that ultimately resulted in both their deaths was driven by the enraged prattling of egoistic demands for respect and acknowledgment to an ego-story that resided in their own minds—*F-you! You cannot do that to ME!* This is foolish, egoistic nonsense.

Besides the angry response to the disrespect and disregard directed toward our ego-stories, when others—family, friends, neighbors, co-workers, society-at-large, the government—do not conform to our expectations of the way we want things to be, we become irritated, disappointed, and impatient. ANGRY. But, why should we expect others to conform to our view? Our expectations are based on nothing more than our personally fabricated, dualistic worlds of personal opinions, no? To angrily demand that others conform to our own dualistic world-view is pure egoistic arrogance.

Finally, there is the anger arising when events remind us of how little control we have over the physical world, and we are confronted with the truth of impermanence. If our machines and electronic gadgets fail to function to our expectations, we become frustrated, annoyed, and upset—angry once again. We curse and become agitated when our possessions break down, when we have accidents, or when we suffer from ill health, not to mention when we perceive others as responsible for our possessions breaking down, our having mishaps, or our suffering physical harm.

All of our anger, when you contemplate it to its source, arises from the desire to protect or legitimize either the physical body or the egoistic conceit. Expressing anger is not only stressful and unhealthful but also a drain of mental, emotional, and physical energy. An argument can be made that if you are protecting yourself from an immediate physical threat, an anger response may be somewhat helpful: Anger can drive you to action. The action, however, will likely be influenced by irrationality, and for the trained and prepared individual, emotional anger is counter-productive to executing the most effective and precise response. Do not lose your head.

When anger arises as protection from a perceived egoistic threat, it is energy wholly wasted on trying to protect a delusion from a mental fabrication, a movement of thought. How can an illusory ego-fabrication suffer harm? Is wanting to protect a mentally fabricated ego-story not nonsensical and plain silly? And how often do we ruminate angrily over past events where we believe pain was inflicted upon us, we were wronged or disrespected? What is this but simply the imagination of memory creating the image of a threat to the delusion of one's mentally contrived ego-story. It is solely in our minds. The emotional struggle and the damage to our wellbeing occurs when, like anxiety, a real, immediate threat does not exist, and the anger response arises from pure imagination. It is an egoistic anger arising to protect a collection of mental elements that have been compounded to create, maintain, and constantly build grander an imaginary ego-story, an imaginary idea of self that is born from emptiness, a delusion and deceit of the mind.

This is not an argument to become passive and non-responsive to life events. Not at all. Contemplate the truth of your phantasmagorical ego-story, and as the truth of the illusory ego becomes more apparent, and the ego attachments are set free, and the monstrous ego-construction, critically examined, crumbles like a clod of earth upon the ground, anger will simply: Begin. To. Fade. And what remains is peacefulness and freedom, a vigorous energy that responds to life events with enthusiasm, assertiveness, intensity, determination, persistence, fearlessness, and a joy to confront challenges.

The irony for the traditionally trained martial artist is that the more the spirit of mushin is habituated to better execute the martial art, the less existent becomes influence of the egoistic rattling mind. The grandiose, mentally compounded ego-story is deconstructed into emptiness and mental stillness. An individual is then less angry, less hostile, less arrogant, and less likely to impulsively and mindlessly fight. Which is not to say that cultivating a calm and peaceful way of being means never fighting without appropriate assertiveness and intensity when it is truly necessary, but the way one takes action is to remain dispassionate toward confrontation and to be better able to ameliorate confrontation without violence. One then begins to understand: the art of fighting without fighting.

THE BUDDHA WAS NOT A BUDDHIST

SEVEN

WHAT IS LOVE?

Ohatu and Tokubei[65]

There is a tricky rhetorical device called a "loaded question" that cannot be simply answered without appearing guilty or implicating yourself in some fashion. It is a question that can cause a moment of fumbling for an appropriate response, a question such as: "Have you stopped beating your children?" A loaded question.

I have always felt fumble-some being asked this particular question: "Do you love me?" While not technically a loaded question per se, it is more like a mostly loaded gun in a solo game of Russian roulette, because if you are in a relationship with someone whom you care about, stuttering out, "No," "No, but . . . ," or even

[65] Suguri F, *Ohatu and Tokubei*, CC BY-SA 3.0, http://en.wikipedia.org/wiki/File:Ohatu_and_tokubei.jpg (retrieved 6/13/2014)

"Yes, but . . . ," are wholly dissatisfactory options, obviously. Three clicks of the trigger. On the other hand, answering "Yes!" releases a Pandora's Box of implications that require clarification. You cannot begin to answer the "love me?" question competently without suggesting: Can we first engage in a rational debate about what love is and the assumptions associated with it? Alas, this is, assuredly, not the hoped for response.

What is love? Love is 愛.

The Chinese character for "love"— 愛 (ài), shows the word for "heart"— 心 (xin), set within the word for "accept" or "receive"— 受 (shòu). Rather inspired, no?

I love my family. I love my dog. I love my car, my job, my house, my country. I love baseball, football, fishing, yoga, spicy food, chocolate, money, travel, and so on. But this is not the kind of love about which people expend their energies romanticizing and poeticizing and fantasizing, is it? The question from your partner—"Do you love me?"—is also not enquiring about feelings of simple lust or even true love (We'll come back to that later). No, the "love" question is referring to a passionate and adoring love that lasts forever and never fades.

Love is Blind

"One of our difficulties is that we have associated love with pleasure, with sex, and for most of us love also means jealousy, anxiety, possessiveness, attachment. This is what we call love."— Jiddu Krishnamurti[66]

The giddy, intense, euphoric, passionate, and joyful romance of "being in love" is referred to, by the love experts, as the honeymoon phase of a relationship. Smitten, we experience the goosey,

[66] Jiddu Krishnamurti, *This Light in Oneself* (Krishnamurti Foundation Trust Ltd., 1999), 50

heart-pounding, breath-shortening, intense longing whenever we simply envision our beloved. It may seem that we cannot help ourselves, and we cannot, because the person with whom we are infatuated is "the one," and our brains reinforce this reverie with a chemical blast of adrenaline, norepinephrine, dopamine (in concert with reduced serotonin levels, note that)[67] and god knows what all else coursing through us, stimulating the brain's pleasure center with an effect similar to that of amphetamines[68] or cocaine.[69] It is true love.

The initial stage of a relationship is, admittedly, a delightful, manic thrill, but, honestly, the reality of it is quite ridiculous. Granted, the primal drive of simple lust is a rollicking biological imperative; from this, however, we proceed to make googly-eyes at the objects of our infatuation as we exalt their virtues and overlook their flaws, all the while having little more than a bare understanding of their true character. At this point, with the relationship being so experientially limited, we are only just gaining a more intimate knowledge of these relative strangers as they, and we, plainly present to one another studied appearances of charm and attractiveness. We cannot conceivably know their true natures (or they ours for that matter) or what kind of persons they are. With whom, then, are we "in love"?

Our new lovers are unquestionably perfect because the objects of our affections are simply our projected fantasies, idealized beings who reside solely in our heads, where we, understandably, cannot get them off our minds. How could we not be infatuated with the mentally fabricated, self-delusional fairy-tales that con-

[67] *What falling in love does to your heart and brain* (Loyola University Health System, Feb. 6, 2014), http://www.loyolamedicine.org/newswire/news/what-falling-love-does-your-heart-and-brain (retrieved 6/13/2014)

[68] Anne Marie Helmenstine, Ph.D., *Love Chemicals and Chemistry of Love*, http://chemistry.about.com/od/valentinesdaychemistry/a/Love-Chemicals.htm (retrieved 3/22/2014)

[69] *The science of love* (The Economist, Feb 12th 2004), http://www.economist.com/node/2424049 (retrieved 3/22/2014)

tinue to detonate a euphoric brew of biochemistry in our brains. We skip and hum and giggle down the street as the people around us politely smile (or scoff) all the while thinking that we are a goofy idiots—and we could care less. We are in love with our own story, and it feels absolutely profound.

Further adding to the egoistic chaos is the enhancement that romantic relationships make to the construct of an ego-story and social status. We feel terrific about ourselves: confident, worthy, smart, accomplished, special—desired. Life is beautiful because our egoistic wellbeing is stroked by the attention and recognition of not only our lovers but also the attention and recognition (real or imagined) of those around us. The passionately-loving-couple relationship can be displayed as some prized triumph for others to notice and envy, a possession of the ego-story, a baby rattle.

Realizing that being "in love" is simply a neurological condition, a temporary state of delusion and madness fueled by our biochemistry, does not mean to suggest we should seek to avoid the experience. No, not at all. Life would certainly be less inspired and exuberant without having experienced the mania of romantic love. Simply recognize, however, that: (1) these feelings of insane joy have less to do with the persons across from us than our own hormonal cravings and egoistic fantasies, and most significantly, (2) an egoistic attachment to a transient delusion is bound to result in anxiety, neurosis, and discontent.

Romantic Love—Self-love

The honeymoon will end. It will. It is biologically destined to be so. Commonly lasting for several months to no more than a few years (closer to two years, according to the love experts), the honeymoon is then over.[70] Kaput. Why does this have to happen?

To begin with, your body works to regulate itself toward a state of homeostasis, which runs counter to the bipolar biochemical ecstasy of romance and its attendant stress and anxiety as you obsess over your newly proclaimed lover. Emotional highs and lows serve no long-term purpose for the dispassionately purposeful nature of your biology. It is not for mere merrymaking and poetic inspiration that you are induced to experience the periodic love-high. No, your sole mission is to acquire a mate and to conceive. Consequently, a few years of crazed passion later, mission accomplished (or so we can presume) and the manic love chemistry naturally begins to peter out; the euphoria dwindles. Your brain has adapted and built up a tolerance to the rapture-inducing stimulants, and thoughts of "the one" no longer generate stomach-fluttering exhilaration. In fact, spontaneous thoughts of "the one" have by now dramatically diminished in frequency, if not having altogether disappeared. Obsessing over your lover is no longer. Tellingly, while a low level of the chemical serotonin in your brain would be linked to an increase in obsessive thought, in marked contrast, your serotonin level has been on the rise.[71]

It is known that serotonin, a neurotransmitter, is present at uncommonly low levels in the nervous systems of sufferers of OCD (Obsessive Compulsive Disorder) as well as in individuals experiencing the romantic passion of infatuation.[72] The apparent effect of low serotonin levels on individuals who have just fallen in love—anxious and obsessive longing for and fantasizing about the beloved—can be compared with the effect of low serotonin levels on the OCD sufferer—uncontrollable, obsessive, and intrusive thought. While treatment of OCD sufferers includes medications that increase the levels of serotonin in the brain (helping to alleviate obsessive thought and compulsive behavior) the distractedly possessed, love-struck romantic can mark his or her natural rise in serotonin levels with termination of the honeymoon phase in a relationship. Clank.

[70] Sonja Lyubomirsky, *New Love: A Short Shelf Life* (The New York Times, December 2, 2012)

[71] *What falling in love does to your heart and brain* (Loyola University Health System, Feb. 6, 2014), http://www.loyolamedicine.org/newswire/news/what-falling-love-does-your-heart-and-brain (retrieved June 13, 2014)

[72] *What falling in love does to your heart and brain* (Loyola University Health System, Feb. 6, 2014

Coincidentally, or maybe not, as the presence of your lover becomes more familiar and the novelty and freshness of your newly beloved becomes the everyday and humdrum, the biochemical intensity of infatuation is fading. The ego-fantasy ends, and you drift quietly back to an earthbound reality. One day you (or god forbid, it is your partner who returns to earth first) turn beside yourself and awaken to the reality that, "Oh my, this he or she individual next to me is just a regular person."

It may seem a bit deflating, but it is all necessarily pragmatic. You cannot float around in euphoric ecstasy for too long; you have things to do, like take care of that baby you just procreated! Fear not. Your biochemistry will not completely abandon your feelings of love. As the obsessiveness wanes, the two neurochemicals oxytocin and vasopressin, being released during sexual activity and insinuating their influence over you all along, become more significant. While not associated with the madness of romantic love, these chemicals have been identified as fostering the loving bonds necessary to become one big, happy, and nurturing family.

Oxytocin has been shown to play a significant role in the development of trust, attachment, and social and parental bonding. It is released when a woman gives birth and breastfeeds, helping establish the tender maternal connection between mother and child.[73] Oxytocin levels also increase during loving physical contact between couples, promoting intimate bonding, long-term attachment, and a sense of calmness and unity with the beloved. In fact, by simply holding hands and hugging, oxytocin levels can rise and induce feelings of closeness and social bonding with others.[74]

Vasopressin, likewise, is considered to have a vital influence on encouraging pair-bonding. Research indicates that vasopressin encourages long-term feelings of possessive attachment to and protectiveness over an individual mate.[75]

At this stage, you are still feeling the love, the pair-bonded at-

[73] R. Bowen, *Oxytocin*, July 12, 2010, http://www.vivo.colostate.edu/hbooks/pathphys/endocrine/hypopit/oxytocin.html (retrieved June 13, 2014)

tachment kind of love, but you are no longer love struck. Calm, cool, collected, loving, and appreciative toward your mate, you are back to your sane and rational self, more or less.

Now, hereby, we can consider the truth of romantic love.

Familiarity Breeds Contempt

Yikes! Such a harsh and cynical thought. Admittedly, it seems reasonable that the more we understand someone, the more likely it is that we will uncover a characteristic that we detest, but is it not just as likely that we will discover attributes that we admire? Yes, of course, because: Familiarity breeds clearer understanding of a person's true nature. Not as pithy, I admit, but more accurate, no?

Once we and our mates no longer affect a deliberately charming and attractive demeanor and we become comfortable enough to display our true natures, we can then begin to see each other in a truthful way. The idealized fairy-tale story is replaced with real life, and the traits that we find annoying in anybody else start to annoy us in our mates, possibly more so. Conflict and doubt may now appear in our relationships because we are no longer blind to the others' shortcomings. Which is how it should have been in the first place anyway, should it not? The not being blind part, that is, because we are not simply seeking a mate with whom to procreate, that would be easy enough. No, what we truly desire is more personal, perhaps a relationship established from something like this: having a commitment to each other based on a spirited friendship, mutual respect, affection, and physical intimacy; providing one another a sense of security, support, warmth, nurturing, and so on.

Regardless of how or why we "fell in love," when we note one day that our partners do not fulfill our physical, social, economic,

[74] John Pickrell, Lucy Middleton and Alun Anderson, *Introduction: Love* (The New Scientist, September 2006), http://www.newscientist.com/article/dn9981-introduction-love.html?full=true (retrieved June 13, 2014)
[75] *The Science of Love, BBC: Human Body & Mind,* http://www.bbc.co.uk/science/hottopics/love/ (retrieved June 13, 2014)

emotional, intellectual, or spiritual demands, the attraction begins to wane. The earlier feelings we had of affection begin to mutate into dissatisfaction, frustration, disinterest, resentment, bitterness, and enmity because, ultimately, the "love" in romantic love is, in truth, an egoistic expression of self-love.

Describing romantic love, Jiddu Krishnamurti states, "So what you are really saying is, 'As long as you belong to me I love you, but the moment you don't I begin to hate you. As long as I can rely on you to satisfy my demands, sexual and otherwise, I love you, but the moment you cease to supply what I want, I don't like you." [76]

Bitingly cynical, yes, but inaccurate? When our partners become less attentive, spend more time with their friends, no longer show us special affection, gaze at someone else, do not give us social face, do not express respect and support, act selfishly, do not maintain their physical attractiveness, express conflicting tastes, desires, and world-views, cannot provide a sense of security or stability, do not help care for the children (or do not want to have children), and so on, we become dissatisfied. As our partners do not live up to our demands, there comes a point when our "love" dissipates. In this, where is the love but in the love of the self and its satisfactions? There is, certainly, nothing unnatural or unseemly about looking out for one's best interests, but there is nothing romantic about it either.

Self-loathing and Fear

On the other end of the spectrum, we might be the type who willingly denies their self-interests and stands fast by their beloved, regardless of how we are treated. Is this how romantic love might be defined? We may suffer our lovers' verbal or physical abuse, disrespect, and ridicule, but, no matter, we cannot leave our jealous and controlling and narcissistic partners because we "love"

[76] Jiddu Krishnamurti, *Freedom from the Known* (Rider Books, 2010), 82

them. Being so lacking in self-worth, the more we are abused, the harder we strive to do whatever is necessary to secure the "love" and affection of our demeaning partners. We are emotionally, physically, and intellectually dependent on our mates, and without the attention and presence of our lovers, we feel incomplete, socially unrecognized and unaccepted, unworthy, and unattractive.

Or, perhaps, we are the ones who stay in unhealthy and inequitable relationships out of fear, the fear of being alone, because being alone means that we are unaccompanied by partners with whom we can together share the joys of, or face the sorrows of, life experience. It means having either to care for ourselves by ourselves or to humble our egoistic conceit and to seek out others for our emotional, physical, mental, and spiritual wellbeing. It means being self-reliant and solely responsible for the consequences of our life circumstances or to be self-effacing and connected to a greater community for support. Is this what we fear? Or is it the fear of solitude, of being alone with our discursive thoughts? Do we fear being alone with our minds that ruminate upon and long for the contrived achievements of happiness and success, minds that are disturbed by the inevitability of ill health and death? Do we not fear loneliness and the absence of a constant companion with whom we can chat to relieve the chatterings of an anxious and disquieted mind?

The Hero and Martyr

Perhaps romantic love has less to do with what we might derive from a relationship and more to do with what we can provide to another. We are sensitive and empathetic, compassionate and caring, able to understand another's needs, pains, and struggles. We have feelings of love emanating from our desire to nurture and protect. We will rescue our lovers from themselves and their self-destructive behaviors, lead them to enlightenment and happiness. We will rescue our beloveds, sacrificing ourselves in the process because they depend on us, and this is the meaning of love. The sacrifice and the selflessness become our ego-story. We are the virtuous hero, the noble martyr.

Romantic Love

A "romantic love" fueled by low self-worth or the need to personify the selfless and virtuous hero-martyr is nothing more than the egoistic desire to fabricate a personal, or socially recognized, ego-story which makes one feel worthwhile and fulfilled.

A person who remains "in love" because of fear clings to the pretensions of a prideful and socially recognized ego-story, desperately striving to avoid the ego-challenging doubts of self-worth and self-sufficiency. Additionally, there is the fear of a mind in isolation, chattering and tormented by the mental constructs of a dualistic world-view and the refusal to recognize the truth of impermanence.

Finally, a "romantic love" that is dependent on one's self-satisfaction is simply an egoistic expression of self-love.

Is romantic love, then, merely egoistic? Yes, certainly. It is born from a love of the self.

Love

Is it possible to truly love a partner? Of course, but true love is not bound by the egoism of romance or desire or need or fear. No, to truly love someone is to wish for one the freedom to express their true nature and to develop the intellectual, physical, emotional, and spiritual growth that leads to wellbeing and contentment. Honestly, though, you can wish this for anyone whom you care about, and then some, no? A lover, a daughter or son, your parents, friends, relatives, neighbors—all of humanity. True love is universal; it is not egoistic, possessive, or exclusive.

The following point, undoubtedly, is then raised (usually by men, unsurprisingly), "If love is not egoistic, possessive, or exclusive, intimate relationships can simply be polyamorous, no?" A reasonable argument can be made for this, certainly.

Polyamory: openly and honestly having multiple romantic partnerships, with knowledge, acceptance, and consent by all parties.

The Coolidge-Effect

Research has revealed a phenomenon that is common to most mammalian species and which proves instructive to the long-term pair-bonding monogamy advocate: having sexual interest in a mate diminishes when lust has been satiated by the one particular partner, but libido is promptly invigorated when a novel and responsive mate is introduced.

The original research experiment went something like this: a male rat was placed with several female rats in heat. After spirited and repeated copulation with the female rats, the male rat eventually exhausted himself. At this point, regardless of the licking and prodding of the still receptive females, the male rat remained fatigued to the point of torpor. Subsequently, a new female was placed in the enclosure, and the male rat promptly perked to attention. Instantly revitalized, he immediately began engaging in energetic mating activity exclusively with the newly introduced female rat.[77]

The neurochemical that is thought to be responsible for this seemingly boorish behavior is the previously mentioned dopamine. Initial engagement in sexual activity is rewarded with a blast of dopamine in the brain's pleasure center. As the activity is repeated with the same partner, however, the dopamine level diminishes until it flatlines. Yawn. Ho-hum. Not so surprisingly, when a new potential partner enters and romps past, dopamine and sexual interest levels instantly perk back up.

The term Coolidge-Effect was coined from a dubious but oft-

[77] Beach, F. A. & Jordan, L., *Sexual Exhaustion and Recovery in the Male Rat* (Quarterly Journal of Experimental Psychology 8: 121–133, 1956)

repeated tale of the 30th U.S. president, Calvin Coolidge, and his wife, Grace, allegedly visiting a government-run experimental farm. The story goes that at some point after arriving, they parted and began touring the grounds separately. As the First Lady was passing the chicken pen, she paused and asked the staff, "How often does the rooster engage in mating activity?"

"Oh, dozens of times a day, ma'am."

Impressed, Grace replied, "Really? Well, please tell that to the President when he passes by here."

Later, as President Coolidge was strolling past, the worker duly recounted to him his conversation with the First Lady. The President thought for a moment and enquired, "Tell me, does the rooster choose the same hen each time?"

"No, sir. It's a different one each time." The President quietly smiled, "Please tell that to the First Lady."

Grace and Calvin Coolidge

Love and Relationship

Returning to the concept of true and non-egoistic love, there are several assertions that appear equally reasonable: (1) You can have several lovers (polyamory), with a truly non-egoistic love for them all; or (2) You can feel a non-egoistic love for everyone and be in an intimate, everlasting relationship with none; or (3) You can feel a non-egoistic love for all while maintaining an intimate relationship with a single partner. Each argument, however, does not come without enquiry.

1) Having Multiple Partners: Is the drive for polyamory not simply the egoistic craving for sensation? That of the dopamine rush associated with discovering novelty in a variety of sexual partners, otherwise known as the Coolidge-effect? Is polyamory fueled by a prideful attachment to the individually and socially fabricated ego-story of being attractive to the opposite sex?

If the responsibilities of raising children are not a consideration, the polyamorous relationship, with its regular dopamine-generating exhilaration, seems rather appealing. The trade-off, however, is having to navigate your own egoistic, discursive, prattling thoughts and dopamine-high cravings along with those of your several other lovers, a time-consuming pain in the arse, certainly. Are ya crazy?

2) Having No (Everlasting) Partner: Is the refusal to have an intimate partner arising from fear that the exposed self-loving ego will become vulnerable? Is this an aversion to intimacy arising from a dualistic mind that defines our natural procreant impulses to be "bad" or spiritually unhealthy? Is there unease because physical desire leads to conflict in an egoistic mind struggling with its discursive and anxious nattering thoughts?

Free yourself of egoistic attachment and aversion arising from dualistic thought and you will have no fear of intimacy.

If you simply have not met or have no necessity to meet a compatible partner, this second scenario seems a natural and reasonable outcome. There is no imperative to having a singular lifelong partner. You can still express love to others, can still feel enthusiasm for the joy of others, and you can still feel grounded and content with yourself and your life.

3) Having a Single Partner: Can you be satisfied in a relationship with feelings that evolve into a tranquil and affectionate love, foregoing a regular dopamine rush of infatuation and novelty? Are you grounded enough to encourage (without egoistic intent) development of your lover's

intellectual, physical, emotional, and spiritual growth, leading to his or her wellbeing and contentment?

*Finally, the third example appears, on the surface, somewhat famil-
iar, though a non-egoistic love for your partner is dissimilar to the
soul-mate fulfilling, live-happily-ever-after, fairy-tale concept of romantic love/self-love. Can you have a non-egoistic, true love for your
partner and wish for him or her intellectual, physical, emotional, and
spiritual growth leading to wellbeing and contentment? Conceivably,
this path may at some point result in a divergence of life direction for
you and your partner, the result being an end to your physical intimacy and togetherness. Or, not so evermore, the separation may turn
out to be impermanent, followed by a later convergence once again of
your life paths. Who knows? Is life not a constant flow of energy and
transformation?*

To love without ego is, among other things, to recognize the truth
of impermanence: there is no clinging to the illusion that an intimate relationship must last indefinitely. An honest, non-egoistic
love between individuals, without possession or exclusiveness or
ego-attachment, can remain constant and true, endless and infinite.

There is no universal, absolute, and dualistic right or wrong
perspective on love and relationships, merely truth and rationale
to consider.

Relationship and Mindfulness

The usual question is how to determine whether some individual
personifies a partner with whom we are most likely to maintain a
loving relationship, a partner who inspires our intellectual, physical, emotional, and spiritual growth, a partner whom we do not
have to struggle to be with.

There is no doubt that starting from the initial spark of hormonal lust, physical attractiveness and the subsequent "chemistry" are relevant, but is our concept of attractiveness not formed

by media and cultural fabrications? How much of our physical attraction to another is driven by our desire for association with a partner who gains for us egoistic social recognition and approval? Before falling in "love at first sight," consider beforehand deconstructing the conditioned thoughts of physical desirability that have been contrived by and derived from commercial and media fairy-tales, alongside social and cultural norms. Liberate your ego from its social conditioning.

Friendship doubles our joy and divides our grief.
— Swedish Proverb

Loving couples who have stayed together for a significant number of years regularly proclaim that their partner is their best friend and someone whom they unreservedly and objectively like as a person. Does having a lover such as this not make utter sense? What is a best friend if not someone for whom we have a non-egoistic love, someone for whom we wish personal growth, wellbeing, and contentment, someone with whom we enjoy sharing laughter, secrets, and time. A truly best friend is one with whom we share a similar world-view and life philosophy. He or she does not "complete" us or enable us but rather confronts us with sincerity and truth so that we are stimulated to grow as individuals, and as we develop, evolve, and thrive, how can we not find one another regularly inspiring and enlivening?

Look for a partner based on true friendship, not merely a friendship founded on a shared history, or on a chance shared interest or common proximity, or on an egoistic neediness and attachment. No, consider a potential partner mindfully and seek out a genuine friend who has more of the characteristics that you would admire in others, and fewer of the traits that would annoy you in others, because, eventually, the infatuation must end and you are one day faced with the simple reality of the person before you.

Live mindfully with this friend and partner and recognize that the allure from the Coolidge-Effect is most often a craving for physical sensation driven by biochemistry and an attachment to a mentally fabricated ego-story, physical sensation followed by egoistic thought compelling one to base action. Observe the truth of your cravings and mental chatter, and you need not live hostage to the deceits of your conditioned mind, your discursive thoughts and compulsions.

Rid of egoistic attachments and cravings, one has no needfulness for a partner who must fulfill, complete, or enable his or her egoistic inadequacies nor does a person feel conflicted by the sensory cravings fueled by the Coolidge-Effect. One has simply infinite non-egoistic love and an inspiring and responsive and intimate best friend, partner, and lover.

EIGHT

EATING MY DOG

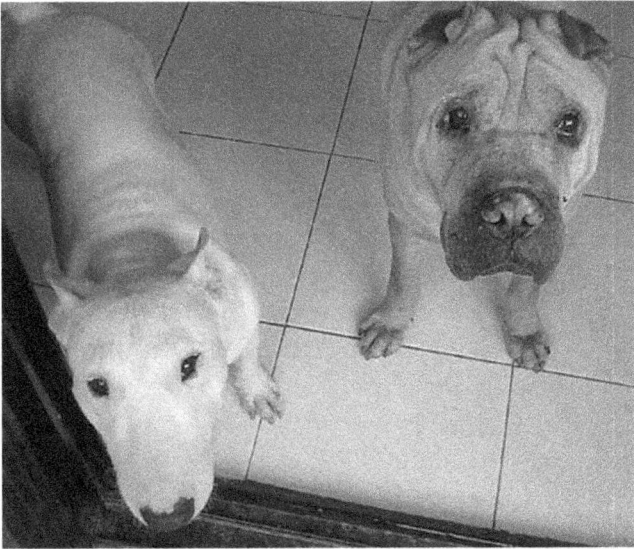

Chubby and Ku-gua

I was looking at my dogs one day and thinking about eating them. I had taken in two strays—Chubby, a peglegged miniature bull terrier, and 苦瓜 (ku-gua, "bitter melon" in Chinese), an über-wrinkly-skinned sharpei—two apparently purebred dogs that I had rescued from the streets around Taipei City. Although mangy and flea-infested when I had found them, both appeared to be young and healthy (Chubby's crippled and immobilized left rear leg notwithstanding). At the time it was not uncommon for Taipei residents to buy a cute and trendy pedigreed puppy and then abandon it in the street after it got too big and unruly for a cramped urban apartment. Great luck for me, a dog-lover.

What would it be like eating one of my dogs? I wondered. I looked at them basking in the sunshine that streamed through my picture window, Chubby curled up and laying on top of Ku-gwa. They were my hiking partners in the mountains surrounding the city and lived like siblings: best friends most of the time, annoying to and snarly at one another on occasion. Could I eat one of them? The answer would seemingly be no, but then again, I rather enjoyed my previous meal of dog.

Dog Food

It was my first ever trip to China. I was in Guilin, following Henry, a bespectacled and collegiate-looking young man who had eagerly approached me earlier that day and offered his services as a local guide. "What you want to do, want to see, you tell me. I take you," he enthused. So there we were, hiking up one of the iconic karst hills of Guilin, where the trail happened to wind around a mountainside restaurant. Passing the back of the restaurant, I spotted a stoic-faced, apron-covered man outside, methodically butchering what appeared to be a furless medium-sized dog, its face frozen into a death grimace.

We have all heard by now that the eating of dog meat, 香肉 (xiang ròu), in Asia is not so uncommon, but being a "dog-person," I was still taken aback to see a canine carcass being hacked into pieces. On the one hand, I was disturbed by the sight, but then again, my ancestors are Cantonese, and what is said about the Cantonese is this: "Cantonese will eat anything with four legs but a table, anything in the sky but an airplane, and anything in the sea but a submarine." When you see a video or read a story of a Chinese person eating an odd-sounding or stomach-cringing meal, it is most likely a Cantonese.

After the initial shock, I was intrigued. Being an adventurous eater, I always felt that if other people could eat something and it didn't make them sick or kill them, I should, at the least, give it a taste. And wouldn't eating dog be a novel experience that I could take back to share with my friends in the U.S.?

After Henry and I finished our trek of the Guilin hills, I asked him, "Do you know where I can try dog meat?"

"You like eat dog meat?"

"Well, I'd like to try it. Can you take me to a local place where people eat dog meat?"

"Okay. No problem."

He led, I followed, as we wound our way through a warren of nondescript, single-story brick structures and ended up in what appeared to be the local neighborhood eatery: a plain, slightly grimy, no-frills room fitted with low-slung wooden tables and chairs. The steam of simmering broths and the earthy aroma of herbs and roots greeted us at the entrance. We took a seat at an empty table and sat half-squatted on the undersized chairs.

After shouting a greeting to a man working behind the counter— a stoic-faced, apron-covered man gripping a meat cleaver, Henry turned to me, "How you want eat dog meat?"

"I don't know. I've never eaten dog before. The usual, I guess."

Henry glanced at the menu and yelled something in the local dialect at the cleaver-wielding man. The stoic-faced man nodded and shouted a few unintelligible Chinese utterances in return. Raising the cleaver, he pushed aside a thin curtain in the back doorway and disappeared into the kitchen.

I looked at the menu, a sheet of paper scribbled with Chinese characters, encased in a plastic sheet cover. I imagined what exotic cuisine the scrawls might represent as the whacking of the cleaver rhythmically clunked from behind the curtain.

A couple of locals at the next table eyed us curiously and began chatting with Henry. I could only speculate as to what they were eating: Noodles? Worms? Brains? It could be anything. We weren't so far removed from the Cantonese province after all. They looked my way and smiled, nodding their approval. Somehow, they seemed a bit too amused. *As long as it doesn't make me sick or kill me*, I reminded myself.

The stoic man returned from the kitchen and set on our table a steaming pot of what looked like stew. Dark chunks of meat were submerged beneath the dense, brown broth. My throat clenched. I thought about my dog, Monster, the mixed breed that I had given to a friend when I had left the U.S. *It isn't like I'm eating my own dog,* I thought, but yet, it felt like I was about to. Since childhood, regardless of where I had moved, I had always had a dog as a pet and companion. I was feeling torn as my dog-loving side conflicted with my Cantonese taste for "anything goes" cuisine. My gastronomic side won out, and I ladled myself a bowl of stew as Henry served me a bowl of rice. "Do you want some?" I offered Henry.

"No, I no eat dog meat." Henry smiled politely, sat back, and poured himself a cup of tea.

While Henry sipped his tea, I picked out a hunk of meat and took a slow bite. It was oily and chewy, the flavor earthy and slightly gamey. It reminded me somewhat of beef, albeit a greasier and chewier beef. I found it quite tasty, dog meat, but then I imagined I was eating my own dog and felt a twinge of guilt to Monster and all the other dogs I had had as pets.

"You like? Dog meat?"

"It's very good, very tasty."

I had to admit, despite the sleight queasiness, that I quite liked it.

Monster

Several years later, looking at Chubby and Ku-gwa in Taiwan, I realized that if I could enjoy the taste of that dog meat stew in Guilin, I could just as enjoyably feast on either of my own dogs. They would likely be equally as tasty; I suppose I would hardly notice a difference. Perhaps the stewed dog in Guilin had also been a stray. Or abducted from its owner and sold to the restaurant? Who knew?

Dog-eating apologists will say, "It's only because we're not socialized to eat dog. We eat cows, pigs, lambs, and chickens. What's the difference?" And this is meant to explain that it is unreasonable to be uneasy about eating dog and cat or to be offended by others who eat dog and cat just because we have been conditioned in our own particular non-dog-and-cat-eating way. I understand the logic, but I now offer a different perspective: I clearly cannot eat my own dogs because I recognize them as sentient creatures whose consumption is not necessary for my survival. If I cannot eat my dogs, of course, I feel uneasy eating any dog because I reasonably view all dogs as sentient creatures. The following logical enquiry then is: How can I eat a cow or pig or lamb or chicken when I recognize that they, also, are similarly sentient beings? There is no difference. Eating a cow, or pig, or lamb, or chicken is no different from eating my own dog. If I cannot eat my own dog because I recognize it as a sentient being, then logically, I should not be able to eat any other animal I recognize as a sentient being.

Well, there is logic, and then there are the pleasures of eating. For a while then, I had been considering the idea of not eating meat. Initially, it was the beef of cows. They seemed such passive herbivores, and to be honest, a friend once commented that Monster looked a bit like a cow. I suppose that's what got me thinking about why we consider some animals acceptable and others unacceptable to eat. At the time, though, I still quite enjoyed eating meat. It tasted good, and besides, the eating of meat is a quite normal occurrence in the natural world. There is nothing untoward about it.

The practice of eating animals had never troubled me in that "have compassion for the innocent creature" kind of way. (Did I mention that I am Cantonese?) If you have ever viewed a pack of hyenas rip apart live a young wildebeest, you will have witnessed the simple, brutal reality of nature. There is no feeling or compassion from predator to prey. It is purely food to be slaughtered and consumed, a perfectly mundane occurrence in the yin and yáng of nature. Why should humans not be a participant in this dynamic?

To see a creature slaughtered before us, however, would make most of us cringe. We are more than happy to eat the animal, just don't make us watch it being killed. It is understandable. Perhaps this has something to do with the mirror neurons in our brains, brain cells that fire not only when we perform an action but also when we see someone else perform the same action. It is speculated that mirror neurons play a role in allowing us to feel what others may be feeling. We empathize.[78]

It follows, then, that if we are determined to eat meat, and we are not sociopathic, we would prefer to butcher an animal in a way that avoids any undue suffering.

If you are a typical meat-eater and purchase your packaged meats at the supermarket or big-box store, do a search online to learn the nightmare of "factory farming cruelty,"[79] and recognize that you are participating in a system that creates misery for around ten billion animals a year in the U.S. alone.[80][81] This is not to say that it is impossible to consume meat humanely. A skilled hunter prides himself or herself on executing a clean kill, which results in an animal living wild and free before its life is fairly quickly and efficiently ended. If you want to consume meat humanely, learn how to hunt, and aim well. Alternatively, you can raise your own animals and learn how to humanely kill them yourself, with as much compassion as you can muster.

At the very least, you should know your supplier of meat and learn how the animals are raised and slaughtered. Factory-farmed

[78] Ronald T. Kellogg, *The Making of the Mind* (Prometheus Books, 2013) 198-201

[79] *Glass Walls*, documentary narrated by Paul McCartney (Free From Harm, 2009), http://freefromharm.org/videos/documentaries/meat-org-the-web-site-the-meat-industry-does-not-want-you-to-see/ (retrieved 06/02/2014)

[80] *Report: Number of Animals Killed In US Increases in 2010*, FARM, http://farmusa.org/statistics11.html (retrieved 06/02/2014)

[81] *What's Wrong with Factory Farming?* The Organic Consumers Association, http://www.organicconsumers.org/foodsafety/shortlist031604.cfm (retrieved 06/02/2014)

meat and poultry? Cross them off your shopping list. There seem to be more and more meat producers enthusiastically promoting their efforts in raising, handling, and butchering their livestock in a humane manner (Note: meat labeled "organic" does not equate to being humanely raised and butchered). Do your research. In the end, all these animals are still led to slaughter for consumption, but by comparing the suffering a farm animal experiences at the hand of a humane rancher with the brutality the wildebeest faces at the natural savagery of the spotted hyenas (or the inevitable old age, starvation, disease, or injury that debilitates wild animals and leaves them vulnerable, once again, to the voracity of predators) it is clear that we can eat meat and still take care to avoid causing undue suffering to the animals we consume.

Yet there are still vegetarians and vegans who will insist that they are somehow more morally righteous because they do not participate in the slaughter of animals for consumption. They are somehow "better" than meat-eaters because they cause less suffering by not eating animals. This sentiment is equally a claim that one is somehow "better" than nature, a nature that is both resplendent and brutally indifferent, a nature of which we all are a part, a nature from which we all have been born. This moral righteousness is simply an egoistic statement fabricated from a dualistic worldview and an ignorance of the natural world.

On the other hand, if you are comfortable eating a cow or pig or chicken, you should be just as comfortable eating your own dog, cat, rabbit, parrot, or any other pet. If you could not make a humanely-butchered meal of your beloved companion because you recognize your pet as a sentient being, then I suggest you open your eyes to the truth that the animals you consume for meat are just as sentient, just as equally conscious, aware, and feeling as your own pet-companion-friend. The act of eating any animal is no different from the act of eating your own pet. As Paul McCartney has been quoted as saying, "When I see bacon, I see a pig, I see a little friend, and that's why I can't eat it. Simple as that."[82]

After acknowledging that my eating of animal flesh was illogical when I recognized that all animals were as sentient as my own dogs and that it was simply unnecessary for me to eat meat to live healthfully, I greatly reduced the quantity of meat I consumed, virtually eliminating beef and pork—virtually. Still, I continued to regularly eat, in moderate amounts, fish, poultry, and various seafood. Although I didn't feel so bothered by the seeming hypocrisy of it all, somewhere in my subconscious existed uncertainty over the illogic of it all.

What I have found instructive about meditation is that as the private mental chatter becomes less prominent, less of a distraction to the focus of your attention, the truth becomes much more apparent and undeniable. Finally, there is a moment of clarity, and there is no more trying. The truth is simply laid bare before you, obvious and without doubt. A thread of egoism snaps, a switch in one's mind clicks, and knowing becomes being.

And so it was. One day—*click!*—I definitively recognized that the eating of any animal was no different from the eating of my own dogs, and that was that. My response to the suggestion of eating meat, any meat, became similar to the likely response a Westerner would give when invited to eat dog or cat: Uh, no thanks!

I was attempting to explain this phenomena to a Chinese-American friend of mine back in the States: "It's as if I were to make a pot of stew, and after trying a bowl, you tell me how tasty it is and ask me for another. As I'm serving you the second bowl, I tell you it is made with dog meat, and, immediately, you have lost all craving and decline to eat more. At one moment you want seconds, and a moment later, you have abruptly lost your appetite, though it is the same stew and still tastes "delicious." It is the certainty of truth. Your attitude and feelings and perceptions change, just like that, directly and effortlessly. Awaken to the truth, and it is possible to transform the way you live, without mental conflict or struggle."

[82] Paul McCartney (Animal Times interview, Fall 1998)

My friend replied in all earnestness, "No, dog meat wouldn't bother me. I'd still want another bowl of stew."

"Oh, all right. I know. You're Cantonese! Well, how about if I told you my neighbor was riding his motorcycle, got hit by a car, and had his leg ripped off? The stew was made with my neighbor's dismembered leg."

"Okay, I probably wouldn't want to eat a second bowl of that."

And, lastly, there is this argument: When we eat plants, are we not still killing and causing suffering?

In order to survive and maintain a healthful, nutritious diet, we have to kill and eat something, plants or animals, or both. There is no argument. It is nature's process through which solar energy can flow through all living things while chemical elements are cycled back and forth throughout the ecosystem. There is no right or wrong, good or bad, about it. The killing and consumption of one by another is a perfectly mundane occurrence in the yin and yáng of our ecosystem. The question here is this: What is the difference between being an herbivore and being a carnivore (or omnivore)?

A Simple Ecosystem Review

The biological system acquires solar energy through the process of photosynthesis: Plants absorb light energy from the sun and convert it to chemical energy. This energy allows plants to grow and is stored in their leaves, roots, and fruits. (Remember this from elementary school?) Plants then provide energy to virtually every living thing on earth. When herbivores (including bugs) consume plants or plant parts, the stored chemical energy from the leaves, roots, and fruits is taken in and allows the animal to store this chemical energy for its own life processes: growth, movement, reproduction, sight, hearing, smell, taste, touch, and so on. Carnivores and omnivores consume herbivores (or each other), and chemical energy (essentially solar energy) in the flesh of the consumed provides for the energy needs of the consumer.

Besides the constant flow of energy throughout the community of organisms in the ecosystem, other chemical elements essential for life are cycled through the soil, water, air, plants, and living community of creatures as these organisms inhale and exhale, consume food and excrete waste, die, and, finally, decompose, once again recycling nutrients through the system, back into the soil for plants.

The various elements of the ecosystem, the elements of the natural world, are in constant movement and interaction, moving in complex flows of energy and matter in a continuum. The physical nature of living, then, is to assimilate the energy of the sun and to cycle chemical elements throughout the ecosystem, with the simplest, most direct, and most efficient way being to consume plants and plant products. The killing and consumption of plants (and animals, frankly) is a perfectly mundane occurrence in the yin and yáng of nature.

Do plants not suffer pain?

The obvious answer is that plants have neither brain nor nervous system, so they cannot suffer from nor even feel pain in any way in which we are familiar, but perhaps that is a bit too apparent.

Consider the rare medical condition called "congenital analgesia,"[83] a disorder of the human nervous system in which the sufferer cannot feel, and has never felt, physical pain. Otherwise normal children with this condition often chew through their tongues and lips, chew through their fingers, break bones, get burned, poke their eyes out, and so on, never feeling pain and not knowing that they are injured (parents of a child with this condition will sometimes have all their child's teeth removed to prevent self-mutilation, e.g., chewing through his or her tongue, or chewing off his or her fingers, etc.). Tragically, the childhood of individuals with this

[83] *Congenital insensitivity to pain* (Genetics Home Reference, 2014), http://ghr.nlm.nih.gov/condition/congenital-insensitivity-to-pain (retrieved 06/02/2014)

condition often ends in physical trauma and an early death.

One adult patient, Steven Pete, describes an incident from his childhood when he broke a leg at a roller-skating rink and hadn't realized that anything was wrong until people started pointing to his pants, which were covered in blood from where the bone was sticking out.[84] Another, Karen Cann, after giving birth through an emergency C-section, recalls the right side of her body feeling stiff. Several weeks later, though feeling no pain and able to walk, she observed the stiffness becoming worse and hampering her ability to get around. Noticing a clicking noise inside her body, she returned to the hospital for X-rays and discovered that she had broken her pelvis during childbirth and was suffering from internal bleeding.[85]

If a person with congenital analgesia can be injured and feel no pain, can he or she "suffer" from physical pain? Logically, no, and they do not. They feel no pain and have no emotional reaction to physical trauma. If a plant has no brain or nervous system, can it suffer from physical pain? I have no idea. I am not a plant after all, but, logically, it seems not. Plants have been observed to respond to chemical and physical stimuli: they might turn toward the sun, they might respond to auditory or physical stimulus, they might "communicate" through chemical signals—but, still, they have no brain or nervous system; they do not and can not react emotionally, as we know it, to physical trauma.

When we observe the function of plants, it is apparent that they occupy a role different from animals in the flow of solar energy and matter throughout the ecosystem. Plants, though part of the biotic (living) community, have a role that lies somewhere between the other biotic elements—animals, insects, microbes—and the abiotic (non-living) elements—sunlight, temperature, wa-

[84] Steven Pete, Congenital analgesia: The agony of feeling no pain (BBC News Magazine, July 16, 2012), http://www.bbc.com/news/magazine-18713585 (retrieved 11/02/2013)

[85] Justin Heckert, *The Hazards of Growing Up Painlessly* (New York Times, 15 November 2012), http://www.nytimes.com/2012/11/18/magazine/ashlyn-blocker-feels-no-pain.html?pagewanted=all&_r=0 (retrieved 11/02/2013)

ter, air, soil, and chemical components. Plants transform sunlight to a chemical energy that we consume and metabolize to fuel our own energy needs; plants take in CO_2 from the air and expel the oxygen that we then breathe; plants take in chemical elements from the air and soil which will nourish our bodies when we consume plant matter. From the organic farming system called biodynamics, we can consider the plant world as made up not of individuated beings, such as animals and humans, but rather as a subsystem that is "part of the larger macrocosmic process," closer to an earth process, more akin to an "organ of the earth."[86]

Plants and animals, though both living organisms, are clearly incomparable. Do plants suffer pain when we harvest and consume them? I imagine not, regardless, if you wish to minimize the trauma caused by the harvesting of the produce you consume, I suggest you grow your own vegetable plot. Otherwise, get to know your local small-scale organic grower. I have never met an experienced gardener or small-scale organic farmer that did not express great care and respect for the plant world.

The Pyramid of Energy

Next, there is the Pyramid of Energy. Once again, we return to our elementary school classroom.

Have you ever noticed that there are so many more plants than animals existing on the earth? This is because green plants (including algae) are the producers; they are able to take the energy of the sun and chemical elements from the soil and air to synthesize their own food and, subsequently, provide food to virtually every living thing on earth. Plants, therefore, make up the foundation of the Pyramid of Energy.

The first level of consumers is the primary consumers: herbivores, animals, and bugs that consume green plants to satisfy their

[86] Wolf D. Storl, *Culture and Horticulture, A Philosophy of Gardening* (Biodynamic Farming and Gardening Assoc., Inc., 2000) 125

energy needs. The next level consists of the secondary consumers, commonly referred to as carnivores (including omnivores). These animals eat primary consumers, the herbivores. The third level of consumers in the Pyramid are the tertiary consumers, animals that eat secondary consumers, e.g., a Great Horned Owl eats a snake that has eaten a mouse that has fed on plant matter. Eventually, there is a top predator with few or no natural enemies.

The significant aspect of the Pyramid of Energy is that only about 10% of the energy from one level, called a "trophic level," is transferred to the next higher level on the Pyramid. The other 90% is "lost" as it is used up to fuel growth and life processes from the original trophic level. When energy is transferred from plant products to a cow (herbivore) for example, only 10% of the original "plant" energy is available for a person (omnivore) who eats the cow. The cow has used up the other 90% for its own energy needs. At the next level—above the cow-eating human— only 1% of the original plant energy is available for the next level of consumers, the tertiary consumers (a great white shark or cannibal, perhaps?), and so on. By the time you get to the end of a food chain, most of the original plant energy that was obtainable at the beginning is no longer available. Consequently, energy is used much more efficiently when humans live as herbivores instead of omnivores. A given amount of grain can supply the energy needs of many more people if the grain is eaten directly by people rather than eaten first by livestock that people would subsequently eat. Additionally, land and water resources would be better utilized and more sustainable because we could: (A) support more people on a given area of land, or (B) support the present number of people on a smaller area of land.

Unfortunately for the sustainability of our natural resources, the U.S. Environmental Protection Agency website states: "According to the National Corn Growers Association, about 80% of all corn grown in the U.S. is consumed by domestic and overseas livestock, poultry, and fish production."[87]

From The American Public Health Association: "Industrial meat production, especially beef, requires the most water—much of it to irrigate feed crops. For example, by one estimate it takes more than 100,000 liters of water to produce grain and hay for each kilogram of industrially produced beef."[88]

A 2003 article in the American Society for Clinical Nutrition reports that the weight of U.S. raised livestock was about five times greater than the weight of the total U.S. human population and that livestock "consumed more than seven times as much grain as is consumed directly by the entire American population. The amount of grains fed to U.S. livestock is sufficient to feed about 840 million people who follow a plant-based diet."[89] (The U.S. Census Bureau website has estimated the 2013 U.S. population to be around 316 million.)[90]

Finally, there is the relationship between what we eat and greenhouse gas emissions. The four greenhouse gas emissions influencing the vast majority of global climate change are CO_2, methane, nitrous oxide, and fluorinated gases. While carbon dioxide is well-known as a greenhouse gas, two by-products of the livestock industry, methane and nitrous oxide, are two major and more potent (pound for pound) greenhouse gases.

As part of their normal digestive process, the approximately 100 million cows in the U.S. produce massive amounts of methane and release it into the atmosphere by belching from one end or passing gas from the other. Then we have manure, from not only cows but also the billions of chickens, turkeys, and pigs in the

[87] *Crop Production*, Ag 101, U.S. Environmental Protection Agency, http://www.epa.gov/agriculture/ag101/printcrop.html (retrieved 11/12/2013)

[88] *Toward a Healthy, Sustainable Food System* (The American Public Health Association, Policy Date: 11/6/2007, Policy Number: 200712), http://www.apha.org/policies-and-advocacy/public-health-policy-statements/policy-database/2014/07/29/12/34/toward-a-healthy-sustainable-food-system (retrieved 12/17/2013)

[89] David Pimentel and Marcia Pimentel, *Sustainability of meat-based and plant-based diets and the environment* (American Society for Clinical Nutrition, September 2003 vol. 78 no. 3 660S-663S), http://ajcn.nutrition.org/content/78/3/660S.full (retrieved 10/18/2013)

[90] *Annual Estimates of the Resident Population: April 1, 2010 to July 1, 2013*, U.S. Census Bureau, Population Division, http://factfinder2.census.gov/faces/tableservices/jsf/pages/productview.xhtml?src=bkmk (retrieved 06/08/2014)

livestock industry. As the manure is stored or managed in acres of lagoons, holding tanks, or heaps, methane and nitrous dioxide are emitted as the feces sits and rots.

Again, from The American Public Health Association: "Meat production is a particularly powerful contributor (to greenhouse gas emissions); the Food and Agriculture Organization of the United Nations (UN FAO) estimates that approximately 18% of all greenhouse gas emissions worldwide come from livestock production."[91]

In fact, the United Nations Food and Agriculture Organization reports that livestock production generates more greenhouse gas emissions as measured in $CO2$ equivalent than transportation[92]

Well then, is it "better" to eat plants than animals? Decide for yourself based on truth and reason.

Reasons for being a non-meat eater: You can have a perfectly healthful, balanced, and nutritious diet that provides for all of your energy and nutritional needs (do not forget the B12 supplement) with no need to kill another sentient creature and eat its flesh. Ideally, grow your own produce or purchase it from a small-scale organic farmer, and you will be participating in a food production system that causes less land and water degradation, is more sustainable, and contributes much less to greenhouse gas emissions than industrial livestock production.

Reasons for being a meat eater: Meat tastes good.

[91] *Toward a Healthy, Sustainable Food System* (The American Public Health Association, Policy Number: 200712, 11/06/2007) http://www.apha.org/policies-and-advocacy/public-health-policy-statements/policy-database/2014/07/29/12/34/toward-a-healthy-sustainable-food-system (retrieved 06/26/2014)

[92] *Livestock a major threat to environment* (Food and Agriculture Organization of the United Nations, 2006), http://www.fao.org/newsroom/en/News/2006/1000448/index.html (retrieved 10/18/2013)

From Carl Sagan:

> "Humans—who enslave, castrate, experiment on, and fillet other animals—have had an understandable penchant for pretending animals do not feel pain . . . The limbic system in the human brain, known to be responsible for much of the richness of our emotional life, is prominent throughout the mammals. The same drugs that alleviate suffering in humans mitigate the cries and other signs of pain in many other animals. It is unseemly of us, who often behave so unfeelingly toward other animals, to contend that only humans can suffer."[93]

[93] Carl Sagan, co-written with Dr. Ann Druyan, *Shadows of Forgotten Ancestors* (Random House, 1992) 371-372

NINE

NON-DUALITY AND THE MORAL DILEMMA

"Everything happens for a reason."

Certainly.

Or, maybe not.

The above well-worn phrase is commonly uttered when one needs comfort following an unfortunate event: failing a test, wrecking a car, losing a job, a partner's cheating, becoming ill, or perhaps, a prized horse's running off. Of course, Zhuang-zi's farmer would likely reply, "Bad luck? Sure, I guess so. Maybe. I don't know. What is bad? Excuse me, I'm busy. I have to mend my fence." He is more apt to conclude: Oh, well. Shit happens.

Events occur, we acknowledge them, deal with them, other things happen, and we continue to live. Can fortunate and unfortunate, good and bad, success and failure exist without the mental conditioning that causes us to project dualistic judgments and characterizations? Of course not. The universe maintains no concept of dualistic or non-dualistic anything. The natural order is beyond concepts and simply exists.

Here We Live—What is the Point?

Crowfoot, Chief of the Blackfeet Indians

"What is life? It is the flash of a firefly in the night. It is the breath of a buffalo in winter time. It is the little shadow which runs across the grass and loses itself in the sunset."— Crowfoot, Chief of the Siksika Nation (1821–1890)[94] Photograph: Crowfoot, Chief of the Blackfeet Indians – Library and Archives Canada

We are seemingly headed down a path toward nihilistic views that will claim our lives in this universe have no divine meaning and that morals are purely artificial, mental contrivances. A bit disquieting perhaps, but shall we claim these propositions to be otherwise? Look skyward, observe and contemplate for a moment that in the brilliance and radiance and gloriousness of a vastly immense

[94] T. C. McLuhan , *Touch the Earth* (Promontory Press, March 1971) 12

cosmos, we are mere specks, and our nattering, discursive thoughts little more than, well, fleeting electrochemical speckles. The truth as we know it is that if all life on our planet were destroyed by a wayward asteroid, worldwide nuclear conflagration, global climate change or whatnot, the wondrous, expansive universe would hardly flicker.

Of course, I am not going to assert that other possibilities do or do not exist. It may very well be true that fairies and spirits and elves exist unnoticed among us, secretly compiling lists of who is naughty and who is nice. I cannot prove that they do not. To definitively state that one knows, one way or the other, requires a leap of faith into an imaginary narrative. Myths, fables, legends, and holy books, created by people for people, have existed and been passed down for ages. A normal human endeavour, imagining stories can suit a variety of purposes: to allay the fear of or grief over death; to explain natural phenomena absent the understanding of science; to maintain control, social order, or the status quo; to entertain and amuse, and so on. Many of these stories, however, based not on evidence but rather creative contrivance are irrelevant to the bare truth of life's existential meaning.

Acceptance of the nihilistic view, though, suggests that life is ultimately pointless. How could this sentiment not draw one toward melancholy and despair? If life is meaningless, what is there to inspire and motivate us? The inevitable result, it seems, is a life of apathy, boredom, and disinterest. Sounds quite a dreary existence, I admit.

Yet there is another view. Although, as far as we can know, this universe has no existential purpose, regardless, we can still live reveling in the beauty and wonder of simply being alive with the warmth of the sun on our faces, the delight of our children's carefree laughter and loving smiles, the gustatory satisfactions of a home-cooked meal, the comfort of a tender embrace, the exuberantly wagging tail or soothing purr of a beloved pet, the blissful glow of a sunrise and sunset, the sublime luminosity of a full midautumn moon, the exhilaration, vigorousness, and crisp, fresh air of a mountain hike, the stir of emotion when experiencing expressive, soulful music, and so on. Without the superfluous egoistic striving and craving, the pride, conflict, and fear, can the value of life not be the simple moment to moment joy of celebrating, as Chief Crowfoot has expressed, "the flash of a firefly in the night . . . the breath of a buffalo in winter time . . . the little shadow which runs across the grass and loses itself in the sunset"? Is experiencing joy not a great enough value and meaning for living? After opening one's eyes to recognize the beauty and magnificence of the natural world, how could a person ever suggest that rising to greet each morning is pointless?

Before we get to all that, however, if you need something to do, great, there are things to be done. Our first priority, unquestionably, is to get out and secure water, food, shelter, and clothing to maintain our basic needs. Whether we hunt and grow our own food, build our own log cabin and stitch our own clothes, or more contemporarily, train to be a nurse, truck driver, biologist, accountant, school teacher, or shopkeeper, and generate the income that employs others to supply us our primary necessities, our fundamental purpose is to rise each morning and take care of the physical survival requirements of ourselves and our families. There is no time for boredom, apathy, and despair. Get up! We need some food!

Once our basic needs are secured, we are free to simply experience the beauty and joy around us. But this would be insufficiently ambitious for a species such as we. Modernity instructs us to direct time and energies toward fabricating grander egoistic visions of ourselves, constructed upon identities of material possessions or social recognition and prestige. Or less grandiose, we can invent individualized life goals which provide us a sense of personal fulfillment and accomplishment. Perhaps we may live as ordinary a life as watching television and perusing the internet, playing video games, and indulging in unwholesome foods, beverages, and intoxicants, pure pleasure, amusement, and enough sensory distraction to while away the time.

And, finally, if there is no inherent purpose for existence and no objective foundation for moral values, we may as well consider the carnal life of the narcissist or the wholehearted hedonist. Quite understandable, yes, but follow these sensorial pursuits, and while you may find moments of temporary satiation and pleasure, a rush of dopamine or some other biochemical fix, certainly you will not find contentment when your mind is most often in an agitated state (obsessive and constantly craving, self-absorbed and distracted, anxious and bored) between one intoxicating rush and the next.

Well, regardless, we should be free to choose for ourselves, because, ultimately, it makes little difference, right? To many of us, though, it does make a difference. Although the nihilistic logic and non-dualistic view seem coolly rational (and we are all so rational, no?) we feel unlike purely primal beasts bound to instinctively and unmindfully follow the natural laws.

Most everyone, religious or secular, will attempt to contrive reasons why we should be compassionate and caring, as opposed to greedy, murderous, self-absorbed sociopaths (as if the universe or the natural order would care). This mental impulse to imagine a "correct" world-view and life construct truly distinguishes our species from other creatures, but for what purpose? In nature there can be found rape and murder and thievery, all within the natural order. Why should we humans distinguish these behaviors to be unsavory and objectionable? And we do. One might argue that good will towards and cooperation with one another is related to some Darwinian advantage that has allowed our species to survive the fiercer and more savage predatory beasts of the wild. Point taken, but brutality and violence and ruthlessness can just as well have its effective Darwinian utility in our survival and dominance, no? In a non-dual world, both paths are equally legitimate. We continue to ponder the possibilities: aggression-passivity, selfishness-compassion, greed-generosity, creation-destruction; is there a "correct" path?

Regardless of how conservative or liberal, religious or non-theistic, rich or poor, apart from the sociopaths, most of us like to believe that underlying everything we are and do, we, each one of us, represent some dualistic distinction of "good" and "righteous." We are not creatures purely responding to primal impulses after all; we are rational minds, and from this arises our dilemma: While transcending brute animalism, our rational minds also refuse falsity, which means there is an uncertainty towards living conditioned and robotic, marching mechanically in line to some arbitrarily fabricated, contrived and dualistic dogma of right and wrong, good and bad. And so it appears, in the background of our ordinary thoughts, there is doubt, lingering like a splinter in our minds: Are we living lives that are grounded in any meaningful truth, lives that have any true value, lives that are just and legitimate?

The Moral Dilemma

It would be pure freedom and autonomy to live strictly according to the plain fact of nihilistic logic and non-duality. We could then live in whichever way brings us individual, personal fulfillment. Living with no moral code would allow for a life of greed and thievery and violence to be no more or less desirable than one driven by love and compassion and kindness. We could abuse and kill and plunder; we could be caring, altruistic, and compassionate; we could conserve natural resources and reduce our destructive impact on the environment; we could be wasteful and frivolously over-consuming, degrading and contaminating the earth; we could be expressive and create art and music; we could be purely hedonistic, concerned only with satiating our carnal lusts and cravings; or perhaps, more banally, we could pass our days being narcissistic, self-centered, inert blobs, and it would make no difference.

Although the modern environment our species has contrived for itself promises life opportunities of ease and virtual satisfactions—sensory comforts and convenient survival systems, services and resources to indulge and satiate cravings, electronic gadgets and vacuous media to stave off boredom, etc.—a life of entertainment, satiation, and mindless distraction is, in fact, not wholly fulfilling. As individuals, something more than these purely base motivations tug at our sensibilities as we reason and contemplate, seeking to free ourselves from mere beastly ignorance and live a life inspired with purpose.

Many turn to dogmatic moral codes and customs inherited from the past; but are these not simply contrived fabrications meant to constrain our primal behaviors? (Oftentimes enslaving us, by the way.) Alternatively, we can live by the bare truth of the natural laws, but this can be repulsive and terrifying when we observe that during the course of predation and competition for resources, mates, and territory, pure nature is replete with conflict, aggression, and brutality. Living solely by the natural order, what would prevent us from tearing each others' eyes out? Well, nothing, it seems, because the indifferent and oftentimes violent cycling of nature's forces and elements could simply care less how we conduct our lives.

Can we not recognize moral values, a world-view, a way of life in some non-dualistic truth that exists between the human contrivances of social and cultural dogma and the harsh brutality of nature? Because who desires to live by the dogmatic (and, usually, archaic) contrivances of some past other or the harshness of our animalism?

mo • ral • i • ty (noun): a system defined by principles of behaviour in accordance with standards of right and wrong

By definition, morality is grounded in some dualistic "standards of right and wrong," so at this juncture we can discard completely the notion of it. Morality is a contrivance that is wholly unnecessary. There is no moral dilemma.

This returns us to the question of whether rational and uncontrived principles of behaviour can emerge from the non-dualistic, indifferent, and oftentimes brutal reality of the natural world.

What we seek are principles of behaviour in accordance with

some truth. Note that this must encompass not only the effect our actions have on other people but also on the natural world around us, because an investigation into principles of behaviour is also an enquiry into our world-view and way of life. So, is there a way we "ought" to live?

The yin and yáng energies depicted in the tàijítú (the yin-yang symbol) suggest there is no "ought to" nor "ought not to." There is simply the transformation of complementary forces creating a balanced and single whole.

In fact, the yin-yáng symbol is too simplistic to describe the more ordinary fluxing of life forces and depicts only the relationship of energies in extremis. This is inadequate for depicting the everyday, in which extreme fluctuations are not the norm, nor are they necessary nor ideal for living systems. A more complete representation of the natural order would include a healthy, natural state of equilibrium, without extremes, regulated by complementary forces interacting within a narrower range, the center, for optimal harmony and balance. The harmony of the everyday natural order can be found where the interplay of energies maintain total equilibrium.

Only when this balance, the center, is lost do the natural forces become excessive and migrate outside the harmonious, eventually culminating at a point where complementary forces finally and decisively reassert balance.

Imagine a musical string that must be constantly tuned as physical conditions, constantly in flux, affect its pitch. The sound of the string becomes too flat or too sharp and must be regularly tightened (increasing yáng, decreasing yin) or loosened (increasing yin, decreasing yáng) to maintain the perfectly balanced pitch. The ideal balance between yin and yáng qualities creates not a stillness of energy, but a unity of complementary forces that maintains the energy of a life force in harmony with the natural order.

In nature, when a symbiotic balance is maintained in the eco-system, say between the size of a deer herd and a sufficient number of predators relative to the (ever fluctuating) physical conditions, the result is a comparatively sound, untroubled, and enduring environment in which all life forces can exist with limited conflict, a relatively stable state of dynamic equilibrium. If this natural order is disrupted, however, and one of the complementary forces approaches its extreme limit, greater suffering and privation will appear before either upheaval occurs or, somehow, the various life forces are decisively brought back in tune with the natural laws.

At every level of our existence, we must respect our symbiotic relationship with the totality of life forces, we must avoid causing imbalance, excessive yin or yáng energies, or we will certainly suffer the consequences of complementary forces arising to reassert the natural order: a dynamic state where all living systems trend toward equilibrium and homeostasis.

If it is true that living systems constantly trend toward equilibrium and homeostasis and it is also true that we care about our own wellbeing as well as the wellbeing of our families and communities (not to mention our species), then the way we "ought" to live is this: respecting our symbiotic relationship with the totality of life forces and avoid causing imbalance, excessive yin or yáng energies. Otherwise, we will create the conditions for our privation and misery.

Consider the living systems that are essential for individual and collective wellbeing:

1. The environment and ecology of the natural world
2. Family and others in the community
3. Our physical body and health

1: The Natural World

The state of energy and matter in the natural world is impermanent and in a constantly transitioning process of achieving dynamic equilibrium, maintaining relatively uniform conditions, a
vibrating string tuning itself to its perfect pitch. If the natural
order becomes imbalanced, however, too excessively yin or yáng,
the inevitable result is drastic, revolutionary transformation driven
by complementary forces that will finally, dispassionately, and indifferently reassert equilibrium while causing suffering and privation for the habitat's sentient creatures. These creatures include us,
our mammalian species, because we are not unlike all creatures
bound by the natural order.

Of course, we humans do possess unique qualities that distinguish our species from other creatures: abstract thought and reason; the potential to recall the past and imagine the future; the
capacity to create symbols, narratives, music, and art; and the ability to contemplate, share, and record complex ideas. These several
traits mark us as distinctly human and allow us to heighten our life
experience; to build systems that make our physical survival more
convenient, productive, and efficient; to create new forms of stimulation to evade boredom; and to enable us to be more successful
and prolific as a species.

We have this incredible potential, and yet, while we have used
these unique qualities to shape our environment and relationship
with other creatures, thereby improving our quality of life, on the
other hand, we, as a species, disregard these same intellectual ca-
pacities when we fail to recognize the symbiotic relationship we
human creatures have with all other organisms and elements of
the ecosystem. While it is simply obvious to any one of us that
with a scarcity of predators, a herd of deer will soon proliferate
and strip their habitat of food resources, whereupon the deer will
starve and suffer, along with other creatures that depend on those
plant resources for sustenance, regardless of this insight, we con-

tinue to live in a way that is unrestrained and, ultimately, blindly animalistic. We have become the mindless herd of deer, living in our species-centric system created with an arrogant disregard for the natural order.

Instead of visualizing the truth of the natural laws and moderating our behavior to avoid creating the conditions for the harshest yin and yáng phases of the natural order to arise, instead of consciously regulating our own energies and intentions to live mindfully in tune with nature's forces, instead of supporting conditions for an ecosystem that is less chaotic and more enduring, we contrive our egocentric human world without conscientious respect for the natural order. We are no different from other unmindful creatures that are wholly bound to and hapless against nature's indifferent and often brutal cycling of energy and matter. Our fate will be not unlike the predator-free deer herd that proliferates and consumes unabated until all resources are depleted and the habitat is destroyed. Ignoring our interdependence and interconnectedness to the totality of the natural world, we will create the conditions for our species privation and misery.

While we have the distinct intellectual capacity to recognize, plan for, and avoid this fated misery, it seems more and more likely that we will not, as with increasing effectiveness, we deplete limited natural resources and befoul our habitat. Perhaps we are simply bound to the natural order as a species, and that is that. Like other animals, we are hapless elements in nature's indifferent cycling of energy and matter. We can proceed no other way. It is the Tao, and our species is no different from the herd of deer without the wolf as predator, proliferating unabated, unmindful participants bound to the natural laws.

2: The Community

A community, a family, a group of people is a vibrant state of symbiotic energy like any other collection of interdependent organisms found in the natural world. Constantly in flux, a society evolves and trends toward a state of dynamic equilibrium, relatively steady and uniform, because a community derives little benefit from living in a state of conflict and disunity; on the contrary, a collective group desires to exist in harmony and peacefulness. If there is imbalance, the inevitable result is either drastic, revolutionary transformation or eventual collapse.

To maintain a group that is harmonious and enduring necessitates moderating individual behavior to avoid imbalance and a culmination of extreme yin or yáng forces. It is no different from our relationship to the natural world. You might individually choose to plunder, rape, and murder, and who can prove that you should not? It is simply obvious, however, that to anyone with the intellectual capacity to recognize the symbiotic relationship one has with other members of a group, you are a menace to the natural order, an extreme of energy that need not be defined as right or wrong, but simply a sociopathic energy form creating imbalance in the harmony of the natural order. You are free to behave in this manner, but complementary forces, certainly, will arise to reassert balance. And those forces may be the rest of us, those who recognize the truth of interconnectedness and strive to maintain not a purely individual energy but an energy in tune with the dynamics of equilibrium.

Whether you are an ordinary member of a group or an individual who possesses power and influence, ignoring the interdependence and interconnectedness to the totality of the communal energy will create the conditions for disunity, conflict, and collapse. When you live in a state of disconnectedness, with concern for only yourself, your interests, and your fabrication of a greater egoistic illusion of individuation, your life will be one of fear, anxiety, conflict, and stress as complementary forces will regularly rise before you to reassert equilibrium.

We do not require a moral dogma of right and wrong to guide our behavior, instead, we need only avoid excesses that create imbalance. Strive to remain in tune with the natural order of equilibrium. There is no dualistic dogma of one quality being "better" than another. All energies have their place and necessity. At times it is necessary to be passive, other times to be forceful. Sometimes it is meaningful to give, at other times to receive. It may be constructive to speak out, sometimes it is more helpful to remain silent. Sometimes it is beneficial to build, other times it is better to dismantle. It may be incumbent upon us to fight, other times to retreat. We produce and consume, gather and discard. The point is to avoid the emergence of extreme conditions by regularly moderating our energies—increase yáng, decrease yin; increase yin, decrease yáng—to regulate and harmonize and live in tune with the dynamic forces of the natural order. We call this the Tao.

3: The Physical Body

While the desire for moral values displays concern for the behavior we express between one another and the external world, we are equally accountable to our physical bodies. Our bodies require balance to sustain health, vigor, strength, and wellbeing, because they are no less energy forms belonging to the natural order. When the body maintains equilibrium, life continues. When equilibrium is lost, sickness and death follow.

American physiologist Walter Cannon (1871 – 1945), author of the book *The Wisdom of the Body*, originated the term "homeostasis" to describe the dynamic equilibrium of internal physiological conditions that our bodies maintain for healthy survival. It is natural and without intention, a biological system of organized self-government, the Tao.

The body constantly monitors, adapts, and maintains a relatively steady equilibrium of internal physiological conditions even as it is in constant interaction with an external world that is continuously undergoing fluctuation and change. Ordinary examples of internal conditions that must be regulated within a narrow range for optimum health are body temperature, water concentration in the bloodstream, blood glucose level, blood pH

level, blood pressure, etc.; all the while various organ systems are: transporting food and water into our bodies and eliminating wastes before they build up to toxic levels, bringing in oxygen and removing carbon dioxide, protecting against disease, and so on. Homeostasis is the body's system of regularly adjusting yin and yáng properties to avoid the emergence of extreme internal conditions that can lead to imbalance, weakness, and ill health. It is not unreasonable to claim that "most disease can be regarded as a result of its (homeostatic) disturbance, a condition called homeostatic imbalance."[95]

Your body arises each morning simply to maintain homeostasis and live healthfully. If you care at all about your physical wellbeing, be mindful of the elements you allow to cycle through your body. Not only are you what you eat, but you are also what you breathe, drink, and absorb through your skin. The air, the water, the food, toxic or wholesome, make up the totality of chemical compounds you allow into your body. Stop and look around. Consider the quality of air you are breathing and the water that you drink. Look at what you are eating. Consider how natural and whole it truly is, or is not. Does it look like part of a plant or, more likely, something that has been (wet) milled and pulverized, the dregs processed, reconstituted and spit out of a machine? Your body has not evolved to metabolize refined and processed psuedo-foods. Your body has evolved to consume and metabolize fresh, natural whole foods. Foods that look like something recently harvested from nature provide everything necessary for optimal health, body function, and for the the body's proper maintenance of homeostasis.

Your body is the object that connects you here, to this physical existence. It is reasonable to assume that your first priority, each and every day, would be to maintain your physical health, because once homeostasis is lost, you are either sick or dead. Without your

[95] Elaine N. Marieb and Katja Hoehn, *Human Anatomy and Physiology*, 7th ed. (Pearson Education, Inc., 2007) 8-12

body, you have no existence in this physical world.

It is not so difficult to live healthfully. Simply allow your body the health it naturally seeks out. Do not be hostage to the constant jibber-jabber of having to satiate sensory cravings or to habitually seek idle and listless comforts. As with your relationship to all living systems, avoid excesses that create imbalance. Do not assault your health with the toxic abuses of nicotine, alcohol, drugs, processed psuedo-foods, and so on. Remain in tune with the natural order of equilibrium. Exercise, get adequate sleep, and give your body what it is designed to consume and metabolize—real, natural whole foods.

The Middle Path

The concept of "having no desire" is oftentimes misconstrued as to suggest that the path to contentment can be found by living an ascetic, austere lifestyle, eschewing all worldly pleasures and comforts. This is simply ill-informed—and what a dull life that would be.

Whether you have cravings (are preoccupied with satiating carnal lust and desires or aspire to some egoistic notion of identity) or aversions (live in self-denial and abstention), it amounts to the same thing: movement of thought, an ever growing junk pile of discursive and agitated mental prattle arising from mentally contrived dualistic distinctions of good and bad, right and wrong.

There is another direction, however, and that is following the true nature of existence, what the Buddha might describe as *The Middle Path*. That is, we can recognize our interconnectedness and interdependence to the totality of nature as we experience all aspects of life; we can acknowledge the truth of compounded phenomena and observe the deceits of our grasping, dualistic minds and their attendant egoistic chatter, all the while having no mental attachments to any of it: the cravings, aversions, thoughts, concepts, ego-stories, baby-rattles, and so on.

When you see the truth, there is no dualism. There is only

being, being and an interconnectedness to other sentient creatures and the totality of nature. Meditate on and contemplate this, and the path to living with meaning and purpose will come freely, naturally, and without effort. Acknowledge the truth and recognize the Tao, and you will understand that there is no moral dilemma; your mind will awaken to a life filled with novel and compelling choices, each day, until you find that choices no longer need be made because there is no more thought. You have been transformed, or rather, deconditioned, and simply live in tune with the natural order.

Four points for consideration:

1. The true nature of egoistic cravings and the deceits of our conditioned minds;
2. the true nature of non-duality;
3. the true nature of compounded phenomena and impermanence;
4. the true nature of our interconnectedness.

If we contemplate behavior that causes others to suffer or leads to ruin, we will find that it is driven by not only egoistic cravings or the attachment to a contrived ego-identity but also a disregard to the truth of our interconnectedness with other sentient creatures, each other, or the environment, thus begetting greed, thievery, violence, overconsumption of resources, degradation of the ecosystem, the self-centered satiation of lust, and so on. In turn, whatever destruction or misery we create ultimately becomes a part of the environment in which we live and will eventually affect the character and quality of our own physical and mental wellbeing.

So why can we not see the truth of it? Perhaps it is the lack of immediacy between cause manifesting the effect. We can pollute and contaminate the environment, discharging toxins into our air, our water, our soil, and our food for years before it sickens and weakens us and our children. We can disregard the wellbeing of our community for generations before social decay and disorder begin to degrade our own safety and quality of life. We can smoke, overeat unhealthful processed junk foods, and live a sedentary lifestyle for decades before we notice the effects of ill health. We can live self-absorbed, conceited, arrogant, and egoistic for much of a lifetime before we recognize that we have become anxious, fearful, narcissistic, angry, greedy, and neurotic, lonely wrecks. We do not see the result of our actions plainly causing the effect, and, subsequently, we live disconnected from the truth, blind to our symbiotic relationship with the totality of the external world and oblivious to how our intentions and behaviors create the reality in which we individually and collectively find ourselves.

If you are in search of "moral values" as a guide to behavior, you need not rely on the inventions of (presumably) well-intentioned but nevertheless fanciful, contrived moral dogma. Simply consider the truth. Focus the intention of your actions to arise without the the contrivances of mental deceits and egoistic cravings or the falsity of permanent and unchanging compounded phenomena (conditions, experiences, and physical objects). Liberate the intention of your actions to arise with a recognition of a thorough interconnectedness to the external world (which clearly includes other people and sentient beings) and the physical environment. Whenever you are confronted with a "moral dilemma," contemplate and meditate with these intentions derived from the true nature of our existential reality, and you will discover a way to proceed that will be driven not by greed or hostility or hatefulness or egoism or arbitrary dogma or delusion but rather rationale, compassion, honesty, and understanding.

Contemplate the Tao, i.e., the non-duality of the natural world and the impermanence of compounded phenomena. Observe the world around you and acknowledge the truth of our interdependence and interconnectedness. Live recognizing the unity of complementary forces that form the life force of which you are a part, both in nature and in community. Live in tune with the natural order, not a hostage to your egoistic cravings or the deceits of your conditioned mind, and you will follow a path toward harmony, contentment, and wellbeing.

> "All a musician can do is to get closer to the sources of nature, and so feel that he is in communion with the natural laws. Then he can feel that he is interpreting them to the best of his ability, and can try to convey that to others."—John Coltrane[96]

[96] Bill Cole, *John Coltrane* (Da Capo Press, 2001) 11

TEN

THE MYTH OF INDEPENDENCE—THE ORIGINS OF CONFLICT—COMPASSION

Luther Standing Bear, Oglala Lakota Chief

"The old Lakota was wise. He knew that man's heart away from nature becomes hard; he knew that lack of respect for growing, living things soon led to lack of respect for humans, too. So he kept his youth close to its softening influence."—Luther Standing Bear, Oglala Lakota Chief (1868-1939)[97] Photo: Library of Congress[98]

Go outside to a city street or public square. Stop and observe the people around you, and the thing you surely have already noticed is that the world is looking down and inward, down toward their

[97] T. C. McLuhan, *Touch the Earth* (Promontory Press, March, 1971) 6

[98] *Luther Standing Bear, Dakota chief,* 1868-1939, Library of Congress (digital ID cph 3b04255), http://hdl.loc.gov/loc.pnp/cph.3b04255 (retrieved 06/02/2014)

shoes, into their electronic gadgets, into the virtual reality of their private mental discourse.

Now look upwards and outwards, into a bright blue sky or a clear moonlit night. Contemplate without the distraction of discursive thought, and you will experience awe and wonder recognizing that your presence is part of this mind-boggling cosmic creation.

Mountain Moonset — Photo by Jessie Eastland[99]

We choose our worlds to be expansive or insular. At what level do you focus the attention of your life's reality? Starting with the universe as a whole, we can descend into ever smaller worlds: our galaxy, our solar system, our planet earth, our country, our state or province, our city or town, our neighborhood, our street, our residence packed with household baby rattles, then on to our rooms jammed with personal objects, to our physical persons affixed to electronic gadgetry, and further still, all the way into our illusory and fabricated ego-stories.

Admittedly, a world-view concentrated on the cosmos is not an everyday practicality. Instead, our usual attentions are concentrated upon individual ego-story lives of contrived dramas, passions, ambitions, desires, comforts, pleasures, troubles, challenges, inter-

[99] Jessie Eastland, Mountain Moonset, Wikipedia, CC BY-SA 3.0, http://en.wikipedia.org/wiki/File:Mountain_Moonset.jpg (retrieved 6/7/2014)

ests, boredoms, and routines. Is there anything wrong with that? Well, as a matter of fact, yes, there is.

Except, perhaps, for our fantasies and sleep-time dreams, everything we find enjoyable about life would not occur without elements of the external world: other people, art, music, food, weather, animals and other creatures, nature and the natural environment, our baby rattles and electronic gadgetry—everything. Our lone, singular selves are not all that intriguing. Nevertheless, we have been habituated to move through life with a sense of prideful individuation, a mental fabrication of being a separate, self-sufficient entity, having control and feeling empowered, failing to recognize that at every breathing moment, we are not at all independent. While our bodies do maintain a physical boundary with the external environment and we are not rooted to the soil, our physical existence is merely a participatory event in the manifestations of the sun's radiant energy and the ecosystem's cycling of chemical compounds.

Physically and egoistically, our existent reality is founded on what the Buddha describes as compounded phenomena. That is, a synthesis of elements and external conditions arise a unitary state of experience or material form. As conditions inevitably change, the assembled and once unified state will once again separate into its constituent parts. It is this interconnected and interweaving of various elements that gives rise to the reality of our world.

Interconnected to what?

"Behold, my brothers, the spring has come; the earth has received the embraces of the sun, and we shall soon see the results of that love! Every seed has awakened and so has all animal life. It is through this mysterious power that we too have our being, and we therefore yield to our neighbors, even our animal neighbors, the same right as ourselves, to inhabit this land."—Sitting Bull, Hunkpapa Lakota Chief (1831–1890)[100] Photo – Library of Congress[101]

Have you ever contemplated what energizes you to get up and out the door every morning so that you can experience joy, purpose, friendship, accomplishment, fulfillment, and all the rest of it? Do you know the source of your movement through life? It gives you the power to live and be present at every moment. No, it is not money or love or God. It is the sun. This is the brilliant, simple, and humbling truth: Our bodies are flowing with and driven by the energy of the sun. With-

Sitting Bull, Hunkpapa Lakota Chief

out the sun, we become utterly dead, inanimate matter, compost. Almost all of the movement and energy around you, living, mechanical, as well as technological, is powered by energy derived from the sun.

Solar energy indirectly flows through and animates nearly all living things. Recall that through the process of photosynthesis, we are fueled by the energy of the sun. Without the capability of plants to allow us access to the sun's energy, we would not exist. It is the energy of the sun, converted by plants into chemical energy, that fuels our life processes and the creation of every mouthful of food that we consume. The energy necessary for our every action, every emotion, and every thought is provided by the sun's energy being made available to us through the lives of plants.

Now wherever you are, take a moment to observe your environment. Go ahead, take a look. The world around us, all matter: liquid, solid, and gas, is composed of chemicals or chemical com-

[100] T. C. McLuhan, *Touch the Earth*, 90

[101] *Sitting Bull*, 1868-1939, Library of Congress (digital ID cph 3c11147), http://hdl.loc.gov/loc.pnp/cph.3c11147 (retrieved 6/2/2014)

pounds. Look in the mirror, because we are, of course, included in this material world, the six basic elements that make up roughly 99 percent of our body mass being oxygen, carbon, hydrogen, nitrogen, calcium, and phosphorus. A variety of other elements and trace elements make up the rest. That's it.

Since the earth is a materially closed system (except for the occasional meteorite), all the chemicals and chemical compounds that make up our bodies and maintain our life processes constantly cycle through us and the biosphere of the earth, the "global ecosystem." Haven't you noticed? From moment to moment, waking or not, we inhale the oxygen produced by plants. Without oxygen, we pass out within ten seconds and will, usually, be dead within 15 minutes. Water is vital for most bodily functions, and since the body cannot store water for long, we need a regular and fresh supply daily. Without water, bodily functions begin to deteriorate, and after several days (normally 3-5), we are, once again, deceased. Dust in the wind. The rest of the nutrients for our healthy survival can be consumed from plants that cycle the necessary chemical elements from the soil, atmosphere, or water (well, okay, you still need that B12 supplement). Without food, we have roughly three or four weeks, then, sayonara. We are bound to and in constant interaction with our environment as we not only metabolize elements necessary for survival but also excrete waste products that are used in turn by other organisms and once again cycle through the system, back into the soil, back into the atmosphere, back into the plants, back into us.

A healthy ecosystem is fundamental for our physical wellbeing because as we constantly consume, we are interacting with the chemical elements of our environment. We are physically interconnected to our ecosystem, and what happens to it, happens to us. If we abuse the environment, we abuse ourselves. When the air is polluted, we inhale the same pollutants. When water is fouled with toxic materials, we ingest and are fouled with the same toxic materials. When the soil, plants, and animals are contaminated with unhealthful chemical compounds, we consume and are contaminated with unhealthful chemical compounds. What we do to the environment and other organisms, we do to ourselves. This is no revelation.

"The air is precious to the red man, for all things share the same breath—the beast, the tree, the man, they all share the same breath. The white man does not seem to notice the air he breathes."

"What is man without the beasts? If all the beasts were gone, men would die from a great loneliness of spirit. For whatever happens to the beasts, soon happens to man."

"Whatever befalls the earth, befalls the sons of the earth. If men spit upon the ground, they spit upon themselves."

"This we know. The earth does not belong to man; man belongs to the earth. This we know. All things are connected like the blood which unites one family. All things are connected."

"Man did not weave the web of life; he is merely a strand in it. Whatever he does to the web, he does to himself."

"Continue to contaminate your bed, and you will one night suffocate in your own waste."

These quotes were claimed to have come from an 1854 speech made by Chief Seattle, chief of the Suquamish tribe, when the Native American tribe was conceding native lands to the settlers. Later details revealed that in 1971, the screenwriter Ted Perry, using a dubious translation of Chief Seattle's original speech, was inspired to pen these quotes as part of a screenplay for a movie on ecology called "Home," produced for the Southern Baptist Radio and Television Commission.[102] Although it has been established by historians that this commonly cited movie adaptation of the speech is not historically accurate and originates more from the poetic license of Ted Perry than the oration of Chief Seattle, the sentiments are still moving, thoughtful, and compelling.

Every moment we take a breath, enjoy a meal, and quench our thirst is testament to our ecological interconnectedness through the energy of the sun and the material elements of the earth. Our life processes, energetically or materially, are not at all independent from the physical, external reality of the earth's plants, creatures, water, atmosphere, and soil.

Consider another aspect of interconnectedness: our dependence on the community of people who provide us our essential material and physical needs. Unless one is a pioneer or homesteader and can forage and hunt for or grow his or her own food, secure a potable water supply, build shelter, and stitch his or her own clothing, one is dependent on the skills, experience, and efforts of others to supply these essentials. If the infrastructure that supplies these necessities, whose ready availability we normally take for granted, were to break down at this moment and we had solely our survival skills and the available resources of the immediate environment, most of us would certainly perish. Relatively quickly and quite pathetically, I might add. Our confident arrogance and mental delusions of being independent and self-reliant would soon collapse under the reality of being too ignorant and feeble to maintain our primary and basic physical survival without the knowledge, experience, and aid from a community of others.

Witness natural disasters and catastrophic events where the infrastructure is utterly destroyed, living shelters are wholly obliterated, personal electronic gadgets and collections of baby rattles are washed away or transformed into piles of rubble. How long could one then survive on their own? Witness a day hiker getting lost in the woods. How many nights could one survive in the wild,

[102] Timothy Egan, *Chief's Speech of 1854 Given New Meaning* (and Words) (New York Times, 21 April 1992), http://www.nytimes.com/1992/04/21/us/chief-s-speech-of-1854-given-new-meaning-and-words.html?pagewanted=all&src=pm (retrieved 10/2/2013)

independent and alone? How independent and self-reliant are we, really? How much do we take for granted our connection to and interdependence on the community of people locally and globally who contribute to our basic survival needs, our non-essential electronic gadgetry needs? Stop and look around you. Choose any one of your basic possessions. Pick it up. Look at it. Where did it come from? It was not simply spit out of some factory machine and dropped into your world. How many hands touched this object along the way so that it could end up in your possession?

Finally, how do we become the moment-to-moment "selves" that we express to the world? Is our demeanor and expression of personality in society not a consequence of being interconnected with the emotional energy of, attitude toward, and relationship with the others in our presence?

We move through our daily lives constantly shifting from one mood to another, one personality to another, one facade to another, never one singular person but rather a collection of various characters constantly in flux. Much of who we become at any particular moment relies on social context. You have surely found yourself assuming different roles, behaving differently depending on the persons around you: friend, acquaintance, spouse, family, sibling, child, professional something-or-other, colleague, supervisor, rival, stranger, neighbor, and so on. Is the very expression of self, at any particular moment, not interconnected with and influenced by those with whom we are interacting?

And what of the emotional and instinctual response we have to another's gesture or look or word or attitude? Is our very person, our mood and demeanor, not interconnected to the emotional presence of others as we are instantly affected and transformed by their hostility or kindness, rudeness or politeness, selfishness or generosity, ingratitude or appreciation, unlikeness or familiarity, evasiveness or honesty, disinterest or attention, arrogance or humility, and so on. Our emotional state, mental wellbeing, and sense of security and comfort are, certainly, significantly influenced, because our emotional energies are interconnected with the community of people around us, no?

If one of the infuriated participants in the previously mentioned road rage incident had offered a conciliatory gesture, a nod of humility, a recognition of responsibility, would that not have affected the other and changed the outcome into something less tragic than a violent assault and a fatal shooting? Yes, undoubtedly so, because the behaviors, attitudes, and moods of others affect our own as well.

Recognize the truth of your interconnectedness to the external world and lay bare the illusory, contrived, imaginary ego world into which you would otherwise isolate yourself, certainly in what would be a lonely and cynical and fear-filled existence.

When will it end?

I was sitting and chatting with a group of American friends one evening when Frank, a decent, well-meaning Caucasian guy, apparently prompted by some recent political discourse on race and ethnicity in the U.S., asked with all sincerity and an apparent hint of impatience, "When is it going to end? African-American, Mexican-American, Asian-American? Does everyone need a hyphen? What should I call myself? White-American?"

Since I had had a couple of beers by then, which never fails to impair my sense of mindfulness and presence, I reframed the issue in racist implications and replied obnoxiously, but not at all angrily, "What's the problem? If not Asian-American, what should I call myself? Chink?"

"What?" said another friend, slightly taken aback, "Where'd that come from?"

That was a bit of a straw man, I suppose, a fairly common, misleading logical fallacy whereby you misrepresent and distort a person's argument—the "straw man"—and you then proceed to attack this easier-to-discredit exaggeration (i.e., implying that Frank's enquiry was somehow racist) without ever addressing the original position.

"No, what I mean is: Can't we all just say we're American?" Frank tried again.

"Yeah, well, we don't all have the same American experience. I grew up Chinese in America, and that's a lot different from growing up White. Chinese in America have a different history. People treat me differently, perceive me differently, stereotype me differently, discriminate against me differently. The same way a Black person in America has a totally different experience from either you or I. When people think 'American,' they don't think: Chinese guy. The hyphenated terms describe a unique and particular American experience and—blah, blah, blah."

Afterwards, I realized I never did answer Frank's question since I was too enthusiastically beating up on the straw man as if it were a Las Posadas piñata. The original question comes to this: When is it going to end? The "it" being the creation and fierce attachment to an ego-story of a distinct ethnic identity. An excellent question, come to think of it, a question whose answer addresses the origins of conflict.

The Origins of Conflict

Failing to recognize the truth of our interconnectedness, we cling to our fabricated and individuated ego-stories, identities of self that instigate the conditions for mental conflict: "I" opposed to "other." The result is inevitably pride, arrogance, greed, defensiveness, self-righteousness, narrow-mindedness, and the subsequent fear of and apprehension toward other. With the arising of psychological insecurity, we seek out groups to whom we can belong, a place to feel togetherness and sameness and security. We are now a gang, a clan, a village, an ethnicity, a country, or we find approval and belonging through a religion, a movement, a philosophy, a political party, a school of thought . . . a sports team? The mental leads to the physical, and we follow a path to where hatred and violence and war erupt.

So when will it end? It can end when we stop identifying. When we no longer define dichotomies, cling to ideas, have a need to be right, create psychological and egoistic division and conflict. Yes, regardless of ethnicity, we are all American or whatever other nationalistic identity, but this is nothing more than another ego-story, another mentally fabricated construction, another seed for conflict: American versus non-American. To say "I am this" is to say "some other is not." We become egoistic and individuated: a vegetarian versus a carnivore; a vegan versus a vegetarian; a true vegan versus a pseudo-vegan; a Christian versus a Muslim; a Fundamentalist Christian versus a Progressive Christian; a Republican versus a Democrat; a patriotic American versus an unpatriotic American; a Theravada Buddhist versus a Mahayana Buddhist, and so on. The conflict does not end until the fabricating of and the identifying with fairy-tale ego-stories end.

> "Most of us take pleasure in violence, in disliking somebody, hating a particular race or group of people, having antagonistic feelings towards others."—Jiddu Krishnamurti [103]

It is true, no? Egoistic pleasure is experienced when every demeaning utterance, every hateful intention, every hostile, arrogant thought and smug put-down of others elevates the profile of our own pridefully fabricated and individuated ego-stories. And as we fabricate ever grander and more brilliant ego-stories for ourselves, we develop more prideful attachments to them, resulting in a kind of mental self-reinforcing feedback loop whose primary consequence is to keep us attached to and in love with our imaginary, singular selves: the greater our attachments are to our ego-stories, the more we love and nurture them; and the more we love and nurture them, the greater our attachments are to them.

[103] Jiddu Krishnamurti, *Freedom from the Known* (Rider Books, 2010) 47

Compassion

com • pas • sion (noun): a sympathetic feeling of sorrow and pity for the suffering or misfortune of another, often accompanied with a desire to alleviate it.

I hear a lot about compassion these days, but I'm still not sure what it means to practice it.

When we recognize our interconnectedness to the earth and the sun and the various living and non-living forms of our ecosystem, when we recognize our dependence on people nationally and globally whom we rely on for the conveniences and comforts of our lives, when we recognize our reliance on the local community that maintains the infrastructure and everyday supply of goods and services that are vital to our physical survival, when we recognize our interconnectedness to those around us who contribute to our overall wellbeing, and as we deconstruct the mental fabrications of our illusory ego-stories and we become grounded in the truth, will compassion not then occur as a natural consequence? How could it not? Work on yourself. See past your delusions and mental fabrications; recognize the truth. As attachments to our individuated ego-stories diminish, and our awareness and consciousness becomes more expansive and inclusive, compassion will arise as a matter of course.

There are those who believe that living with a sense of compassion means to be motivated to, literally, reduce the suffering of all sentient beings in the cosmos, thereby achieving some special state of being, some idealized image of sainthood. Besides being utterly impractical and unrealistic, is a desire to achieve some unique metaphysical state or some contrived idea of a compassionate being not simply another example of fabricating an identity, an ego-story to which you can be attached?

Have no expectations nor desires nor ideas to be or become anything, but, simply, live grounded in the truth, and compassion will arise. That is all. No hopes, no cravings, no purposeful becoming of anything. Let it happen. Allow your behavior to be natural and uncontrived, 無爲 (wú wéi: non-striving or non-becoming), as the Taoists would say. Deconstruct the egoistic fabrications of self and, no doubt, your world-view will be different, your direction in life will take a different path. When we live recognizing the delusion of our illusory ego-stories as well as our interconnectedness to the external world, our daily and life choices will be decided with a concern for how we affect other people, other sentient creatures, the environment around us, and everything else. Living with a sense of our interconnectedness, perhaps, is the "practice" of compassion?

> "Compassion can be roughly defined in terms of a state of mind that is nonviolent, nonharming, and nonaggressive. It is a mental attitude based on the wish for others to be free of their suffering, and is associated with a sense of commitment, responsibility and respect towards the other."— His Holiness the Dalai Lama[104]

If having compassion means a wish that others are free of suffering, we must first understand what it means to suffer. Physical suffering is inevitable when there is a lack of basic necessities: clean water, food, shelter, clothing, and health care. Considering that "more than 2.8 billion people, approaching half the world's population, live on less than the equivalent of $2 per day,"[105] the idea that one can alleviate literally all of human suffering, let alone the suffering of all sentient beings, appears futile and is clearly impractical and unrealistic. This is not to say that cultivating "a mental attitude based on the wish for others to be free of their suffering" is impractical and unrealistic. No, not at all. Although having a compassionate world-view will lead a person to a greater

[104] His Holiness the Dalai Lama and Howard Cutler, M.D., *The Art of Happiness* (Riverhead Books, 1998), 114

[105] *Hunger: Vital Statistics*, United Nations website, http://www.un.org/en/globalissues/briefingpapers/food/vitalstats.shtml (retrieved 6/11/2014)

awareness and knowledge of the misery, suffering, degradation, and violence that countless people and other sentient creatures must endure, along with recognition of global industrialization's ceaseless environmental destruction, one should not feel overwhelmed. All conditions belong to the natural laws, and we are mere participants in it. No, you are not going to save the whole of earth or humanity, but you always do have opportunities to cultivate a "state of mind that is nonviolent, nonharming, and nonaggressive," and you are regularly faced with making choices that can enable you to alleviate the suffering of other sentient beings in some way, small or large, sometimes by simply changing your daily habits. At some moment a sense of caring and empathy and compassionate action will be realized in one's everyday behavior, in one's habits, one's values, one's goals and life purpose. Contemplate, regularly, the truth, and knowing will become being. Allow compassion to develop without emotion or the desire for personal achievement. Avoid being motivated by sentiment or moral righteousness or self-satisfaction; otherwise, your actions become yet another egoistic pursuit to which you can attach or with which you can fabricate identity. Let compassion develop based on your recognition of the truth, and you will act without striving or expectation, without contrived dualistic notions to elicit disillusionment or self-righteousness or pridefulness. You simply are in tune with the natural order, your actions grounded in rationality and truth.

If absolutely nothing else is realized, at least recognize the need of basic necessities for human survival anywhere on this earth: clean water, food, shelter, clothing, and healthcare, and then acknowledge the physical suffering and misery you, personally, need not endure. Note the fortuitous life circumstances you benefit from, whatever good fortune and privileges you do possess. Confirm the freedoms and opportunities you are allowed, and this alone should leave you grateful and appreciative for the conditions of your life. Perhaps by simply practicing to live with the perspective of a compassionate mind and interconnected world-view, a person can achieve some personal level of happiness and contentment and gratitude, without having to raise a single finger.

Beyond the physical aspect of suffering, there is suffering of the mind, an affliction of the human condition. While physical suffering can be relieved with the necessary resources, relief from the causes of mental suffering exist nowhere outside of the mind of the sufferer (unless you have some underlying neurological condition perhaps). Regardless of wealth, status, possessions, and recognition (or lack thereof) we all face or have faced the torment of a mind conditioned to its deceits. Memory of past experience, apprehension of future events, the illusory "self" fabrication, a clinging to cravings, conditioned dualistic views, all are mere mental impulses that exist nowhere but in private thoughts and images that give birth to fear, anxiety, anger, hatred, jealousy, loneliness, shame, insecurity, self-loathing, discontent, and everything else.

Even if you have somehow escaped the normal occurrence of everyday anxiety, uncertainty, frustration, disappointment, and self-doubt, even if you have had until now the perfect life, live long enough, and you will, assuredly, experience the same blunt truth of impermanence and physical suffering that Siddhartha Gautama, the Buddha, witnessed as he left his palace—illness, old-age, and death—and the subsequent mental distress that results from having to face these realities.

Cultivate a sense of compassion for the physical suffering of other sentient creatures by recognizing that they experience, on some level, a fear and distress similar to what you might experience. Cultivate a sense of compassion for the egoistic mental suffering of others by recognizing that all of humanity—your partner, relatives, friends, neighbors, teachers, colleagues, enemies, everybody—suffers the torment of an egoistic mind filled with discursive mental prattling. Everyone. Note the distress that your own voice of ego can create for you and know that every other person you see and meet and know is also imprisoned, on some level, by a mind held hostage to its incessant ruminations.

Does this understanding not move you to feel some measure

of universal compassion for all: friend, acquaintance, stranger, enemy? If not, the Buddhist tradition has an ancient practice called metta (or maitri) meditation, also commonly referred to as loving-kindness meditation. In this exercise, one meditates on radiating unconditional and selfless love, goodwill, care, and friendship to all sentient beings.

Metta Meditation

The basic technique is to repeat a series of verses and concentrate these intentions toward particular individuals. The phrases (or something similar) are:

1. May you be safe and protected.
2. May you be happy and content.
3. May you be healthy and strong.
4. May you be at ease and at peace.

Starting with a typical sitting meditation, you settle your mind and focus on having an honest and sincere heart. Visualize an image of yourself feeling joyful and carefree, and then recite toward yourself, to your mental image, the four verses, repeating them at a constant and comfortable pace. Allow the intention of these feelings to infuse your mind, heart, and body.

In succession, visualize and offer these wishes to the following individuals:

• yourself,
• a person whom you respect (a teacher, mentor, supporter, etc.),
• a loved one,
• a good friend,
• a neutral person (an acquaintance, neighbor, or colleague, etc.),
• a difficult person,
• all beings in the entire universe.

THE MYTH OF INDEPENDENCE—THE ORIGINS
OF CONFLICT—COMPASSION

It is an innocent, wholesome, and altruistic meditation, a tad touchy-feely perhaps, but the intention is sincere. I imagine it is quite effective in enabling one to be filled with a sense of caring and universal love, and how could this not lead to becoming a kinder, calmer, and more compassionate individual, one who is less angry, judgmental, and spiteful. A positive effect on a person's wellbeing, no doubt.

Of course, it is not terribly difficult to wish loving thoughts to those whom we respect or care about, even those towards whom we have neutral feelings. Most challenging is extending goodwill and care to those who treat us with ill will and harmful intentions. When we have thoughts of these individuals, it is natural for feelings of anger, distrust, anxiety, or stress to arise. Is this the remedy, then, to imagine your "enemies" and visualize their joy and contentment? Continue to offer your care and compassion? That simply?

There are those who further suggest that we can radiate loving-kindness thought-energy and directly influence the wellbeing of others. Really? Beams of radiant goodness and universal love streaming out of our hearts to permeate other sentient beings? Who knows? Perhaps radiant thought-rays truly are spurting from us in all directions, healing the cosmos. I have no idea, but it begins to sound a bit egoistic, dubiously straying toward conjecture and a belief that necessitates some leap of mystical faith.

Honestly, isn't the true purpose not to initiate an effect on others but to work on ourselves, to break down the fabricated illusions of ego-identity, those prideful and conceited delusions which cause conflict and separation from the world around us? Only then are we able to clearly understand the truth of our shared condition, recognize the truth of our interconnectedness, and, finally, live with a collective respect and care for this worldly existence of which we are all a part.

While the intention of the metta meditation is admirable, the practice is somewhat mechanical, formulaic, and contrived. Does the systematic and excessive thought, the mental nattering, not generate striving and the desire for becoming? Can we not directly deconstruct our mental fabrications and live grounded in the truth, without further mental contrivances? In fact, simple recognition of the truth is immediate and practical, and can also bring you to cultivate a feeling of goodwill and compassion for all beings, live with a sense of equanimity, and harbor no anger or hate.

Love Thy Enemy?

I do not claim to be a Buddhist, but I can imagine that an individual who practices metta meditation would be a genuinely pleasant person—kind, gentle, and caring. I also am quite certain that I would not call on this person for assistance if someone were breaking into my house some late night, I were being threatened by a pack of stray dogs or predatory street thugs, my city were being overrun by a hostile army, or other such grave situations.

As a minority growing up in the U.S., I was regularly the target of racist taunts. Though I felt anger from the belittlement, I faithfully followed the teachings of the religion in which I was brought up and dutifully "turned the other cheek." Outwardly, I remained unperturbed, smiling and accepting the insults, while inwardly, spitefully, I questioned why I should.

What I learned about turning the other cheek and being passive in the face of aggression is that it often leads to your getting punched in the face. When you are perceived as weak, you become a more likely target for physical threats and bullying. My solution, then, was to learn how to fight and to face down my aggressors, a preferred alternative to getting beat up, certainly. I was not at the time familiar with the idea of sending metta to my tormentors, and it is probably for the best as I imagine it would have resulted in my dodging punches to the face on a regular basis.

The main drawback to becoming more confident at defending myself was that I began to enjoy the energetic and physical expression of hostility and aggression. Nurture aggression in the self and you are likely to feel empowered while becoming combative and antagonistic, arrogant and egoistic, hostile, and—a little nuts. This is not so pleasant, for yourself, who will live irritable and in constant mental conflict of "I" opposed to "other," and for those around you, who must witness and be oppressed by your belligerence.

For the time, however, my strategy of confrontation worked out well enough, because it turns out that if you can confidently face down a bully, he or she, unsurprisingly, will often retreat and look for an easier target. This is all utterly predictable, as it follows the natural laws: Those perceived to be weaker and more vulnerable are singled out for attack, and those considered a more formidable foe are much more likely to be left alone. Additionally, is it so unnatural to protect oneself when attacked? Not at all. Fight is as instinctive as freeze and flight. Observe this in the natural world.

Can we follow the natural laws, protect ourselves from the aggression and antagonism of others, while also recognizing the truth of our interconnectedness and stay unattached to the mental fabrications of our ego-identities that produce anger, hatred, violence, and mental conflict? Is it possible to be assertive and ward off hostility, perhaps physically, without enmity but with compassion?

The practical effectiveness of metta when we might be engaged in physical conflict with a hostile aggressor is unlikely. No doubt, it is always best to handle conflict with composure, understanding, and humility (self-defense skills and a weapon could prove a useful Plan B as well), but we cannot always expect an individual who behaves threateningly toward us to be especially rational or easily persuaded by loving thoughts or placid dialogue. More mundanely, we may have to contend with ill-natured individuals who are unavoidable aspects of our lives: a family member, relative, colleague, neighbor, perhaps even our partner, people who seem to enjoy provoking others, or perhaps are too completely self-absorbed and crass to be concerned with how others feel or what others have to say. Can we extend compassion to these individuals without suffering their ill will?

There is nothing false or unseemly about protecting oneself

from harm and the destructive intentions and toxic behaviors of others, and it is possible to take action without the movement of thought and emotion—"mushin no shin" (無心の心), "mind without mind," mindfulness. Whether conflict is verbal or physical, it is possible to act without undue anger, without undue fear, without undue emotion. Respond assertively and decisively with whatever is necessary to neutralize the aggression, and no more. It makes no difference if you use evasion, redirection, a direct strike, or non-action. Act, however, without egoistic intent, because underlying it all is the recognition of our collective humanity and a sense of compassion. Have no intention of causing undue harm.

The point of metta, after all, is that if we can recognize our interconnectedness and illusory ego-fabrications and our shared human condition, we should naturally have compassion for our "enemies." Certainly, we can, but this does not mean that we disallow the natural laws of self-protection. Compassion does not mean that we allow others to beat us up and beat us down. No, we defend ourselves, dispassionately, at any moment of hostility. It is when the hostility has ended, and we consider the motivations of our aggressors, that we can more sincerely extend compassion, and in so doing, we refuse to harbor enmity or spite or animosity.

Let us imagine you, your family, and your loyal canine companion are camping, and you go for a hike in the woods. Un-fortuitously, you stumble across the path of a mother bear with its cub. The bear is startled and threatened by your presence. It charges to attack. Do not believe that you can outrun it. You cannot. You might consider climbing a tree or curling up and playing dead, but you still have the rest of your family to look after. Fortunately, you have your hunting rifle, but before you can raise it and take aim, your devoted and fearless canine pet rushes to confront the bear and is fatally injured. Do you shoot the bear? Of course. Are you trying to kill the bear? Most definitely. You fire. The bear has been injured. It charges again and you fire a second time. The bear is dead.

You have killed the bear. Your family is safe. Your dog is dead.

Do you hate the bear? Most probably not. Can you feel compassion for the mother bear protecting its cub? Very likely, yes. Would you have the same response if you were again under the same circumstances? Of course, but before that happens, would you not first consider how your actions may have contributed to the initial incident and how you might be able to avoid it from happening again? It is a rational and natural and compassionate approach to dealing with hostile conflict.

The question that arises is this: Why should I have compassion for people who deliberately, or even unintentionally or indifferently, cause me distress? They're irritating and obnoxious. They are negative and condescending. When I think about them I feel anger and hostility. I imagine punching him or her in the face. I wish them misfortune as a form of karmic vengeance. Is it possible to understand their behavior so that I feel for them compassion?

I am not suggesting the solution is to hold hands with unpleasant people and together sing campfire songs. You do not have to tame the bear, neither do you need to slay it. Consider your own actions, and, specifically, do not carry your "enemies" with you, in your mind, ruminating about what they have done or said, fantasizing hatefully and vindictively about what you will say to them the next time you meet, how you will gain your revenge and cause them to suffer. Do not do it. Because not only does this cause disturbance in your mind, the truth is this: They are already suffering.

Think about it. People who are truly content do not bring upon others unpleasantness, discomfort, anger, jealousy, pettiness, disparagement, ridicule, condescension, rudeness, and all the other joyless energies to weigh heavy and drag down one's spirit. People who are happy and comfortable with themselves and their lives have no need to bring others down to lift themselves up. You may know well-grounded people like this. They are loving and loved, can laugh at themselves and are not so concerned with others' opinions; they are not judgmental toward themselves or others;

they are supportive, honest, and good listeners; they live with less fear and anxiety, or the need to always feel in control; they live with an appreciation, gratitude, connection, and compassion toward others, as well as nature; they are spontaneous and joyful, laugh freely, and so on.

If somebody irritates you, first consider how much of the annoyance arises from your own egoistic conceit, because in some measure, it is your egoistic mind's reacting that causes irritation. Nevertheless, some individuals may seem to purposely bring you uneasiness and discomfort, even as you harbor towards them no ill will.

Think of a person with whom you do not get along well. Toward you they are rude, condescending, small-minded, and antagonistic. The practice of putting others down indicates the fear and insecurity of an ego seeking empowerment by making others feel low. A bully. Listen carefully to what they say or reflect on what they have said and you will realize that they are merely projecting their own ideas and values, revealing more about their own fears, shame, and self-doubt than they are anything about you.

Consider the attachment they have to their ego-stories and imagine the mental chatter of dissatisfactions and failures and insecurities and anxieties and fears that they live with, tormenting them, day by day.

Have you tried by now meditation? Have you noticed throughout the day the mental jibber-jabber of your discursive thoughts? Have you noticed replaying in your head previous (or, just as likely, anticipated) conversations or stressful events or dissatisfactions? Have you noticed ruminations over the mental deceits of your conditioned mind? Have you noticed the stress, the anxiety, the discontent, the fear, the anger, the jealously, and all the unsettling rest of it that arises from a mind living in egoistic illusion and craving, and denial of the truth.

If you have observed this yourself (and you are likely an individual who has some level of self-awareness, insight, and recognition of the truth), then you certainly understand how much focus and mental presence and mindfulness is necessary to live grounded in the truth and not to get swept away in the discursive chaos of your thoughts. It takes substantial effort to stay unattached to your thoughts, no? They are constantly streaming to your attention, agitated thoughts that cause endless rumination, egoistic thoughts that give rise to anxiety, displeasure, anger, craving, fear, conceit, pride, and all the rest of it.

When we consider how much struggle is necessary for an aware person to remain mindful, imagine the amount of torment the malcontents who are not in the least bit mindful will suffer from the discursive mental prattle of their conditioned minds as he or she struggles to regulate and maintain the fabric of their illusory, egoistic fairy-tales. They end their days returning home to sit in their rooms, where they ponder, deliberate, and brood over the events of the past days or days yet to come, anxious and yearning, never fully content with the conditions of their existence.

Or perhaps the antagonists appear not at all dissatisfied. Smug and self-important, proud and arrogant, conceited and vain, desirous of recognition and envy, they have a constant and egoistic need to display their good fortunes, successes, and material possessions, a collection of baby rattles, while taking pleasure in comparing and belittling others in order to lift themselves higher and feel better about themselves. Theirs is not a world of discontent but rather of vainglory—and fear.

What is vanity but the glorification of and fierce clinging to an ego-story. Every accomplishment, every accolade, every baby rattle becomes yet another fabrication in an imaginary and abstract ego-story to which one fervently clings and aches to eternally possess. The entirety of one's life becomes manufacturing an egoistic castle of sand taller, grander, and more magnificent for all to admire and envy, all the while purposefully ignoring the faint and fleeting but ever present fear of it all one day washing away. And it will, as the truth of our impermanence is inevitably made manifest through illness, old-age, and death.

Observe your antagonist with deliberation, and you will witness an egoistic voice yearning and searching for the recognition of others, a recognition that serves to validate and reinforce the illusion of actuality to an ego fabrication that is not merely the story of one but a progressively more vibrant and dynamic mental aggregate of the collective many. In the end, however, acute mental conflict surely arises in the vainglorious, self-important, and conceited, because the greater and more grandiose the ego-story, the greater and more distressing is the fear and clinging that emerges as the truth of impermanence becomes more apparent, year by year, and day by day. The intensifying, disquieting fear that accompanies the truth of impermanence is our commonality, an immutable aspect of our shared humanity.

Extending Compassion

"To 'love our enemy' is impossible, because the moment we love him, he is no longer our enemy."—Thich Nhat Hanh [106]

When confronted by a person with toxic energy and ill intent, it is illuminating to stay mindful and non-attached to your egoistic reaction, to remain silent and egoistically disengaged. Practice this and you will notice that antagonistic individuals appear quite disturbed, mentally, emotionally, and physically. The more animosity they display, the more apparent it is that their chattering mind is full of unease, discontent, and agitation. Do not participate in their inanity and become dragged into the misery of their illusory ego world. Do not allow another's egoistic nonsense to metastasize in your consciousness and become a cancer of irritated nattering in your mind.

Be mindful of your thoughts, especially if you feel yourself impulsively reacting to hostility in kind. Note that when your own

[106] Thich Nhat Hanh, *Living Buddha, Living Christ* (Riverhead Books, 1995) 85

mind becomes still, you begin to lose the urge and impetus to react, at all, and it is quite simple to step back and observe the madness around you.

When we understand how each of us is subject to the torment of an agitated mind, an agitated mind that adversely affects contentment and wellbeing, and we can recognize that this mental suffering causes people to act out in odd, irrational, and impulsive ways, then perhaps we can begin to feel compassion for everyone around us, friend and foe.

The value of having understanding and compassion is that it frees us of hatred, anger, and mental conflict. And to the pragmatist, I reiterate that this does not at all mean that we passively lay down and allow ourselves to be eaten by the bear. No, we protect ourselves from whomever or whatever may harm us. We follow the natural laws to administer decisively forms of protection from the killers, rapists, pedophiles, and whatever other predatory threats may exist, but with understanding and compassion, we can act, decisively, without harboring hatred and anger.

ELEVEN

THE ILLUSION OF FREE WILL

"How can a will, or anything for that matter, arise
without conditions, away from cause and effect,
when the whole of existence is conditioned and
relative, and is within the law of cause and effect?"
—Walpola Rahula[107]

Captive Monkey – Chiayi, Taiwan

English Student: "I just drank this milk tea. I can't to drink
green tea because no have any free will."

Me: "Okay, don't use 'to' after the modal verb 'can.' Say
'can't drink,' not 'can't to drink,' and use 'there' as the subject of the 'because' clause and say, 'because there is no free
will.' 'No have any' is the Chinese way."

[107] Walpola Rahula, *What the Buddha Taught* (Grove Press, 1974) 54

As an English teacher in Taiwan, I became acquainted with a great variety of students: high school and college students, housewives, businesspeople, researchers, doctors, teachers, professors, government employees, office workers, retirees, and anybody else with a desire to improve their English, which was pretty much everybody. The topic of the day could end up being anything under the sun, and it is no exaggeration to say that I learned as much from my students, about a variety of topics, as they may have from me.

On this particular day, I was having a discussion with a doctoral student of philosophy. Continuing the conversation, I asked, "But if I thought about drinking milk tea, and then thought *No, I think I'll have green tea*, I just decided that of my own free will, didn't I?"

"Your thoughts are come from brain activity. If you want to drink milk tea but change green tea, then drink green tea, of course, you can only to drink green tea. How you can milk tea? No have free will . . . sorry, I mean, there is no free will."

Between correcting his grammar and pronunciation, the thought arising from my brain activity at that moment was, *What the hell are you talking about?*

What I later discovered is that it is now commonly proposed by psychologists and neuroscientists that free will is an illusion[108]: We do not freely choose to do what we do. The thought of it seems counterintuitive. We make choices every day, freely. No one is coercing me when I decide to drink green tea instead of milk tea, right? But these are scientists after all, so they no doubt have a rational, logical argument to be considered. First there are the lab experiments using functional magnetic resonance imaging (fMRI) to measure brain activity. The experiments show that it is possible to detect brain activity that reveals which of two buttons a participant will choose to push seven to ten seconds before the person decides to push it.[109][110] It seems that our brains have already chosen what we are to do before we decide what we are going to

[108] Sam Harris, *Free Will* (Free Press, 2012)

do. We might feel we are making freely formed conscious decisions, but our brains have already decided for us.

This seems somewhat unsettling, a threat to our autonomous and self-governing conceit. But observe that thoughts appear randomly and without conscious intent. It may feel as if we are directing our thoughts, but do we will ourselves to think what we are thinking or do thoughts simply arise?

Perceiving, responding, reacting, remembering, emoting, our minds are a swirling narrative of memories, images, ideas, opinions, observations, prejudices, judgments, fears, desires, etc., and this constant, ongoing narrative is what we think of as "me," our sense of being. From moment to moment, it may feel as if we are not only the agents of our thoughts, but we are the thoughts that we think, and we are freely deciding to think what we think and then do what we do. This, the scientists say, is an illusion.

It is practically instinctive to feel that we are the thoughts that we think, but if you have ever practiced meditation, or some type of mindfulness, if you have ever taken the time to focus your attention on the arising of discursive thought, you have surely experienced creating space from these thoughts, stepping back from and being a

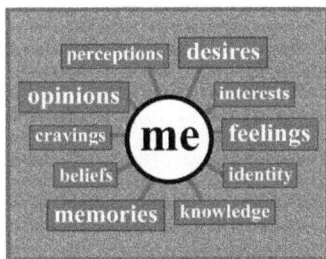

conscious witness to thoughts that arise as a result of impulses, emotions, and cravings. The illusion of free will then becomes more apparent, because as thoughts and images spontaneously arise, you can silently observe them, and it is obvious that you are not willing yourself to form these rambling, discursive thoughts and

[109] Chun Siong Soon, Marcel Brass, Hans-Jochen Heinze, & John-Dylan Haynes, *Unconscious determinants of free decisions in the human brain* (Nature Neuroscience, Volume 11, Number 5, May 2008), 543-545
[110] *Unconscious decisions in the brain* (Max Planck Society, April 14, 2008), http://www.mpg.de/567905/pressRelease20080414 (retrieved 06/16/2014)

images; they simply appear in your conscious awareness.

Try this simple experiment and note that your conscious mind does not willfully direct your brain to arise specific thoughts. Imagine that you are at home and hear a knock at your door—*Knock! Knock! Knock!*

Hello! I have arrived for a visit. You graciously invite me in and prepare to offer me something to snack on. Now take a moment and guess what you think I would enjoy eating, something you have in your refrigerator or pantry. Anything?

Sorry, not so fast. Of course, it has to be something you are fairly certain I would like to eat, some particular thing that you have in your kitchen. Will it be junk food or something healthful? Oh, and don't forget, I am Cantonese. Go ahead now, guess what you think I would like from your kitchen.

Now imagine getting up and going in to get it. (By the way, I don't eat meat, and I don't really like salad or tofu.)

All right then, what are you ready to offer me? Say you first thought to offer me a chocolate chip cookie. Your conscious mind did not instruct your brain to think this thought: *Arise a thought or intention about offering a cookie.* No, the idea simply pops up and your conscious awareness is a witness to it. Of course, many people like chocolate chip cookies, as I certainly do, but there are surely a number of other things in your kitchen worth snacking on. Why a chocolate chip cookie? Why not chips, or a piece of fruit? Who knows? The decision occurs in your subconscious, beyond the level of conscious awareness. Neural activity occurs in your brain, a thought or image appears in your consciousness, and you then move to act. Or not. Because perhaps you reconsider, *No, he'd probably like an apple.* (I am not so fond of apples, by the way.) Once again, it is not your conscious mind directing your brain to arise the thought: *Think about not offering a cookie and instead think about offering an apple.* No, the thought, *He'd probably want an apple*, simply arises, and your consciousness is a witness to it. Even if you had rationalized a thoughtful reason why one choice might be preferred over another—*he is a vegetarian and seems health conscious, and an apple is more healthful,* for instance, still, while you may become aware of these thoughts, you are not commanding these particular thoughts to emerge.

Now you go to the refrigerator to retrieve the apple, open the door, and spot last night's leftover homemade organic pizza—pesto, sun-dried tomatoes, eggplant, mozzarella and goat cheese. *Hmm, yes, the pizza,* you think. (Thank you. Sounds delicious! I'd say.) Of course, you have not consciously instructed your mind to think: *Offer pizza.* The thought simply appears, you become aware of it, and then act upon it.

If you took the time to notice, the thoughts or images of whatever snack you considered appeared randomly, with no conscious intention as to what you should think of. You did not purposefully will yourself to think of a cookie or an apple or anything else; the thoughts just appeared, and you became aware of them. And why did you think of them and not others? Who knows? Your brain makes neural connections, and there you are, a thought or image arises. There is no free will or intention behind any of it. Thoughts and images arise, and you simply become aware of them as they occur.

The point is that the notion of being free to decide anything is constrained by the state of your brain and whatever limitations it may have at any particular moment. For instance, you could not have considered offering the pizza initially because your brain neglected to recall it was in the refrigerator. It was not an option until you got up to get an apple, opened the refrigerator door, and your brain state changed when you spotted the previous evening's pizza. In fact, how many other choices in your kitchen were available to you that simply did not come to mind at the time? And your brain could not have come up with offering something like, say, "balut," because you likely have no idea what that is (a popular Filipino and Southeast Asian snack consisting of a partially developed duck embryo that is boiled alive and eaten in the shell).

If our choices are constrained by the state of our brains, if thoughts and intentions arise prior to conscious awareness (including that rejecting one decision in place of another is still a neural activity that emerges prior to conscious awareness), if our making decisions is simply an electrochemical process of our physical brains and free will is an illusion, what are the implications?

We are not so troubled by the idea that we the lack the free will to push one random button or the other or to decide what kind of snack we might offer our guests. The unease comes from concluding that we are lucky or unlucky participants in a genetic lottery that determines what kind of character we have and that we have no personal or moral responsibility to behave in any particular way—and neither does anyone else. We are simply bound to whatever inherent nature we are born with, and whatever choices we make, whatever actions we take, are not of our own volition.

The argument, while difficult to embrace, becomes increasingly reasonable when we can hardly dispute that our thoughts emerge subconsciously, from the brains residing in our heads. And these physical brains and their processes, which give us our personalities, thoughts, opinions, ideas, abilities, cravings, and everything else, are material that is subject to material damage, malfunction, and failure. Destroy regions of the brain through injury or a disease like Alzheimer's, and we can lose the cognitive abilities that make up the "I, me, my": language ability, recognition of familiar people and objects, memory, reasoning, behavioral abilities, etc.[111]

We are born with a particular genetic make-up that allows us certain potentials (physical, mental, and emotional), and these potentials then may or may not develop, based on whether they are inspired and encouraged and allowed to flourish by our external environment.

Consider Ludwig van Beethoven, celebrated German composer

---

[111] *Alzheimer's Disease Fact Sheet* (U.S. Department of Health and Human Services, September 2012), http://www.nia.nih.gov/alzheimers/publication/alzheimers-disease-fact-sheet (retrieved 06/13/2014

and pianist. If he were born in an era before the piano and classical music were created, would his musical genius have been realized? If he were born to pioneers or homesteaders in some far-flung countryside, would he have been able to develop his musical potential? At the end of his life, Beethoven went almost completely deaf. If he had been born deaf, could he have been able to express his musical capabilities? Regardless, he would certainly not have become the renowned Ludwig van Beethoven that we know of today. How much credit can he take for his social, environmental, and historical background? How much credit can he take for his genetic inheritance? How much credit can he take for becoming the great classical composer he became? Virtually none. If he were born the deaf son of 15th century explorers living in some remote region, having never seen or heard a piano, would he have had thoughts and intentions of composing piano sonatas? Most assuredly not.

Whatever capabilities or potentials your body and brain were born with, whatever background environment you were born into, it is pure happenstance that you have them. If some other person were born with the identical genetic make-up you inherited from your parents: the physical appearance and physique, intellectual and emotional tendencies, personality traits, and whatnot, and this person also had your exact life experience and background growing up: country, city, neighborhood, schools, family, friends, media, cultural values, natural environment, and so on, he or she, thinking and behaving exactly like you, would, in fact, be you, reading this book. How could he or she not be?

Since a synthesis of the brain's genetic make-up and its lifetime of external inputs arise thoughts and intentions from the subconscious, you, the "conscious self," cannot claim authorship for any of them. Even if you imagine that you have been inspired by some reincarnated consciousness or soul guiding your thoughts and intentions, or claim that: all my neural activity, conscious or subconscious, is, in fact, ME, regardless, because thought creation and intent occurs beyond conscious awareness, you can claim none of it as freely and deliberately and willfully chosen. At each particular moment, whether you are deciding to do something or not to do something, you think what you think and then do what you do because you cannot think and do, or not do, otherwise.

Moral and Personal Responsibility

To those who champion freedom, independence, and self-determination, the illusion of free will can be a challenge to certain moral and social principles. Two issues regularly raised are: (1) holding someone accountable for their life predicament and behavior, and (2) being able to take credit for the hard work and sacrifice one endures to become successful.

When one is asked to consider the notion that free will is an illusion, the initial questions are of this nature, "So the rapists, killers, and sociopathic financial industry executives cannot help their predatory instincts and should not be held accountable? We should sympathize that they were unlucky enough to have been born with a combination of "bad" genes and a less than altruistic upbringing? We should then be more concerned with their rehabilitation than punishment?"

Hardly.

While it is true that these individuals are the result of their "unlucky" genetics and background environment, a common assumption is that conceding the absence of free will absolves people of their destructive or harmful behaviors and that is that. Of course not. In fact, the necessity for having a system of punishment is that it makes up a part of the background environment of which we are a part, and this input of negative consequences for disharmonious behaviour is presented to our neural processes to affirm, where they consequently become part of our subconscious minds from which emerge thoughts and intentions. Or not, because it is also possible that our neural processes have some competing, more compelling drive, or we lack the capacity to accept this input because we happen to be genetically-inclined predatory sociopaths.

THE ILLUSION OF FREE WILL

This is no suggestion that we dismantle a system of justice that includes punishment, fairly imposed, but absent the illusion of free will, rehabilitation is as much a legitimate consideration (since rehabilitation is simply another form of external inputs). Just as coherently, we can apply punishment with some level of compassion, and, still, when necessary, permanently remove from society certain individuals who threaten the wellbeing and harmony of a society in tune with the natural order.

The emotional response is not unlike one we would have towards the previously mentioned mother bear attacking us to protect her cub. It makes no sense to hate the bear, which we are under no illusion has free will. In the end, by recognizing that free will is an illusion, justice and punishment can be delivered rationally, fairly, compassionately, and decisively while avoiding intentions of vengeance and hatred.

Another implication people find irksome is to consider that a person does not have the free will to change his or her self-sabotaging behaviors and therefore cannot help repeating actions detrimental to their health and wellbeing. We all know these people: the relative who feels purposeless and self-medicates by getting high or drinking to excess; the friend who goes from one miserable relationship to another because he or she cannot help being attracted to irresponsible, immature, and unstable partners; the acquaintance who is an unrestrained compulsive shopper or an excessive gambler; the colleague who has disruptive and irrational outbursts, and so on. After hearing of the same non-constructive behavior being habitually repeated to a level of detriment and near ruin, we finally roll our eyes and think, "Get your act together! Don't be so pathetic!"

We want to believe that we choose of our own free will, and it is difficult to accept that we do not, with at least part of our resistance stemming from egoistic conceit, because we would rather believe that we freely and willfully decide to like what we like and do what we do and live as we live and be as we want to be, and that our unique individualism, our sense of style, our cool attitude and affect are wholly our original egoistic creation. To maintain that free will exists is to believe that we are responsible for and can take credit for the personal successes and accomplishments that make up the ego-story of which we are so prideful. Comparatively, we self-righteously and disdainfully conclude that the substance abuser and the homeless indigent and perhaps the simple disgruntled malcontent are equally responsible for their less fortunate lot in life. They made bad choices of their own free will, and we made good ones.

To acknowledge that free will is an illusion, on the other hand, strikes directly at the core of our egoistic swagger. It means to surrender the egoistic illusion that we are the agents of our own success. It means to concede it is pure luck and happenstance to have been born with the genetics, the historical and cultural background, the social environment, and the state of the cosmos that have allowed us to develop our genetic potentials so that we may experience a sense of success and accomplishment. It means to be grateful and humbled for the propitious circumstances of our lives. It means to be less judgmental toward the malcontent and the maladjusted, who unluckily possess less than ideal genetics or have had an uninspiring and deficient background environment, perhaps both. It means to have compassion for those who have not been or were not able to develop the neural processing necessary to avoid the negative outcomes that cause their suffering. By the same token, it also means to be kinder and more compassionate toward ourselves, less judgmental of our own neurotic impulses and shortcomings. It is not our choice. We have no free will.

Fate

The other assumption people make is that this is all so fatalistic. That is, if we have no free will and we are powerless to consciously alter our destinies, we are resigned to accept that all thoughts, intentions, decisions, and behaviors are predetermined by some notion of fate. This implies two things: (1) If we have no choice to be any different from what we are, any conscious desire for self-improvement is futile, so we may as well sit here, eat potato chips, and play video games; and (2) If something is meant to happen, it will happen; we cannot willfully determine our life purpose, so we may as well get high and eat more potato chips.

Self-improvement—Unrealized Potential

"You cannot teach a man anything, you can only help him to find it within himself."—Galileo Galilei (1564-1642)

Without free will, we have no choice; our lives could not have been lived, to date, any differently, nor could we have willfully changed ourselves to be anything other than who and what we are. The non-existence of free will also seems to suggest that, from here on, "self-improvement" or the ability to live differently from the way we have been conditioned to live is not possible. On the face of it, however, this cannot be true when existing conditions and compounded phenomena are impermanent and constantly subject to flux and transformation. Conversely, to claim that one can deliberately and willfully become some other, an individual closer to what he or she hopes to become, is a falsehood when free will is an illusion.

Although we may not have the free will to decide what we will become, unrealized potentials reside within each one of us. The dilemma is that we can never be certain of what potentials might be realized. We are one day driven to eat organic whole foods, exercise, meditate, and create, and another day we indulge in chocolate ice cream, judgmental gossip, prurient cravings, and sloth. Regularly torn by competing desires and impulses, are we simply held hostage to the seemingly random, subconsciously derived thoughts and impulses arising from our environmentally conditioned, genetically encoded minds? Do we have no influence over whether we realize the potential of a greedy, selfish, angry narcissist; a caring, compassionate humanitarian; a troubled substance abuser; a carb-loading couch potato; a physical exercise guru; a multi-tasking overachiever; a pious renunciate; a hedonist, and so on? Can we not deliberately cultivate particular innate potentials of our own choosing, or is it purely random chance and luck that they are inspired? Do we not have any say in the matter of what we do and become?

More relevant than the question, "What can I become?" is the question, "What is contentment?" because is a desire to become something other not simply a dissatisfaction with what is, a struggle and constant striving between what one is: the not-so-perfect ego-story, and what one "should" be: the conforming, ideal, and righteous ego-identity.

The determination to become something different, something better, something more virtuous and noble, is a purely egoistic conceit, a display of egoism that certainly results in a mind conflicted as a person clings to the idea of having a free will that drives the "I, me, my" to decide the kind of person one should be, which is nothing other than an ambitious, prideful, and egoistic display of a craving for achievement and recognition.

Contentment—being, without mental conflict—on the other hand, emerges from a mind that has been liberated from the egoistic striving and craving to become anything, which certainly does not mean to sit and do nothing. Not at all. An egoless mind, free of its delusions and conditioning, wholly awakened to the truth, is inspired to live dynamically, enthused with honesty, certainty, and purpose.

Purpose

Unless simply getting stoned, accumulating baby rattles, and eating as many potato chips that one lifetime will allow is what inspires you, you more likely want to live with some meaningful purpose. You hope to encourage others, reduce suffering, create a more harmonious and equitable and sustainable society, contribute to others wellbeing, make the world a better place, make the earth a healthier earth, and teach your children to do the same. Unfortunately, regardless of what you do, if others simply follow their own individual genetically-coded and non-willful path, your efforts make little difference, no?

Bien au contraire. Because you are the background environment for the people around you, your behavior and example and teaching can and does trigger the neural potential of others. You make up the inputs from the external environment to which everyone else is exposed. Love, friendship, concern for your fellow human and the environment, simple politeness, all are external inputs that foster the potentials in those around you to create a sense of security, harmony, and wellbeing for all.

In the end, your life purpose is just as meaningful whether free will exists or not, the only difference being that without the illusion of free will, you live without the egoistic conceit of acting from conscious and deliberate "goodness" or "righteousness" or "virtue." You simply do what you do because your background environment has allowed your genetic potential for this behaviour to develop and flourish. It is not of your own volition. This rationale leaves your behaviour unchanged, the difference being that the illusory ego has been removed from your intentions.

What we express, ultimately, is genetically inherited potential inspired by external inputs, and as we do this, we make up the background environment for those around us, the external inputs from whom others might develop and realize their own potentials.

We have no free will; we are driven by subconscious thoughts and impulses over which we have no control; we cannot attempt to change ourselves without the egoism and struggle of mental conflict. Driven by competing thoughts and impulses, what can inspire our subconscious to lead us on a path to contentment? Well, of course, nothing other than: The truth.

Engaged Meditation—Truth and Transformation

It is not enough to simply know and acknowledge truth. Honest and effortless transformation occurs only when the truth is wholly embraced into one's being. Say I am an avid omnivore who considers becoming a vegetarian. I might understand how forgoing the consumption of animal flesh can contribute to physical health while reducing the suffering of other sentient creatures and the degradation of the environment, but it is quite another thing to be liberated from the impulse and desire to consume meat when pleasurable thoughts of meat-feasting memories and gastronomic sensory cravings emerge from the subconscious neural processes of my conditioned brain. Most challenging is being among others who are merrily partaking in a carnivorous repast. Resisting the sensory stimuli and the memory of meat-eating gustatory pleasures becomes an outright mental struggle. It is only a struggle, however, because I have still not embraced the truth of it.

To think *No, do not eat the steak* or *Yes, go ahead and eat the steak* is no different; they are both the neural process of thought emerging from my one singular brain. I do not consciously initiate either thought to arise. I do, however, act upon one and not the other. Why? Is it because of my momentary mental state, emotional state, physical state, the state of the cosmos, the weather, the kitchen gods? One day it is one decision, the next day another. Who knows why? What I do know is that if these thoughts had not subconsciously arisen, I would not have acted upon either of them. Regardless of which action I take, I am forever constrained by whatever thoughts happen to emerge subconsciously from my brain.

Aha, but now you say, "You may not have arisen the thoughts to do or not to do, but they have appeared in your conscious awareness, and you can now consciously choose one over the other." Yes, and furthermore, I can describe my rationale and beliefs as to why I want to do this and not that.

Do not fail to consider that these "rationales and beliefs" that command our choices are founded on contrived knowledge or

224

ideas, emerging from our minds that have been conditioned by some other. We conform to a pattern of thought that we have been conditioned to believe is the normal, the good, the correct, the ideal, the noble, the virtuous. There is no personal freedom in this. The fact that one is compelled to make a choice, at all, displays a mind in conflict between the truth of what one is and the conforming wish of becoming what one should be.

To wholly embrace the truth is to have a mind without conflict. There is no desire nor craving nor egoistic thirst of becoming one thing or another. There is no consideration nor choice to be made. There is only a total acceptance of the truth, and simply being. The extent of mental conflict in the mind of one who has embraced the truth is akin to someone asking, "Would you like a glass of water?" when one is not at all thirsty. Without thirst, there is no mental struggle. There is no choice to be made. There is simply: "No, thank you," free of any opposing thought or consideration emerging and compelling a person to do or not to do.

They say your answer to the old rhetorical question, "Is the glass half empty or half full?" can be used to determine your worldview. Are you an optimist (half full), or a pessimist (half empty)? There is, however, a third response, and it is this: "It matters not, for I have no thirst." Without the attachment to cravings and impulses and self-delusion, without the attachment to conditioned knowledge and dogma, there is no thirst. There is no duality. There is no mental conflict.

By believing the illusion of free will, believing that you can choose to be one thing and not the other, believing that there is what you are and what you should be, believing that you can become good or better or more righteous or more correct is nothing more than an egoistic trap. You are merely going from one egoistic fairy-tale to another, where you will be bound to live enslaved, conflicted, and craving by the deceits of some other dogmatic conditioning. Awakened to the truth, we naturally and spontaneously originate subconscious thoughts and intentions free of this discord.

While the necessity to outline a process might appear to be a method of practice, it is not. It is not a technique to practice or to perfect. It is a way of being.

1: Acknowledge the Truth

Let us say that I regularly enjoy consuming pasta, bread, chips, cookies, and soda, but I now understand that ingesting such large amounts of refined carbohydrates throws my blood glucose levels out of homeostatic balance and has also lead to my being overweight. Now at risk of type 2 diabetes, I want to modify my diet by replacing these toxic processed food-like products with natural, whole foods so that not only will I have a healthier, more appropriate weight, but my body will regain its homeostatic state of health and I will be able to maintain the fitter and leaner physique that has always existed, hidden beneath the accumulated layers of a bad diet and a sedentary lifestyle.

2: The Set-up

I put a few cans of my favorite soda in the refrigerator and leave some of my favorite snack foods on the table, kitchen counter, desk, even in my car. Of course, I do not want to consume any of these unhealthful psuedo-foods.

3: The Arising of Thought

At some moment during the day, I am going to notice one of these objects nearby, the cookie, say, and I think, *Mmm. Eat cookie.* Almost immediately I think, *No. Don't eat!*

Taking a moment, I notice how these thoughts have arisen. I did not will the thought "Eat cookie" to arise. I simply became consciously aware of it. Instead of acting on it, however, another thought immediately arose, "No. Don't eat!" and I acted on that thought by not reaching for the cookie. While this may seem like I have displayed free will by following one thought and not another, there is no difference when action (or inaction) follows subconscious thought and intention.

I can soon observe my thoughts in conversation: *Go ahead and eat it. This is silly ... Don't eat it. Prove you're strong ... Those cookies are delicious. Who cares? ... Don't give in. Focus on your breath ... It won't kill you. Have one ...*

Finally, I act: eating the cookie and feeling somewhat guilty, or not eating the cookie and feeling good about myself. It makes no difference. Either way, I have experienced the same mental conflict and struggle, a struggle that emerges from the mental chatter of an egoistic mind conditioned to project the contrivances of good and bad. It is the egoistic delusion that I am the conscious agent of my "success" or "failure" that reinforces the deceit that I possess the free will to choose. And this finally culminates in a stronger and more pretentious (or frustrated and self-loathing) ego-identity.

4: Stillness, Openness, Freedom

A thought or sensation arises and we naturally have a fleeting awareness of it. When egoistic attention focuses our conscious awareness upon and pursues this movement of thought, a stream of related mental activity is triggered—a dialogue, a narrative, a story, a mental fabrication—at least for a a while, until other discursive thoughts intrude. It is this focused, egoistic attachment to the subconscious arising of thoughts and images that clutters the space and openness and freedom of our minds and distracts us from recognizing truth.

It is another day and a thought arises, *Drink soda.* I become aware of the thought, recognize and observe the movement of thought, and nothing more. Other thoughts follow, and I note whatever else might arise in my mind. As I observe these mental contrivances emerging, I let them pass unimpeded through the silence of my mind; I let them dissipate. It makes no difference what type of thought or image appears. I observe dispassionately;

I am neutral, with no attachment to or clinging to or judgment about the discursive chatter of my craving and dualistic and egoistic conditioned thoughts. There is no intention to do or not to do. Eventually, there are moments of stillness. Without seeking and striving to become, there is no conflict or struggle. This absence of thought can be compared to the musician or athlete or martial artist "in the flow," an absence of striving and intention, a state of pure stillness and openness of mind. There is clarity, and the capacity and freedom to be imbued with and to embrace the truth.

5: Embrace the Truth

I can recognize the truth and I can acknowledge the truth, but when the truth is not part of my being, there is a disconnect, and when there is a disconnect between the truth and my behavior compelled by a craving, desirous, deceived and conditioned mind, there is the basis for mental and emotional conflict, i.e., emerging thoughts and images and intentions that are discordant with what I know as truth.

To contemplate the truth does not mean to recall words or ideas. Although words are used to communicate, words are not truth; ideas and thoughts are not truth. Truth is a state of mental clarity and being, free of knowledge and conditioning. It is, therefore, not necessary to repeat in my mind thoughts and words and images. I simply acknowledge the truth and focus with a clear and silent and unoccupied mind. That is all.

In this example, acknowledgment of the truth is this: The typical manufactured food item is made from plant products that are first pulverized, stripped of essential nutrients (soluble fiber, antioxidants, and "healthy" fats, for instance), and separated into various elements. These substances, still possibly tainted with toxic pesticide, herbicide, and fungicide residues, are then reconstituted and combined with factory-created additives for texture, flavor, and color. They are also sweetened, salted, preserved, and, finally, shaped into conveniently handled food-like objects.[112][113][114]

These "foods," neither whole nor natural, are not substances that our bodies have evolved to consume. Consequently, as we metabolise these manufactured materials, our physical systems are thrown into homeostatic imbalance, and when we objectively observe the state of our physical conditions by looking in the mirror, walking up several flights of stairs, checking our blood chemistry test values, etc., it is clear that consuming these contrived consumer objects as a regular part of our diet is toxic for and abusive to our health. This is not real food.

If this truth has been embraced as part of my being, will I continue to arise thoughts and cravings to mindlessly ingest these toxic foodstuffs? Certainly not. Until then, though, regardless of whether I continue to eat or do not eat these unwholesome food objects, there is no succeeding nor failing. There is no egoistic struggling nor striving to become. This is not a practice to establish the egoistic conceits of fanatacism, dogma, righteousness, mental discipline, nor ego-identity. No, there are simply two intentions: (1) sitting with the observation of, non-attachment to, and dissipation of discursive thought, and (2) fostering stillness, clarity, and openness of mind to embrace the truth.

At some point, a neural potential is stirred. The truth is clear, unquestionable, and certain. A switch in our minds clicks, thoughts and intentions fade, and volitional struggle vanishes. We are not able to consciously will particular thoughts to arise, but free and open minds, quiet and uncluttered, wholly embracing truth, result in subconscious thoughts and intentions emerging out of truth

[112] *Food Processing*, (Teaching the Food System, A Project of the John Hopkins Center for a Livable Future), http://www.jhsph.edu/research/centers-and-institutes/teaching-the-food-system/curriculum/ (retrieved 06/22/2014)

[113] Marion Nestle, *How Ultra-Processed Foods Are Killing Us* (The Atlantic Monthly, Nov 4 2010), http://www.theatlantic.com/health/archive/2010/11/how-ultra-processed-foods-are-killing-us/65614/ (retrieved 06/22/2014)

[114] Ronnie Cummins, *Millions Against Monsanto: On the Road to Victory* (EcoWatch, July 22, 2013), http://ecowatch.com/2013/07/22/millions-against-monsanto-road-victory/ (retrieved 06/22/2014)

and reality, finally arising into our conscious awareness. We have awakened to the truth, and it is of our being. There is no more struggle.

At every cosmic moment, your brain has the potentials to be triggered and developed into the thoughts and intentions of a person who lives in contentment and without mental conflict. What does this person look like for you? I have no idea. Perhaps the perspectives presented here are the external inputs that somehow allow you to realize your potential to live free of egoistic delusion and conceit. Perhaps they are not. Perhaps you will think, "What rubbish!" and then go on to the next thing, unfreely and unwillfully, and that is that.

Of course, if you prefer to live with less anxiety, frustration, craving, anger, resentment, jealousy, fear, and all the egoistic rest of it, and you are inspired to live connected to the truth and reality of our presence in this earthly realm, open and free and still your mind to wholly embrace:

1. The true nature of egoistic cravings and the deceits of our conditioned minds;

2. the true nature of non-duality;

3. the true nature of compounded phenomena and impermanence;

4. the true nature of our interconnectedness.

To believe that you have free will is to live with regret and sorrow. It means to unproductively and uselessly rue the misguided decisions and behaviors of the past as you fantasize that as some previous cosmic moment, with the exact same physical state, emotional state, mental state, genetic make-up, and life experience, you could have had a different thought or intention or could have acted upon some thought or intention differently than you actually had. And how could that be? Because at the time, if you could have, you would have had the strong enough impulse to, but you did not, and thus could not have.

"Will is a form of ambition, and from will arises a desire to control—to control one thought by another thought, one activity of thought by another activity of thought."—Jiddu Krishnamurti[115]

[115] Jiddu Krishnamurti, *This Light in Oneself* (Krishnamurti Foundation Trust Ltd., 1999) 72

THE BUDDHA WAS NOT A BUDDHIST

TWELVE

THE OBSERVER AND THE OBSERVED

Alleyway along the Ganges River - Varanasi, India

The French mathematician, philosopher, and scientist René Descartes famously proposed, "Cogito ergo sum," usually translated as, "I think, therefore I am." I imagine a meditator would respond with, "I do not think, therefore I can be."

Like many people beginning a practice of meditation, I practiced focusing attention away from my discursive stream of mental ramblings. Sitting comfortably cross-legged on a cushion, I first turned my concentration to physical sensation: the weight of my body, the contact of my legs upon the cushion, the release of tension in my shoulders and legs, the suspension of my head and spine, and then the act of breathing: slowly contracting the diaphragm, feeling the leisurely expansion of space in my lungs, releasing tension as my diaphragm relaxed and forced air out in a long, easy, soothing exhalation. Whenever I noticed my attention distracted by a thought or an image, I would quietly return it to the sensation of breathing. As discursive thought seemed to diminish, other sensory perceptions became more apparent: a distant dog's barking, a car outside whooshing past, the ticking of a clock, the laughter of neighbors in conversation, the warmth of the sun on my hand and leg, the slight, periodic breeze from an open window, the hum of the refrigerator, a ringing in my ears, spontaneous tingles and twitches, and so on. At each instance when I became aware of a sensation, I would again return my attention to the process of breathing. After a while, I learned to simply observe the arising of thoughts and sensations dispassionately, allowing them to easily drift off. This experience in meditation made apparent the distinction between the observer (the self?) and what was observed: discursive thoughts, images, intentions, feelings, memories, sensations, etc. It was all quite calming and relaxing and, dare I say, "blissful," as my mental activity became quiet, and the "me" of my mind less agitated and distracted. Was this "me," the observer of mental activity, what the Hindus refer to as the essential and fundamental Atman?

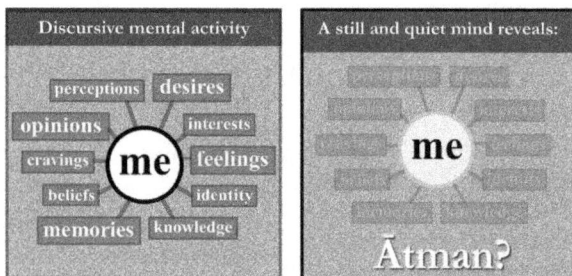

Atman: the Hindu concept of a universal and non-material "self," the eternal soul or spirit. "Says the Bhagavad Gita: When through the practice of yoga, the mind ceases its restless movements and becomes still, the aspirant realizes the Atman."[116]

I was feeling rather good about practicing meditation, and it was becoming more apparent to me that "I" was not my thoughts. Of course, my attention might still become distracted and attached to some fleeting thought or image, and my mind would, quite unwittingly, get temporarily carried away on some discursive narrative, but it was becoming more often that I would remain mindful and stay relatively non-attached to randomly arising thoughts and sensations. Observing and recognizing that mental activity was simply the movement of thought and nothing more, I became less agitated by mental discord and felt I was gaining discipline over the chaos of my mind.

Meditation became a way to practice calmness and relaxation, temporarily ridding myself of agitation and mental dissonance, but it seemed no better than a drug, a tranquilizer, a momentary escape from truth and reality. The limitation was that while I could feel calm and centered during meditation, in my everyday movements, I, the "me," continued to feel somewhat impatient and irritated, dissatisfied and distracted, judgmental and condescending, prideful and egoistic. And there remained a regular craving for something more to acquire, something better to become. Although I may have become more effective in controlling my impulses and behavior, the practice of mental discipline was nothing but one more egoistic conceit: becoming better, more self-controlled, more empowered, stronger willed, and so on.

When reading teachings attributed to the Buddha, I remained a bit baffled, "Mere suffering exists, but no sufferer is found; The deeds are, but no doer is found," the point being that, " ... there is no thought behind the thinker. Thought itself is the thinker."[117]

What?

And there were also other writings of J. Krishnamurti stating that, "the observer is the observed,"[118] and, "I, who am very

[116] Pravrajika Vrajaprana, *Vedanta: A Simple Introduction* (Vedanta Press & Bookshop, 1999) 29

[117] Walpola Rahula, *What the Buddha Taught* (Grove Press, 1974) 26

[118] Jiddu Krishnamurti, *Freedom from the Known* (Ebury Publishing, 2010) 99-100

earnest, want to dissolve the self ... The moment I say 'I want to dissolve this,' and in the process I follow for the dissolution of that, there is the experiencing of the self; and so, the self is strengthened."[119]

Huh? More riddles to untangle.

The Observer is the Observed

What does it mean that the observer is the observed? If we acknowledge this as true, does it not imply that there is no observer, there is no experiencer? There is no Atman?

So what, then, might the instinctive sense of self—the observer, the experiencer, the thinker—be? Perhaps we should consider the following:

Is the observing of thought not simply another form of mental activity?

If, as "the observer," I can observe my mental formations as merely the movement of thought, I must also recognize that the sensation of "being the observer" is nothing more than a further movement of thought, i.e., the observer observing is mental activity: *okay, concentrate on breath ... good ... breathe ... what? ... wait, return to breath ... breathing ... stillness ... stop, don't think about that ... feel breath ... yes ... nothingness ... what time ... huh? ... breath sensation ... no thinking ... joy ... compassion ... om ... what? ... let those thoughts go ... breathing ... bliss ... love ...* and so on. The sense of being the observer—I, as well as the objects of our observations—discursive mental formations, are both, equally, the movement of thought, mental creations that exist nowhere outside the activity of the mind.

The observer and the observed are non-dual in nature

[119] Jiddu Krishnamurti, *Krishnamurti Foundation Annual Gathering Compilation 1990* (Krishnamurti Foundation Trust Ltd., 1990) 26

That is, they are interdependent. Inner thoughts and images that can "be observed" do not manifest unless there is an observer, and an "observer" exists only when there are phenomena to be observed. The psychological observer and the observed make up a singular whole of mental activity. One does not exist without the other.

The Illusion of Self

The Buddha recognized the "I" as "a combination of ever-changing physical and mental forces or energies"[120]—compounded and impermanent phenomena. This sense of "I," the "me," the "self," is not an individual and enduring entity but rather an image, a mental apparition emerging from an aggregate of thoughts, memories, sensations, experiences, perceptions, beliefs, feelings, opinions, habits, knowledge, ideas, impulses, ambitions, cravings, desires, fears, and all the rest of it. From "the observed" is compounded the "observer," hence the observer *is* the observed.

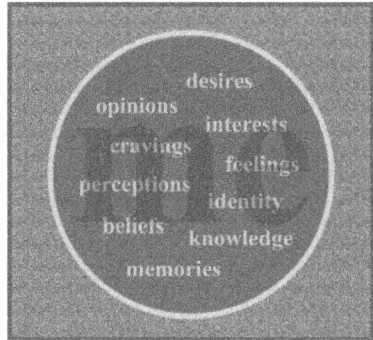

Since compounded and constantly changing physical and mental forces cannot make up an entity that is permanent and everlasting, the sense of an "eternal I"—the Atman—is simply irrational, thus, we recognize anatman, or anatta (Pali)—the illusion of self.[121]

If, having observed your thoughts in meditation, you have ever focused attention on the movement of thought so that mental activity became still, you will certainly be able to reason that the self, the "me," a fabricated aggregate of thought, can also be stilled. It is notable that scientific research is ever clearly demonstrating

[120] Walpola Rahula, *What the Buddha Taught* (Grove Press, 1974) 20

A still and quiet mind reveals:

anātman

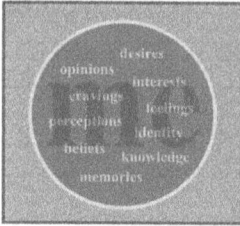

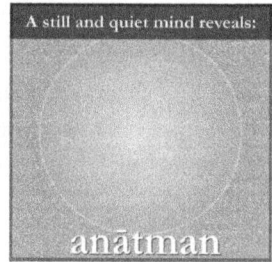

there is no primary individual entity in your head, shifting the gears and steering the wheels of your thoughts and intentions. Rather, "different mental processes are mediated by different brain regions, and there is nothing to suggest the existence of any central controller."[122] In short, the sense of self does not originate from a singular location in the brain but emerges from a collective network of regions distributed throughout the brain, creating the illusion of self.[123]

Three Views of Self

There are two common and seemingly common-sense views of the self (or the soul): (1) the eternalist, who believes man has a "self," an entity distinct from the body, and (2) the annihilationist, who believes the "self" is simply a process of the material brain.

1) The Eternalist (Dualistic View): "I have an eternal Self."

The eternalist maintains a dualistic view of the body and spirit as two distinct entities. Man has a physical self—a body, and a non-physical self—an eternal spirit.

[121] Rahula, *What the Buddha Taught*, 51-66

[122] *In search of self, Nature Neuroscience 5, 1099* (2002) doi:10.1038/nn1102-1099, http://www.nature.com/neuro/journal/v5/n11/full/nn1102-1099.html (retrieved 3/21/2014)

[123] Turk DJ, Heatherton TF, Macrae CN, Kelley WM, Gazzaniga MS, *Out of Contact, Out of Mind, The Distributed Nature of the Self* (Ann. N. Y. Acad. Sci. 2003 Oct; 1001:65-78, PMID: 14625356), http://www.dartmouth.edu/~bil/pubs/turk_2003_annals.pdf

The self or spirit or soul, the Atman, is not only intimately interconnected to the processes of our physical bodies while we are living but will continue to exist after death, transcendent and in communion with a sublime and cosmic entity: God, the Divine.

2) The Annihilationist (Materialist View): "I have no eternal Self."

The annihilationist believes that man consists only of matter, and that thought and our sense of self arise solely from physical processes. When we die, any and all sense of self and knowledge are extinguished, wholly annihilated along with the physical body (not so poetic, these rational annihilationists).

The Aggregate Self: "The 'Self' is a mentally projected aggregate of various elements."

There is a third view, presented by the Buddha, which avoids the extremes of the eternalist and the annihilationist: There is no separate observer entity who experiences thought or sensation because the observer *is the aggregate* of thought and sensation. In this instance, there is neither desire for immortality nor fear of annihilation, thus there is neither craving nor aversion; there is no mental conflict. There is merely living awakened to the true nature of the illusory "I"—the "observer," being a projected aggregate of mental formations—"the observed." When we encounter the sheer truth of it, we experience emptiness and simply being, and the free and uncluttered space to wholly embrace our existential truth:

1. The true nature of egoistic cravings and the deceits of our conditioned minds;
2. the true nature of non-duality;
3. the true nature of compounded phenomena and impermanence;
4. the true nature of our interconnectedness.

THIRTEEN

DEATH

Night cremations at Manikarnika Ghat - Varanasi, India

In the woods, you can always smell a days-old dead body before you see it. It is the distinct odor of putrefaction that first seizes your attention; the fetid stench is one you can hardly forget.

My dogs and I were hiking along a narrow mountain road near where I lived in Tu-cheng (土城, literally, "Earth, or Soil, Town") outside the capital city of Taipei, Taiwan. Nearing a fork in the path, I had a momentary whiff of something I knew was surely a dead something. Searching more deliberately and guided by the not-so-pleasant scent, I spotted it: a weeks-old puppy laying dead a few feet off the trail. I had seen this puppy and its feral siblings in recent days, playfully popping in and out of the underbrush. Now clearly dead, it appeared otherwise normal, seemingly at rest, still in its "fresh stage" of decomposition, the first of five stages.

This first stage of decomposition begins after the heart stops beating. Without circulation, the body begins to cool and blood begins to settle. Within several hours, the muscles become stiff, "rigor mortis." As cells die, they release enzymes which begin to break down surrounding cells and tissue. Within a few days, although the creature is quite dead, the body remains teeming with life as intestinal bacteria begin busily digesting their way out from the inside. Soon they are advancing and spreading, breaking down other organs and tissues in a process known as putrefaction. As the bacteria digest tissue and multiply, they produce various gases that create the foul stench of death.

I called my dogs away from the dead puppy and we continued on. As the dogs bounded ahead, exploring for new smells, I thought of how we, humans, define odors as good or bad, fragrant or rank, the whole duality thing. Dogs, on the other hand, enthusiastically greet one another with a sniff at the other's backside, non-dualistically apparently, and I have hosed down many a reeking dog that had just been merrily wriggling and squirming atop a stinking pile of animal droppings or the remains of some disgustingly putrid, dead creature (a bit of dualistic attitude may not be such a bad thing after all).

The following day as we again approached the fork in the road, I was intending to walk on the opposite side of the trail and to avoid the sight and smell of the decomposing puppy when I thought, *I wonder what it looks like, a body breaking down into bits of organic matter and returning to the ecology of the soil. What the heck . . .* the dogs and I all crossed the road to take a look. Our puppy was still there, in a similar state to the day before. Perhaps slightly different in color, not much so.

For the next couple weeks, we walked past the small puppy each day to observe the process of decomposition. There was not much noticeable change the first few days, besides a worsening odor and a gradual discoloration, from a greenish hue to dark purplish. Ants had arrived, along with small swarms of flies gathering around the puppy's eyes mouth and anus, depositing eggs, no doubt. As I watched the line of ants marching toward the remains, I imagined my own physical body one day resting in the same state of decay.

The second stage soon became apparent: the "bloat stage." The puppy had now blackened and appeared inflated. This was the result of the internal army of bacteria proliferating, digesting and liquefying the remaining tissues and organs, simultaneously releasing putrid gases that were accumulating in the body cavity and causing the puppy's belly to distend. Liquid began seeping from the orifices and staining the soil. The offensive odor was becoming an obvious-from-a-distance stench.

Days later the body seemed to have burst open. The surrounding soil was darkened with wetness. It was now in "active decay," stage three. Reeking of rot, the deflated remains were host to masses of writhing maggots consuming the moist, decaying flesh. After several days, visible activity at the carcass subsided, as did the foul odor. The remains turned to a dark, leathery, puppy-shaped silhouette upon the soil. It had entered the fourth stage: "advanced decay."

The final stage is "dry decay," stage five. At this point not much remained, a few scattered bones and a layer of shriveled skin. It resembled nothing more than a large, dried leaf. Several days later, grasses began to grow over the spot, and you would have never known the poor puppy had ever been there.[124][125][126]

To the dualistic-minded, the topic of death evokes feelings of gloom, sorrow, disgust, and fear. Contemplating death is some-

[124] Molly Edmonds, *The Body After Death in How Dying Works*, (HowStuffWorks.com, 12 January 2009), http://health.howstuffworks.com/diseases-conditions/death-dying/dying.htm (retrieved Feb. 8, 2014)

[125] Jo Marchant and Lucy Middleton, *Introduction: Death* (New Scientist, October 2007), http://www.newscientist.com/article/dn12759-introduction-death.html?full=true#.UvMtZEDE1K0 (retrieved Feb. 8, 2014)

[126] Hyde ER, Haarmann DP, Lynne AM, Bucheli SR, Petrosino JF, *The Living Dead: Bacterial Community Structure of a Cadaver at the Onset and End of the Bloat Stage of Decomposition* (PLoS ONE 8(10): e77733. doi:10.1371/journal.pone.0077733, 2013), (retrieved Feb. 8, 2014)

thing to be avoided, and from day to day, it *is* easily avoided, because in this modern world, we live disconnected from our true nature. Of course, we clearly understand, intellectually, that all that is born must die and materially return to the earth, but like teenagers, we live as if we are immortal, not at all acknowledging the reality of impermanence and our own death, and why should we? We have faith that modern technology and science will cure all of our ills. As long as we have enough money to spend, we can hire the experts to fix, rebuild, and renovate our aging appearance, our neglected health, our outdated houses, and our rattling automobiles. This fabricated reality assures us that all we desire is available: ageless youth through cosmetic surgery; eternal health and energy through pharmaceuticals, medical technology, and the latest exercise fad; a convenient and seemingly infinite supply of food, water, and energy resources through industrial production and an incredibly engineered infrastructure, and all the rest of it. All this modernity, we trust, can indefinitely maintain the homeostasis of our humanly contrived ecosystem and the homeostasis of our physical bodies. It fools us into denial, leading us to perpetually disregard the true nature of our interconnectedness to the natural world and of our material impermanence.

To the non-dualistic, death is an ever-present and intrinsic element of earth's ecological homeostasis, an ordinary aspect of the Tao. Death is nature's constant, commonplace, and complementary yin to an early morning sunrise, a springtime burst of wildflowers, and a newborn's smile (nature's yáng). Acknowledging death means living with a knowing of the true nature of compounded phenomena, impermanence, and our interconnectedness to the external world. It does not, however, mean to have an affinity toward or morbid fascination with death nor does it mean to find our material bodies to be repulsive or ugly. It does not mean to mull over and brood upon death, annihilation, and rotting corpses nor to become apathetic and morose and suicidal, not in the least. It is merely accepting death's inevitability and necessity, and embracing this truth not just intellectually but in our being. For this, however, we must first resolve the fear of death. Simply put, understanding where the fear of death originates allows one to accept death's inevitable reality and reveals a path toward a life with meaning, purpose, and simple joy. Embrace the truth that one day your material existence will end, and you can begin to cherish your moment-to-moment life experience, to live with a greater sense of freedom and gratitude, and to have much less fear—of everything.

> "Like everyone else you want to learn the way to win, but never to accept the way to lose—to accept defeat. To learn to die is to be liberated from it. So when tomorrow comes you must free your ambitious mind and learn the art of dying."—Bruce Lee[127]

When the reality of our impermanence and eventual demise is mentioned, the initial reaction is typically one of unease. So gloomy and depressing a topic, who would want to ponder this? We would rather think about living, about being busy and accomplishing and creating, about celebrating, merrymaking, and carousing, certainly not dying.

Considering the actuality of death, however, may very well change the way you live. This is not to say that you will renounce the accomplishing, creating, and merrymaking but that you will know a way to live that is not a distraction from a life lived with purpose and meaning and presence.

Why fear death?

A fundamental discomfort with death comes from the physical fact of it. Stumbling upon a fetid corpse in rot and decay would be an unpleasant experience for most everybody. But this is not a fear of death; this is more revulsion, a natural, evolutionary survival response to steer us away from pathogens and disease.[128]

[127] Bruce Lee, *The Way of the Intercepting Fist* (Longstreet TV Series, 16 September 1971), http://www.youtube.com/watch?v=_GDWkVRK8kQ (retrieved 05/25/2014)

There is also the inherent fear we have of experiencing pain and suffering at the moment of death. Since our instinctive fear response is part of a survival mechanism that helps us to avoid injury and death, it is reasonable that the thought of death arises fear, and, subsequently, expectations of pain and suffering. Still, this does not wholly explain our aversion to death, because if we could administer medications that allowed one to die "peacefully," would we not still harbor some dread toward our cessation of life?

Death presents the fear of the unknown when what we crave is the known, and we crave the known because it affords us security and a sense of control. Fearful, many faithfully and blindly adopt some fabricated dogma, a vehicle that offers false comfort and assurance, a contrivance anointed as "the Known." This, however, is yet another fairy-tale, because the truth is that death is always of the unknown, as long as we are living.

The fear of death, however, does not exist simply because the truth of death is unknowable. Say we imagine that dying is like falling into a sleep state and never waking, and that is that. What is there to fear? Every night as we sleep, we lose conscious awareness, do we not? Imagine the experience of death being no different: the end of conscious awareness—a deep, eternal sleep. Rationally, it sounds rather pleasant. Has the fear of death now been alleviated? I think not, because there is something more.

You Can't Take It with You

Other common concerns are wholly related to the mentally fabricated story of self:

> *"I have worked so hard to acquire all my material possessions, and I will no longer be able to enjoy them."*

---

[128] Steven Bedard, *Smells Like Death* (California Academy of Sciences, November 19, 2013), http://www.calacademy.org/sciencetoday/smells-like-death/5513085/ (retrieved Feb. 8, 2014)

Both the prideful ego-identification with possessions and the attachment to memories associated with our collection of baby rattles arise from our ego stories and our vanity's attachment to fairytales that have been contrived and conditioned into our minds by a materialist culture (not to mention that such an attachment to physical objects reveals an ignorance toward the true nature of impermanence).

"There are still things I would like to do and experience."

Let us say that reincarnation is a fact, and your essence, your soul if you will, is reborn into another human body after being stripped of your present self/identity (all history, memory, knowledge, experience, opinions, interests, and so on). This new and virgin "you" can then experience all the things you have missed in the previous life. Would this bring contentment? Of course not, because what you truly desire is your present idea of self, your existing fabricated and compounded ego-story, your own particular ego-identity: Mr. or Ms. XYZ, to have these experiences. In fact, you do not truly desire further experiences at all. No, what you truly desire is to have your ego-story continue to exist. You crave permanence, the eternalism of the illusory self.

"I will have to leave my loved ones behind."

Of course, it seems natural to long for loved ones, but is not some, if not most, of the fear of leaving loved ones really a craving for what they provide our egoistic selves: companionship, affection, attention, care, security, relevance, recognition, admiration, love, and all the rest of it? Not only do loved ones fulfill an egoistic need for our feeling wanted, needed, loved, and protected, but they also make up a significant part of our elaborate ego-stories and our attachment to the contrivances of memory and recognition, the support for our egoism. Does the sorrow of separation arise out of a concern for the wellbeing of others or does it emerge from our own egoistic self-love? If there is a true concern for the welfare of loved ones, the main issue is to ensure that their essential needs and a healthful environment in which they can continue to live are provided for them. Get to work with that.

"The possibility of total non-existence for eternity, complete annihilation, is terrifying."

This is not a fear of physical death but rather an extreme attachment to the illusory ego. What you crave is reassurance that your "soul" or "self" or "ego" will continue to live for eternity. The irony is that the fear of "eternal non-existence" emerges from a fabrication of self that is and always has been non-existent in any tangible way, residing purely in one's private, singular, mentally compounded universe. This is the story of an illusory self in terror of recognizing that it is an illusion. And this is of no minor concern.

Is the primary reason for the dread of death not simply the distress over our "ego-story of self" coming to an end? Our memory-based histories, our relationships, our accomplishments, our unique identity, our acquired knowledge, our opinions, abilities, ambitions, and interests, our material possessions, everything that goes into making up our ego-stories, all dissipating to nothingness. Is this not what truly frightens us about death? And the irony is that while we devote our waking hours assembling this ever inflated ego-identity to feel better about ourselves, we are, ultimately, fabricating an empire of fear, because the greater one's ego-story, whether it is mental or material, the greater the fear of death and annihilation of the fabrication.

Regardless of what anyone may believe or claim, we cannot be certain of what may or may not occur with our self, soul, consciousness (whatever you want to name it), after our death. As far as I have heard, not a single person has been proved to die, rot in the ground, and come back to tell us what death is like.

Yes, I know, you are thinking: *What of near-death experiences?*

While these may inspire the imagination, are they nothing more than adventures somewhere near *the threshold* of death? Even if these anecdotes were proved to be true, do they not come from individuals who are "seemingly, pretty much, as-far-as-we-can-tell" deceased but, of course, not, because deceased means, well, dead, as in a doornail. Can one be completely, undeniably dead and then undead?

> "One is never afraid of the unknown; one is afraid of the known coming to an end."—Jiddu Krishnamurti[129]

No hope, at all?

Regardless of how coldly logical we are, I imagine we all harbor a bit of hope that death is not the unequivocal end. Although we can rationalize that the neural activity giving rise to our memories, ideas, thoughts, intentions, feelings, and knowledge ends with the physical demise of our brains, we still like to imagine that some kind of consciousness or spirit-thing that makes us *us* will continue on.

Personally, I am getting used to the idea of "death of the self." I "die" every night, slipping into an unconsciousness of awareness and then vanishing, feeling (or maybe non-feeling) absolutely and altogether gone, out, kaput, non-existent, a bit amazed and amused when I happen to awaken the next morning. Death, I imagine, must feel much like nevermore arising out of your slumber, which, in fact, must feel like nothing at all. The ancient Greek philosopher Epicurus referred to the needless concern for the experience of death thus: "When we exist, death is not; and when death exists, we are not."

Of course, we still hold out hope, just a bit, of something more, do we not? If not out of necessity, then out of wonder and imagination, because, well, it is what our minds do.

[129] Jiddu Krishnamurti, *You are the World* (Krishnamurti Foundation India, 1972) 76

Three Views of Death

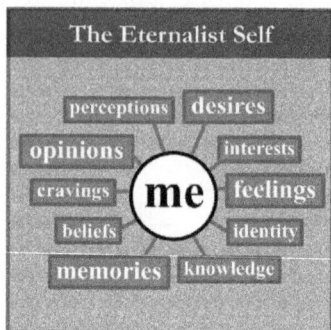

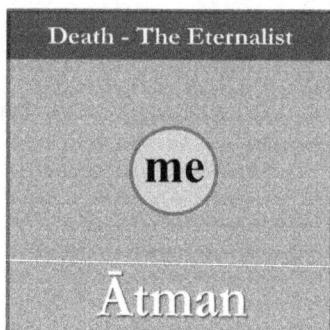

The Eternalist Self

perceptions desires
opinions interests
cravings **me** feelings
beliefs identity
memories knowledge

Death - The Eternalist

me

Ātman

The Eternalist (Dualistic View): In the eternalist view, the self or soul or Atman continues to exist in some form after death of the physical body.

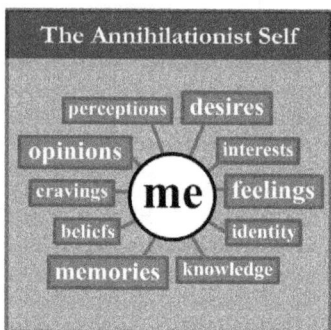

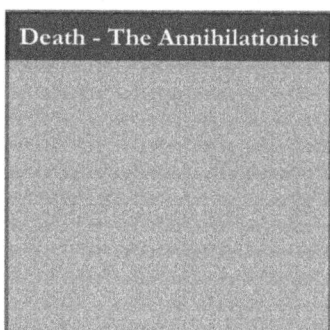

The Annihilationist Self

perceptions desires
opinions interests
cravings **me** feelings
beliefs identity
memories knowledge

Death - The Annihilationist

The Annihilationist (Materialist View): The annihilationist believes that because man consists of only matter, when the body and brain die, any sense of self or being is also destroyed.

The Aggregate Self: Rejecting the claim that there is an eternal Self or Soul or Atman, the Buddha might appear sympathetic to the view of the annihilationist, but this is not so because, in fact, there is no actual Self to be annihilated. The Self is an imaginary, false belief, a mental projection, a fabricated aggregate of memories, sensations, beliefs, knowledge, cravings, desires, fears, and all the rest of it. Can something that does not exist be annihilated? The Buddha is unique in that he could deny the extreme views of both the eternalist and the annihilationist, explaining that an aggregate self of compounded phenomena is indeed no enduring and eternal Self; thus, both eternalism and annihilation of the Self are utterly irrational concepts.[130]

And what, then, might this infer about the phenomenon of death? Walpola Rahula suggests to first consider how we experience living. Observe that although the Self is illusory, no more than a constantly transforming mental projection, we can still live exuberant, spirited, and invigorated with life energies even as we are "without a permanent, unchanging substance like Self or Soul." Once we can observe this as true, "why can't we understand that those forces themselves can continue without a Self or Soul behind them after the non-functioning of the body?"[131]

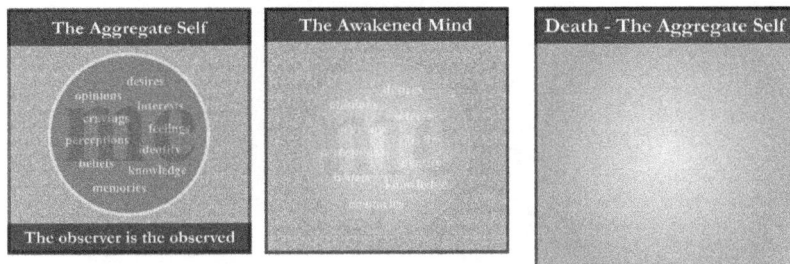

Of course, this is simply one more theory, a hypothesis, a hopeful speculation based on what we can observe to be true.

Well, I suppose it is better than nothing.

Note: Apparently, there are some Buddhist scholars who debate the authenticity of the Buddha's teaching the fundamental concept of anatman or "not-self."[132] But really, it makes no difference. The question is not which scholar's display of erudition is the most impressive but rather what can we observe and experi-

[130] Walpola Rahula, *What the Buddha Taught* (Grove Press, 1974) 51-66
[131] Rahula, *What the Buddha Taught*, 33

ence to be true. Through a practice of mental awareness and focus, we can observe that the "self" is merely an aggregate of various mental processes, or as science demonstrates: the sense of
self is not originated from a singular location in the brain but
emerges from a collective network of regions distributed throughout the brain.

[132] Christian Coseru, *"1.1 The Not-Self Doctrine" in "Mind in Indian Buddhist Philosophy"* (The Stanford Encyclopedia of Philosophy, Winter 2012 Edition), Edward N. Zalta (ed.), http://plato.stanford.edu/archives/win2012/entries/mind-indian-buddhism/ (retrieved 02/12/2014)

FOURTEEN

ENLIGHTENMENT

Morning Ritual – Photo by Jorge Royan[133]

---

[133] *India - Varanasi baño Ganges*©Jorge Royan, (Wikimedia Commons, 2005), http://www.royan.com.ar, CC-BY-SA-3.0, http://commons.wikimedia.org/wiki/File:India_-_Varanasi_ba%C3%B1o_Ganges_-_0072.jpg (retrieved 6/2/2014)

"If you meet the Buddha on the road, kill him."[134]

This oft-repeated koan is attributed to the Chinese ninth-century Buddhist master Línjì Yìxuán, founder of the Línjì school of Chán (Zen) Buddhism. Here, using his trademark irreverence, he is exhorting his followers to awaken to the way of the Dharma.

Dharma—Truth as set forth in the teaching of Buddha.

Of course, being a koan, Línjì's provocation has been interpreted with various meanings such as: Any concept you have of "the Buddha" or what the Buddha is is simply a mental fabrication, therefore, "kill" these fairy-tales from your thoughts; There is no externally existing Buddha to venerate, so "kill" your craving for a savior; The idea of meeting the Buddha is a manifestation of your egoistic desires, and, naturally, your ego and its illusions must be "killed," and so on.

Seems reasonable enough. Perhaps we should consider, also, the original Chinese version of Línjì's koan:

逢佛殺佛，逢祖殺祖 [135]

Translation: "If you encounter the Buddha, kill the Buddha; if you encounter ancestors, kill the ancestors."

The Chinese version expresses its intention a bit less enigmatically. Of course, this is no incitement to kill anybody, because the "killing," if there is to be any, is only of one's conditioned thoughts. To encounter the Buddha is to first carry in our minds an idealization of the Buddha, which is nothing other than learned dualistic

[134] *Linji Yixuan*, Wikipedia, http://en.wikipedia.org/wiki/Linji_Yixuan (retrieved 6/12/2014)

[135] 臨濟義玄, http://zh.wikipedia.org/zh-mo/
%E4%B8%B4%E6%B5%8E%E4%B9%89%E7%8E%84

concepts of how to be or not to be, how to think or not to think, how to act or not to act. To identify our ancestors is to recognize the traditions we have adopted with unquestioning conformity: our values, our religious beliefs, our dogmas of right and wrong, our prejudices, our conceits, our pride, our ethnocentrism, our nationalism, our cravings, our aversions, and all the rest of it. This is the foundation upon which is constructed a mentally fabricated ego-identity, inevitably leading one to individuation and self-righteousness, pride, conflict, hatred, and violence.

Línjì encourages his followers to release from their thoughts all conditioned knowledge: dogmatic beliefs that obstruct one's openness to the truth, doctrines that compel one to conform blindly to authority, traditions that bind one to the past, and so forth, because when one is free of all conditioned thought, his or her mind is still, creating space to awaken to the true nature of the self and to the true nature of existence: impermanence, non-duality, and our interrelationship with the external world.

Is this, then, enlightenment?

Enlightenment

"The so-called enlightened people are not enlightened, for the moment they say, "I am enlightened," they are not. That is their vanity. It is like a man saying, "I am really humble"— when a man says that you know what he is."—Jiddu Krishnamurti[136]

What is enlightenment? Suppose at some moment you are overcome by a state of euphoric bliss; a shift in your sensory perceptions has occurred and you sit in a state of wonder, as if you have been newly born into this world. Your perception of time is distorted. Sound and tactile sensations are heightened and mesmerizing. You see familiar objects in their totality as if for the first time. You have lost fear, anxiety, and self-conscious inhibition, and you

[136] Jiddu Krishnamurti, *Questions and Answers* (Krishnamurti Foundation India, 2009), 72

feel love, trust, empathy, emotional warmth and closeness toward everyone and everything. You have a profound sense of contentment and wellbeing.[137] Is this enlightenment? Or perhaps, more likely, you have just dropped some MDMA. According to the National Institute on Drug Abuse, MDMA (Ecstasy, Molly, the Hug Drug) can alter the activity of your neurochemistry and create this sensation of euphoria and wellbeing:

"It (MDMA) produces feelings of increased energy, euphoria, emotional warmth and empathy toward others, and distortions in sensory and time perception."[138]

If this is the "enlightenment" you crave: exuberance, feelings of expansiveness and euphoria, an experience of emotional closeness, trust, and warmth with others, enhanced sensory perceptions, distortions in time perceptions, and so on, the use of MDMA might seem a reasonable consideration. Unfortunately, MDMA is not only illegal, it can also have adverse side effects that often include "the development of depression-like feelings, anxiety, restlessness, irritability, and sleep disturbances,"[139] as well as possible long-term neurotoxic effects and the potential for life-threatening complications from an overdose.

In fact, MDMA does not supply you anything. It merely manipulates the neurochemistry that is already present in your brain:

"MDMA acts by increasing the activity of three neurotransmitters: serotonin, dopamine, and norepinephrine. The emo-

[137] *MDMA (Ecstasy) Abuse, Research Report Series* (National Institute On Drug Abuse, NIH Pub Number: 06-4728, Published: March 2006), http://www.drugabuse.gov/publications/research-reports/mdma-ecstasy-abuse (retrieved 3/4/2014)

[138] *DrugFacts: MDMA* (Ecstasy or Molly) (National Institute on Drug Abuse, September 2013), http://www.drugabuse.gov/publications/drugfacts/mdma-ecstasy-or-molly (retrieved 3/4/2014)

[139] *Short-term effects after ecstasy is gone from the body* (National Institute on Drug Abuse, January 2007), http://www.drugabuse.gov/publications/teaching-packets/neurobiology-ecstasy/section-iii/1-short-term-effects-after-ecstasy-gone-body (retrieved 3/4/2014)

tional and pro-social effects of MDMA are likely caused directly or indirectly by the release of large amounts of serotonin, which influences mood (as well as other functions such as appetite and sleep). Serotonin also triggers the release of the hormones oxytocin and vasopressin, which play important roles in love, trust, sexual arousal, and other social experiences. This may account for the characteristic feelings of emotional closeness and empathy produced by the drug; studies in both rats and humans have shown that MDMA raises the levels of these hormones."[140]

If sensation is what you seek, you need not drop MDMA after all, because practiced meditators also report comparable feelings of blissfulness, euphoria, empathy, love, distortions in time perception, enhanced sensory perceptions, and so on. Others, without spiritual or supernatural dispositions, relate similar experiences during unique sensorial events (e.g. Dr. Jill Bolte-Taylor, athletes and musicians "in the flow," etc.). This feeling of "enlightenment," then, is not so remarkable, because the potential is always available to be realized, through the neurochemistry of your brain.

Enlightenment—Bliss—Nirvana

It seems a quest, for some, to have an experience of "bliss" or "enlightenment," to acquire knowledge of the supernatural, of the mystical, to undergo trance-like states beyond time and space, to believe he or she has achieved some contrived state of nondualistic consciousness, to become something, some "thing"— the enlightened one—to be able to claim, "I am enlightened," and to be recognized by this egoistic notion of identity.

It is all so utterly silly.

Does the desire to be "enlightened" not begin with the mental

[140] *Drug Facts: MDMA* (Ecstasy or Molly) (National Institute on Drug Abuse, September 2013), http://www.drugabuse.gov/publications/drugfacts/mdma-ecstasy-or-molly (retrieved 3/4/2014)

fabrication of an ideal to which one must conform? Hence, there is the desire to become, with the practice to be or to become any-

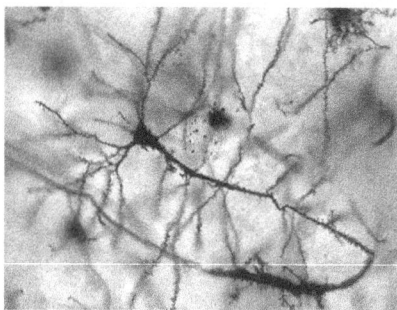

Neuron, 40 times magnification[141]

thing revealing a mind in conflict with what is and what should be, a mind in egoistic pursuit to exemplify an enlightenment archetype that further aggrandizes the mentally contrived and self-important ego-story. For one to claim, "I am enlightened," is wholly absurd, incongruent with the plain logic that one who is genuinely "enlightened" to the truth of his or her being does not cognize the egoistic mental fabrication of a contrived and illusory self, let alone an "I" that claims to be anything, enlightened or otherwise.

Regardless of how it is initiated—drug use, meditation, an exceptional sensory experience—the value of experiencing an altered consciousness that diminishes one's egoistic self-awareness is not the simple feeling of "bliss." No, it is the realization that perceptions, sensations, memories, conditioned thought processes, behaviors, and emotional responses, cravings, aversions, and all the rest of it that make up a sense of self, are transient and mutable, and that a shift in egoistic consciousness can free one from the self-imprisoning attachment to a mentally fabricated and individuated ego-identity, the origin of one's suffering.

Awakening to the true nature of the self and of existence is not concerned with feelings of bliss, is not concerned with knowledge, is not concerned with mystical or supernatural phenomena or achieving any state of anything. It is not something you can accomplish or attain, or even plainly describe. Awakening is not merely seeing and recognizing and understanding. No, it is the inherent and subconscious and innate knowing, that is: being. As Walpola Rahula describes:

> "Truth is not a result nor an effect. It is not produced like a mystic, spiritual, mental state, such as dhyana or samadhi. TRUTH IS. NIRVANA IS. The only thing you can do is to see it, to realize it. There is a path leading to the realization of Nirvana. But Nirvana is not the result of this path."— Walpola Rahula[142]

dhyana—a state of mind achieved through higher meditation
samadhi—concentration attained through higher meditation; mental discipline

Is it possible?

Is it possible to contemplate and wholly see the true nature of the self, an identity derived from memories and conditioned thought? Is it possible to observe that the attachment to and concern for this ego-story results in the involuntary, subconscious, and unwillful arising of feelings, attitudes, opinions, judgments, ruminations, doubts, a constant churn of egoistic jibber-jabber that is prideful, smug, self-satisfied, ambitious, self-righteous, derisive, self-conscious, defensive, anxious, craving, angry, vain, spiteful, jealous, petty, fearful, and all the rest of it, resulting in being incessantly tormented with dissatisfaction, constantly thirsting for others' recognition, approval, admiration, and validation?

Perhaps it is not so difficult to see and understand the notion

[142] Walpola Rahula, *What the Buddha Taught* (Grove Press, 1974) 40

of it, but of what value is knowledge (besides being able to prattle on to others about your acquired intellect)? Knowledge is not the path to realization. Although the nature of the mind and its processes can be observed and conceptualized, experience and knowledge do not lead to truth, the being of it, which is beyond intellectual exposition.

The being of anything is action, without thought, concepts, or intention. One simply is. When the truth that the self is an invention is assimilated beneath the level of conscious awareness, conscious thoughts pertaining to the self no longer arise from the subconscious. This is not conceptual knowledge but an inherent way of being beyond knowing, free of concepts. There is no trying to be or to become. You either are or are not, without the movement of thought. Consider:

- A candle flame is hypnotic and mesmerising, but you do not reach out and touch it, and you need not deliberate over whether to do so. There is no struggle *not to put* your hand in fire, and there is no need to remember why you do not (a long-forgotten childhood experience, no doubt). The truth of it is now part of your inherent nature. Thought need not arise.

- I need not remind myself not to eat my own dog. I simply do not consider it. Neither do I contemplate eating someone else's dog nor killing and consuming any other sentient creature. There is no struggle not to eat meat. The thought, the craving, the interest to feed on animal flesh simply does not arise.

- Having no thirst, there is no consideration for drink. Thought is unnecessary.

Imagine if the truth concerning the nature of self could burst into one's mental universe, the bare actuality of it: that the idea of the self, the ego-narrative, is a purely personal and collective mental fabrication. If the realization of this truth could thoroughly invigorate a person's being, into the subconscious, where thought originates beneath the level of conscious awareness, the illusion of self, like a shadow exposed to brightness, would vanish, along with its associated chatter, its habituated behaviors, its egoistic posturings, and all the neurotic rest of it. The heretofore mentally animated ego-story would not now appear anywhere, at any level of consciousness, and with discontinuance, there would no longer be an identity-story to build up or break down, no more identity-story about which one need feel prideful and arrogant, vain and bloated, no more identity-story about which one need feel insecure, discomfited, or self-conscious. No more uncertainty. No more seeking. No more mental conflict. There would be an "enlightened" awareness, but certainly no enlightened "I am," and this awareness, free from the illusion of self, would also be free from the discursive mental suffering of the illusory self.

Suppose you awake in the morning and, somehow, life feels different. You have been freed from the mental contrivances of your ego and its attendant prattle. You drink your coffee, eat your breakfast, and take your children to school, still going about the day working, running errands, interacting with colleagues, family, friends, and acquaintances, but there is an absence of discursive and reactive thoughts that would otherwise elicit self-righteousness or judgment or prejudice or resentment or envy or greed or perversion or self-loathing or pride or conceit or fear or anger or spite or anything else. When you are drinking coffee, you are drinking, appreciating the aroma and flavor. When you are leaving for work, you are truly noticing your family, wishing them a good day with affection and tenderness. When you are driving, you are maneuvering your car, attentively and patiently, enjoying the warmth of the sunshine through the window. When you are working, you are involved with work, focused and diligent. When you are having lunch with a friend, you are with your friend, attentive and thoughtful. Whether cheerful and warm with a passerby, cool and unperturbed toward another's road rage, or optimistic and supportive of others during a stressful work day, you are mindful of and wholly engaged with the world around you. You are in the flow, fully present, free from the mind chatter of an individuated self, free from conditioned dogma, free from the dualistic concepts that arise cravings and aversions and neurosis.

Annihilation or Nirvana?

"The realization of this Truth, i.e., to see things as they are (yathabhutam) without illusion or ignorance (avijja), is the extinction of craving, 'thirst' (Tanhakkhaya), and the cessation (Nirodha) of dukkha, which is Nirvana."—Walpola Rahula[143]

"We realize that the very root of the self is the movement of thought in time . . . So when thought comes to an end that is a form of death while living."—Jiddu Krishnamurti[144]

Somehow, the idea of enlightenment and Nirvana has been imagined as a tranquil sensation, a euphoric state, an enchanted and happy place, some kind of blissful, romanticized nonsense. It all sounds rather magical and appealing until one considers that seeing the truth, realizing the true nature of the self as illusion might also mean envisioning the self—the precious personal narrative, all that is "I, me, my, mine"—annihilated, destroyed, obliterated, doornail dead. Not so appealing after all when the total cessation of ego-self is the essence of what underlies our utter dread of physical death.

In truth, the ego-self suffers no death or annihilation, because it never truly was. If there is the "death" of anything, it is death to the illusion of the self, the illusion that the self is anything more real than a mental projection, a shadow on the wall of imagination

[143] Rahula, *What the Buddha Taught*, 40

[144] Jiddu Krishnamurti in Dialogue with Buddhists, *Can Humanity Change* (Shambhala Publications, 2003) 34

Bodhi Tree at the Sri Mahabodhi Temple - Bodhgaya, India

that is not and never was any actual and enduring entity.

Illuminated by truth, the self is exposed and revealed as illusory, which may seem like death, but it is not. It is stillness and being. Discursive, egoistic mental activity is no more. There is no longer the narrative, the incessant craving to be or to acquire, the endless, obsessive discourse, the constant streaming of egoistic thought arising from attachment to memories, conditioned ideas and beliefs, the constant thirst for others' validation, confirmation, acknowledgment, and affirmation. Once exposed to truth, the egoistic mental projections and shadows vanish, but are not annihilated, because they had never truly been.

Recognize that you are not your thoughts; you are not your ego-narrative. Live mindfully and wholly engaged with the truth of the "self" as a mental fabrication and with the truth of our existential nature, and you will undoubtedly live with greater wellbeing and contentment: more patient, charitable, and compassionate; less distracted and self-absorbed; less obsessive and compulsive; less judgmental, condescending, and angry; less needy, anxious, and fearful; more self-assured and easygoing, and so on. Find yourself a more contented and self-effacing individual, who laughs easily, is happy for others' happiness, is unassuming, kind, and grateful.

Is this enlightenment? Is this Nirvana? Will one become a Buddha, an arhat, a guru, or some other "enlightened" ideal? I have no idea, and it makes no difference, because to identify as some "thing" means nothing more than to conform to some contrived image. Relinquish conditioned beliefs and awaken to the true nature of the self, and that is that. One can then live with an awareness illuminated by the truth—impermanent, non-dualistic, and inter-connected with the external world.

Regardless of whether one is a Buddha, an arhat or priest, a gardener, banker, scientist, businessman, carpenter, whatever, any-one can live fully engaged in the action of living. And as long as fundamental survival needs are secured—food, water, shelter, cloth-ing, and healthcare—contentment is simply seeing the truth, and living it. When one is free from the delusions of self and sees the truth of our existential reality, he or she can gracefully face life circumstances without the dualistic response of craving or aver-sion. Life can be lived with enthusiasm, conviction, and joie de vivre, and death can be viewed not so fearfully because, well, the self has been exposed and the illusion is no more.

Finally, in the spirit of metta (and an old Irish friend named

Mr. Mac), I offer you this traditional Irish blessing:

May the road rise up to meet you;
May the wind be always at your back;
May the sun shine warm upon your face.

www.thebuddhawasnotabuddhist.com

BIBLIOGRAPHY

Alzheimer's Disease Fact Sheet. U.S. Department of Health and Human Services, September 2012. Retrieved 06/13/2014. Available from http://www.nia.nih.gov/alzheimers/publication/alzheimers-disease-fact-sheet

Amazing Animal Senses. Neuroscience for kids. Retrieved 05/08/2014. Available from http://faculty.washington.edu/chudler/amaze.html

Amos, Amanda, and Margaretha Haglund. *From Social Taboo to "Torch of Freedom" : the Marketing of Cigarettes to Women.* Tobacco Control 9.1, 2000. Retrieved 05/05/2014. Available from http://tobaccocontrol.bmj.com/content/9/1/3.full

Annual Estimates of the Resident Population: April 1, 2010 to July 1, 2013. U.S. Census Bureau, Population Division. Retrieved 06/08/2014. Available from http://factfinder2.census.gov/faces/tableservices/jsf/pages/productview.xhtml?src=bkmk

Anxiety and physical illness. Harvard Health Publications, July, 2008. Retrieved 05/15/2014. Available from http://www.health.harvard.edu/newsletters/Harvard_Womens_Health_Watch/2008/July/Anxiety_and_physical_illness

Anxiety Disorders. National Institute of Mental Health. Retrieved 04/07/2014. Available from http://www.nimh.nih.gov/health/topics/anxiety-disorders/index.shtml

Bedard, Steven. *Smells Like Death.* California Academy of Sciences, November 19, 2013. Retrieved Feb. 8, 2014. Available from http://www.calacademy.org/sciencetoday/smells-like-death/5513085/

Bernays, Edward. *Propaganda.* 1928

Black Bear Biology and Behavior. NJ Division of Fish and Wildlife. Retrieved 05/08/2014. Available from http://www.state.nj.us/dep/fgw/bearfacts_biology.htm

Botvinick, Matthew, and Jonathan Cohen. *Rubber hands 'feel' touch that eyes see.* Nature, Nature Publishing Group, Vol. 391, Feb 19, 1998

Bowen, R. *Oxytocin.* July 12, 2010. Retrieved June 13, 2014. Available from http://www.vivo.colostate.edu/hbooks/pathphys/endocrine/hypopit/oxytocin.html

Brandt, Allan M. *Recruiting women smokers: the engineering of consent.* Journal of the American Medical Women's Association. Retrieved 05/05/2014. Available from http://dash.harvard.edu/bitstream/handle/1/3372908/Brandt_Recruiting.pdf?sequence=1

Brundage, Sandy. *Bad Vibes, Warning: Meditating may be hazardous to your health.* SF Weekly News, 28 Aug 2002. Retrieved 05/25/2014. Available from http://www.sfweekly.com/2002-08-28/news/bad-vibes/full/

Castillo RJ. *Depersonalization and meditation.* Psychiatry, 1990 May;53(2):158-68). Retrieved 05/25/2014. Available from https://www.ncbi.nlm.nih.gov/pubmed/2191357

Congenital insensitivity to pain. Genetics Home Reference, 2014. Retrieved 06/02/2014. Available from http://ghr.nlm.nih.gov/condition/congenital-insensitivity-to-pain

Coseru, Christian. *"1.1 The Not-Self Doctrine" in "Mind in Indian Buddhist Philosophy."* The Stanford Encyclopedia of Philosophy, Winter 2012 Edition, Edward N. Zalta (ed.). Retrieved 02/12/2014. Available from http://plato.stanford.edu/archives/win2012/entries/mind-indian-buddhism/

Costandi, Mo. *Your plastic self.* ThInk, April 7, 2013. Retrieved 04/07/2014. Available from http://thinkneuroscience.wordpress.com/2013/04/07/your-plastic-self

Crop Production, Ag 101. U.S. Environmental Protection Agency. Retrieved 11/12/2013. Available from http://www.epa.gov/agriculture/ag101/printcrop.html

Cummins, Ronnie. *Millions Against Monsanto: On the Road to Victory.* EcoWatch, July 22, 2013. Retrieved 06/22/2014. Available from http://ecowatch.com/2013/07/22/millions-against-monsanto-road-victory/

Diseases and Conditions: Depersonalization disorder. Retrieved 05/25/2014. Available from http://www.mayoclinic.org/diseases-conditions/depersonalization/basics/definition/con-20033401

DrugFacts: MDMA (Ecstasy or Molly). National Institute on Drug Abuse, September 2013. Retrieved 3/4/2014. Available from http://www.drugabuse.gov/publications/drugfacts/mdma-ecstasy-or-molly

Dzongsar Jamyang Khyentse Rinpoche. *What Makes You not a Buddhist.* Shambhala, 2007

Edmonds, Molly. *The Body After Death in How Dying Works.* HowStuffWorks.com, 12 January 2009. Retrieved Feb. 8, 2014. Available from http://health.howstuffworks.com/diseases-conditions/death-dying/dying.htm

Egan, Timothy. *Chief's Speech of 1854 Given New Meaning (and Words)*. New York Times, 21 April 1992. Retrieved 10/2/2013. Available from http://www.nytimes.com/1992/04/21/us/chief-s-speech-o f - 1 8 5 4 - g i v e n - n e w - m e a n i n g - a n d - words.html?pagewanted=all&src=pm

Beach, Frank A., and Lisbeth Jordan. *Sexual Exhaustion and Recovery in the Male Rat*. Quarterly Journal of Experimental Psychology 8, 1956

Fang, Janet. *Snake infrared detection unravelled*. Nature, doi:10.1038/news.2010.122, March 14, 2010. Retrieved 05/08/2014. Available from http://www.nature.com/news/2010/100314/full/news.2010.122.html

Fang, Liu. *Dance of the Yi Tribe*. Retrieved 05/12/2014. Available from http://www.youtube.com/watch?v=yY-xPla0aJU

Food Processing. Teaching the Food System, A Project of the John Hopkins Center for a Livable Future. Retrieved 06/22/2014. Available from http://www.jhsph.edu/research/centers-and-institutes/teaching-the-food-system/curriculum/

Glass Walls. Documentary narrated by Paul McCartney. Free From Harm, 2009. Retrieved 06/02/2014. Available from http://freefromharm.org/videos/documentaries/meat-org-the-web-site-the-meat-industry-does-not-want-you-to-see/

Harris, Sam. *Free Will*. Free Press, 2012

Heckert, Justin. *The Hazards of Growing Up Painlessly* New York Times, 15 November 2012. Retrieved 11/02/2013. Available from http://www.nytimes.com/2012/11/18/magazine/ashlyn-blocker-feels-no-pain.html?pagewanted=all&_r=0

Helmenstine, Anne Marie Ph.D. *Love Chemicals and Chemistry of Love*. Retrieved 3/22/2014. Available from http://chemistry.about.com/od/valentinesdaychemistry/a/Love-Chemicals.htm

His Holiness the Dalai Lama and Howard Cutler, M.D. *The Art of Happiness*. Riverhead Books, 1998

His Holiness the 14th Dalai Lama. *Training the Mind: Verse 2*. Retrieved 05/09/2014. Available from http://www.dalailama.com/teachings/training-the-mind/verse-2

Hunger: Vital Statistics. United Nations website. Retrieved 6/11/2014. Available from http://www.un.org/en/globalissues/briefingpapers/food/vitalstats.shtml

Hyde, Embriette R., Daniel P. Haarmann, Aaron M. Lynne, Sibyl R. Bucheli, Joseph F. Petrosino. *The Living Dead: Bacterial Community Structure of a Cadaver at the Onset and End of the Bloat Stage of Decomposition*. PLoS ONE 8(10): e77733. doi:10.1371/journal.pone.0077733, 2013. Retrieved Feb. 8, 2014.

In search of self. Nature Neuroscience 5, 1099 (2002) doi:10.1038/nn1102-1099. Retrieved 3/21/2014. Available from http://www.nature.com/neuro/journal/v5/n11/full/nn1102-1099.html

Kaplan, Johanna S. PhD, and David F. Tolin, PhD. *Exposure Therapy for Anxiety Disorders*. Psychiatric Times, September 06, 2011. Retrieved 06/02/2014. Available from http://www.psychiatrictimes.com/anxiety/exposure-therapy-anxiety-disorders

Kellogg, Ronald T. *The Making of the Mind*. Prometheus Books, 2013

King, Peter H. *A Moment of Road Rage Changes Lives Forever.* Los Angeles Times, May 27, 2001. Retrieved 4/30/2014. Available from http://articles.latimes.com/2001/may/27/local/me-3290

Kirman, Paula E. *Traditional Chinese Music is in Her Heart and Soul.* Inside World Music, June 24, 2001. Retrieved 05/12/2014. Available from http://www.insideworldmusic.com/library/weekly/aa062201a.htm

Krishnamurti, Jiddu, in Dialogue with Buddhists. *Can Humanity Change.* Shambhala Publications, 2003

Krishnamurti, Jiddu. *Freedom from the Known.* Rider Books, 2010

Krishnamurti, Jiddu. *Krishnamurti Foundation Annual Gathering Compilation 1990.* Krishnamurti Foundation Trust Ltd., 1990

Krishnamurti, Jiddu. *Questions and Answers.* Krishnamurti Foundation India, 2009

Krishnamurti, Jiddu. *This Light in Oneself.* Krishnamurti Foundation Trust Ltd, 1999

Krishnamurti, Jiddu. *You are the World.* Krishnamurti Foundation India, 1972

Lama Surya Das. *Transforming Anger #2*, 05/03/2011. Retrieved 06/02/2014. Available from http://www.surya.org/transforming-anger-2/

Lao-zi. Translated by Gia-fu Feng and Jane English. *Tao Te Ching.* New York: Vintage Books, 1989

Lebow, Victor. *Price Competition in 1955.* Journal of Retailing, Spring, 1955

Lee, Bruce. *The Way of the Intercepting Fist.* Longstreet TV Series, 16 September 1971. Retrieved 05/25/2014. Available from http://www.youtube.com/watch?v=_GDWkVRK8kQ

Little, John, Documentary film: *Bruce Lee: A Warrior's Journey.* 2000

Liu Fang Interview. Retrieved 05/12/2014. Available from http://www.youtube.com/watch?v=lpIyL02dV-g

Liu Fang Interview & Live 2. Retrieved 05/09/2014. Available from http://www.youtube.com/watch?v=wNcs6ZqCy9U

Livestock a major threat to environment. Food and Agriculture Organization of the United Nations, 2006. Retrieved 10/18/2013. Available from http://www.fao.org/newsroom/en/News/2006/1000448/index.html

Lyubomirsky, Sonja. *New Love: A Short Shelf Life.* The New York Times, December 2, 2012

Marchant, Jo, and Lucy Middleton. *Introduction: Death.* New Scientist, October 2007. Retrieved Feb. 8, 2014. Available from http://www.newscientist.com/article/dn12759-introduction-death.html?full=true#.UvMtZEDE1K0

Marieb, Elaine N., and Katja Hoehn. *Human Anatomy and Physiology, 7th ed.* Pearson Education, Inc., 2007

McCartney, Paul. *Animal Times interview.* Fall 1998

McLuhan, T. C. *Touch the Earth.* Promontory Press, March 1971

MDMA (Ecstasy) Abuse, Research Report Series. National Institute On Drug Abuse, NIH Pub Number: 06-4728, Published: March 2006. Retrieved 3/4/2014. Available from http://

www.drugabuse.gov/publications/research-reports/mdma-ecstasy-abuse

Mlodinow, Leonard. *Subliminal, How Your Unconscious Mind Rules Your Behavior.* Pantheon Books, 2012

Nestle, Marion. *How Ultra-Processed Foods Are Killing Us.* The Atlantic Monthly, Nov 4 2010. Retrieved 06/22/2014. Available from http://www.theatlantic.com/health/archive/2010/11/how-ultra-processed-foods-are-killing-us/65614/

Persons With Serious Mental Disorders in Introduction to the Technique. Vipassana Meditation As Taught By S.N. Goenka. Retrieved 05/25/2014. Available from http://www2.dhamma.org/en/code.shtml

Petkova, Valeria I., and H. Henrik Ehrsson. *If I Were You: Perceptual Illusion of Body Swapping.* PLoS ONE 3(12): e3832.doi:10.1371/journal.pone.0003832, 2008. Retrieved 04/07/2014. Available from http://www.plosone.org/article/info%3Adoi%2F10.1371%2Fjournal.pone.0003832

Pete, Steven. *Congenital analgesia: The agony of feeling no pain.* BBC News Magazine, July 16, 2012. Retrieved 11/02/2013. Available from http://www.bbc.com/news/magazine-18713585

Pickrell, John, and Lucy Middleton and Alun Anderson. *Introduction: Love.* The New Scientist, September 2006. Retrieved June 13, 2014. Available from http://www.newscientist.com/article/dn9981-introduction-love.html?full=true

Pimentel, David, and Marcia Pimentel. *Sustainability of meat-based and plant-based diets and the environment.* American Society for Clinical Nutrition, September 2003 vol. 78 no. 3 660S-663S. Retrieved 10/18/2013. Available from http://ajcn.nutrition.org/content/78/3/660S.full

Pipa Soloist Liu Fang. Retrieved 05/12/2014. Available from http:/ /www.youtube.com/watch?v=vD8XsQ8R7o8

Rahula, Walpola. *What the Buddha Taught.* Grove Press, 1974

Report: Number of Animals Killed In US Increases in 2010. FARM. Retrieved 06/02/2014. Available from http://farmusa.org/ statistics11.html

Revel, Jean-Francois, and Matthieu Ricard. *The Monk and the Philosopher.* Random House, 1998

Russell, William F. and Taylor Branch. *Second Wind: The Memoirs of an Opinionated Man.* Random House, 1979

Sagan, Carl, co-written with Dr. Ann Druyan. *Shadows of Forgotten Ancestors.* Random House, 1992

Schacter, Daniel. *The Seven Sins of Memory.* Houghton Mifflin Company, 2001

Short-term effects after ecstasy is gone from the body. National Institute on Drug Abuse, January 2007. Retrieved 3/4/2014. Available from http://www.drugabuse.gov/publications/teaching-packets/neuro-biology-ecstasy/section-iii/1-short-term-effects-after-ecstasy-gone-body

Siong Soon, Chun, and Marcel Brass, Hans-Jochen Heinze, and John-Dylan Haynes. *Unconscious determinants of free decisions in the human brain.* Nature Neuroscience, Volume 11, Number 5, May 2008

Soho, Takuan. Translated by William Scott Wilson. *The Unfettered Mind.* Tokyo: Kodansha International Ltd., 1986

Storl, Wolf D. *Culture and Horticulture, A Philosophy of Gardening.* Biodynamic Farming and Gardening Assoc., Inc., 2000

Taylor, Dr. Jill Bolte. *My Stroke of Insight.* TED talk, February 2008. Retrieved 05/09/2014. Available from http://www.ted.com/talks/jill_bolte_taylor_s_powerful_stroke_of_insight#t-5065

Taylor, Dr. Jill Bolte. *My Stroke of Insight.* Viking, 2006

Thakkar, Katharine N., and Heathman S. Nichols, Lindsey G. McIntosh, and Sohee Park. *Disturbances in Body Ownership in Schizophrenia: Evidence from the Rubber Hand Illusion and Case Study of a Spontaneous Out-of-Body Experience.* PLoS ONE 6(10): e27089. doi:10.1371/journal.pone.0027089, 2011. Retrieved 04/07/2014. Available from http://www.plosone.org/article/info%3Adoi%2F10.1371%2Fjournal.pone.0027089

The charm of ancient traditional music of China. Retrieved 05/12/2014. Available from http://www.youtube.com/watch?v=6k_4DsiM9-g

The Mandarin Superstar. The Pierre Burton Show, 09/12/71. Retrieved 05/25/2014. Available from http://www.youtube.com/watch?v=PFQ7UxUdIH8

The Science of Love. BBC: Human Body & Mind. Retrieved June 13, 2014. Available from http://www.bbc.co.uk/science/hottopics/love/

The science of love. The Economist, Feb 12th 2004. Retrieved 3/22/2014. Available from http://www.economist.com/node/2424049

Thich Nhat Hanh. *Living Buddha, Living Christ.* Riverhead Books, 1995

Toward a Healthy, Sustainable Food System. The American Public Health Association, Policy Number: 200712, 11/06/2007. Retrieved 06/26/2014. Available from http://www.apha.org/advocacy/policy/policysearch/default.htm?id=1361

Turk David J., Todd F. Heatherton, C. Neil Macrae, William M. Kelley, Michael S. Gazzaniga. *Out of Contact, Out of Mind, The Distributed Nature of the Self.* Ann. N. Y. Acad. Sci. 2003 Oct; 1001:65-78, PMID: 14625356. Retrieved Feb. 8, 2014. Available from http://www.dartmouth.edu/~bil/pubs/turk_2003_annals.pdf

Unconscious decisions in the brain. Max Planck Society, April 14, 2008. Retrieved 06/16/2014. Available from http://www.mpg.de/567905/pressRelease20080414

Understanding the stress response. Harvard Health Publications, March, 2011). Retrieved 05/15/2014. Available from http://www.health.harvard.edu/newsletters/Harvard_Mental_Health_Letter/2011/March/understanding-the-stress-response

Voytek, Bradley. *Are There Really as Many Neurons in the Human Brain as Stars in the Milky Way?* Nature Education, Nature Publishing Group, 05/20/13. Retrieved 05/28/2014. Available from http://www.nature.com/scitable/blog/brain-metrics/are_there_really_as_many

Vrajaprana, Pravrajika. *Vedanta: A Simple Introduction.* Vedanta Press & Bookshop, 1999

What falling in love does to your heart and brain. Loyola University Health System, Feb. 6, 2014. Retrieved June 13, 2014. Available from http://www.loyolamedicine.org/newswire/news/what-falling-love-does-your-heart-and-brain

What is dissociation? The International Society for the Study of Trauma and Dissociation. Retrieved 05/25/2014. Available from http://www.isst-d.org/default.asp?contentID=76#diss

What's Wrong with Factory Farming? The Organic Consumers Association. Retrieved 06/02/2014. Available from http://www.organicconsumers.org/foodsafety/shortlist031604.cfm

Wikipedia. *Linji Yixuan.* Retrieved 6/12/2014. Available from http://en.wikipedia.org/wiki/Linji_Yixuan

Wikipedia. *Neuron.* Retrieved 05/28/2014. Available from http://en.wikipedia.org/wiki/Neuron#cite_note-nervenet-28

Wise, Jeff. *Extreme Fear: The Science of Your Mind in Danger.* Palgrave MacMillan, 2009

Wright, David. *Road Rage Leads to Shooting, Suicide.* ABC News, June 19, 2001. Retrieved 4/30/2014. Available from http://abcnews.go.com/US/story?id=93070&page=1&singlePage=true

臨濟義玄. Retrieved 6/12/2014. Available from http://zh.wikipedia.org/zh-hant/%E4%B8%B4%E6%B5%8E%E4%B9%89%E7%8E%84

About the Author

If one points a finger and says, "Look, the moon is beautiful," do you look at the finger or at where the finger is pointing?

Truth and insight, the "moon," are often disregarded and lost when some method, some knowledge, some personality, some dogmatic tradition—the "pointing finger"—is bestowed with undue value and focus and respect. Do not spend your time contemplating and acknowledging the finger.

Where one has been and what one has done, as well as where one plans to go or what one plans to do, is nothing more than a story in one's head. It is all immaterial.

"Do not concentrate on the finger, or you will miss all that heavenly glory."—Bruce Lee